LLOYD GEORGE AND THE COALITION LIBERAL PARTY

Studies in Parliamentary History

Series Editor
Linda Clark (Editor Emeritus, History of Parliament)

This series aims to act as a vehicle for the publication of new research into the history of the representative assemblies of Britain, Ireland and the British Empire, from the medieval period to the present day. It will include monographs and scholarly editions of important texts, and will expand the traditional emphasis on political and institutional developments to reflect current interest in the social, cultural and intellectual history of parliaments.

This series is sponsored by the journal *Parliamentary History*.

Other books in the series

The Early Parliaments of Henry VIII, 1510–1523, Jonathan McGovern, 2025

Lloyd George and the Coalition Liberal Party

The Papers of Lieutenant-Colonel Scovell, General Secretary of the Party, 1919–1922

Edited by G. H. Bennett

THE BOYDELL PRESS

First published 2026
The Boydell Press, Woodbridge

ISBN 978 1 83765 312 6

The Boydell Press is an imprint of Boydell & Brewer Ltd
and of Boydell & Brewer Inc.
website: www.boydellandbrewer.com

Our Authorised Representative for product safety in the EU is Easy
Access System Europe – Mustamäe tee 50, 10621 Tallinn,
Estonia, *gpsr.requests@easproject.com*

A CIP record for this title is available
from the British Library

Contents

Acknowledgements

In the production of this volume, I am indebted to the Lloyd George Archive and particularly to Tony O'Connor. Without the existence of the archive the papers might have been lost to history, and without the archivists' generosity they might not have been shared with the academic community. Tony O'Connor was unfailingly helpful, tireless in his efforts to supply key documents, and wonderfully supportive of the project. I am indebted to Gary Philipps, who provided remarkable assistance in untangling how a deposit of Scovell's papers ended up in the Lincolnshire Record Office, shedding light on the wider story of the documents. I would also like to acknowledge the help and assistance of the staff at the Parliamentary Archives, Churchill College Cambridge, Cambridge University Library, Plymouth University Library, Exeter University Library and the Record Offices at Bristol, Cornwall, Devon, Dorset, Kent, Lancashire, Liverpool, Somerset and Sussex, London Metropolitan Archives and the Scottish Record Office in supplying materials to contextualise and cross reference documents found in the Scovell papers. Particular thanks are owed to Henry Adams in respect of the papers of Commander J.B. Adams, Ruth Nixon for allowing me to reproduce the letter from Frances Stevenson, and the staff at the Parliamentary Archives for providing access to the private deposits in their care and for permission to quote from the McCurdy papers. Despite national advertising, efforts to trace and contact other copyright holders have not proved as successful, but if they should contact me, I shall see that appropriate acknowledgement is made in any future edition or reprint.

Abbreviations

A.E.U.	Amalgamated Engineering Union
B.S.P.	British Socialist Party
EHR	*English Historical Review*
HJ	*The Historical Journal*
I.L.P.	Independent Labour Party
JCH	*Journal of Contemporary History*
JMH	*Journal of Modern History*
L.C.C.	London County Council
LGA	Lloyd George Archive
L.G.L.M.	*Lloyd George Liberal Magazine*
N.D.P.	National Democratic and Labour Party
N.S.P.	National Socialist Party
N.U.W.M.	National Unemployed Workers Movement
PH	*Parliamentary History*
S.D.F.	Social Democratic Federation
T.C.	Town Councillor
Wee Free	Asquithian Liberals
W.N.L.A.	Women's National Liberal Association
W.N.L.C.	Welsh National Liberal Council

Introduction

The Coalition Liberal Party and Its Place in History

In his 1971 chapter entitled 'Lloyd George's Stage Army: The Coalition Liberals, 1918–22' Kenneth Morgan captured the essence of one of the shortest-lived political parties in British history: an unlamented and all but forgotten junior partner in the first British postwar government.[1] A breakaway faction of the Liberal Party, it served the ends of Prime Minister David Lloyd George and those Liberal members of Parliament who preferred to maintain the First World War coalition government into the peace in order to secure the 'fruits of victory' and preserve the established order against the dangers of socialism. Contrary to the image of a 'party without roots', the Coalition Liberal Party did have some substance.[2] It was not formed magically overnight as a result of some order by the 'Welsh Wizard'. Rather, it was the work of several years of development shaped by fluctuations within Westminster politics and by changes across the local political landscapes of the United Kingdom. During its short life it contested just one election, in 1922, and a year later the Coalition (or National) Liberal Party, as it had become, had gone as the Lloyd Georgian and Asquithian wings of British Liberalism came together to reunify under one party banner in the face of the Conservative Party's platform of protectionism in the 1923 general election. Despite the passage of more than four decades, Morgan's chapter remains the only dedicated published study of the life of the Coalition Liberal Party.

This has meant that certain issues about the party, and the way in which it intersected with the political history of Britain in that period, remain virtually unexplored; a period in which the Labour Party supplanted the Liberals as the second force in British politics, and in which the Conservative Party established itself as the 'natural party of government'. Critical questions have not been posed, let alone answered. For example, what was the role of the Coalition Liberal Party in the downfall of British Liberalism? How was it put together and controlled, and what might this tell us about Lloyd George, his colleagues and his government? To what extent did it evolve during its short history, and does that process offer some

1 K.O. Morgan, 'Lloyd George's State Army: The Coalition Liberals, 1918–22', in *Lloyd George: Twelve Essays*, ed. A.J.P. Taylor (1971), 225–6; amplified in Morgan's *Consensus and Disunity: The Lloyd George Coalition Government 1918–1922* (Oxford, 1979).

2 Chris Cook and John Stevenson, *A History of British Elections Since 1689* (2014), 124.

insights into the changing nature of British politics in the early 1920s? What too might the history of that party tell us about developments in the Conservative and Labour parties, and the fluctuating relationships within the Coalition itself? In its processes and methods what can the Coalition Liberal Party tell us about political organisation, patronage and political networks in the early 1920s?

This volume of documents, in addition to providing some answers to these critical questions, also offers a rather different methodological approach to British party-political history. In the 1980s the traditional approach to British politics, in which the great figures like Lloyd George were seen as the driving forces of political developments, was challenged by a new generation of scholars such as Stuart Ball and Andrew Thorpe.[3] Utilising constituency party minute books and the records of political parties (as opposed to the private papers of the leading politicians), they created new understandings about the evolution of British politics, with the low politics of the constituency complementing the high-politics, Westminster-focussed, approach which had dominated the 1970s thanks to the work of Maurice Cowling.[4] The rise of a 'new political history' in the 1990s and early twenty-first century has raised significant issues, with recognition of the roles of class, culture and language in determining long-term shifts and even short-term outcomes in political behaviour. A 'new, new political history' has begun to emerge which stresses the interaction between high and low politics and the agency of women as activists, voters and as Westminster politicians.[5]

To some extent, however, the process of evolution over the past twenty years has remained slow, and the field remains highly politicised in a contemporary, as opposed to an historical, sense as political historians write about the history of parties with which they have at least some sympathy – the Liberal Party's devalued status in modern politics having an impact on the historiography. The Coalition Liberal Party's role in what Robert Self has described as the 'tragedy of Liberal self-immolation' has further counted against interest in the short-lived breakaway group.[6] After Morgan's chapter was written in the 1970s, the Coalition Liberal Party became largely left behind in the decades following as methodologies and understandings of British political history changed.[7] With

3 Stuart Ball, Baldwin and the Conservative Party: The Crisis of 1929–1931 (New York, 1988); Andrew Thorpe, *The British General Election of 1931* (Oxford, 1991).

4 Maurice Cowling, *The Impact of Labour 1920–1924* (Cambridge, 1971); *ibid.*, *The Impact of Hitler: British Politics and British Policies 1933–1940* (Cambridge, 1975); see also, Robert Crowcroft, 'Maurice Cowling and the Writing of British Political History', *Contemporary British History*, xxii (2008), 279–86; Craig David, 'High Politics and the "New Political History"', *HJ*, liii (2010), 240–60; Steven Fielding, 'Looking for the "New Political History"', *JCH*, xlii (2007), 515–24.

5 On the new political history see, amongst many others, David Jarvis, 'Mrs Maggs and Betty: The Conservative Approach to Women Voters in the 1920s', *Twentieth Century British History*, v (1994), 129–52; *ibid.*, 'British Conservatism and Class Politics in the 1920s', *EHR*, cxi (1996), 59–84.

6 R.C. Self, *Evolution of the British Party System 1885–1940* (2014), 140.

7 While the Coalition Liberal Party has been left behind in scholarly terms, continued interest in Lloyd George has thrown light on some aspects of its operation. See, for

such a short-lived (and rather unloved) party, few records appeared to have survived long enough to reach places of safety in archives. Nevertheless, in 2016 a number of documents relevant to the study of Coalition Liberalism were acquired by the Lloyd George Archive, an archive established in 2008, following the discovery of rare artefacts relating to David Lloyd George held in two private family collections. Subsequent acquisitions, notably from members of the Lloyd George family, followed to produce an historically significant collection with papers coming from the estates of Freddie Guest MP, Mr A. J. Sylvester,[8] Lloyd George's chauffeur and the Lloyd George home, Bron-y-de, and farm at Churt in Surrey.[9] The papers acquired in 2016 through public auction came from Lieutenant-Colonel G. J. S. Scovell CBE. Somewhat less than a household name (indeed he escapes mention in most biographies of Lloyd George), Scovell had served as general secretary of the Coalition Liberal Party Organisation from 1919 to 1922. Significantly, much of his correspondence was with Freddie Guest, Coalition Liberal chief whip from 1917 to 1921, and with Guest's successor as chief whip, Charles A. McCurdy. The significance of these materials is evidenced by the fact that when Cameron Hazlehurst compiled his *Guide to the Papers of British Cabinet Ministers* in the 1990s he found only fragmentary deposits for both Guest and McCurdy.[10] The contents of the Scovell papers, read in conjunction with archival materials from other repositories, including the Lloyd George papers at the Parliamentary Archives, document the development of the Coalition Liberal Party from the unusual perspective of the chief whip's office and the head of the party – the chief point of intersection between the high politics of the party in Westminster and the low politics of party organisation in the constituencies and the regions. The present volume, impelled by chance archival survival, targets this critical political intersection.

It is also worth noting that the Scovell papers in the Lloyd George Archive retain the file structure assigned to them by Scovell himself in the early 1920s; the papers have not been rearranged and reclassified by subsequent archivists and biographers, so that through preservation and organisation we have the opportunity to see what mattered, how it mattered and when it mattered to the general secretary of the Coalition Liberal Party. In some cases, papers, often in the form of inclusions, were not found in the archive probably because they were forwarded to the chief whip. Only those papers relating to Scovell's political life and the Coalition Liberal Party have been included in this volume, apart from a few letters to contextualise the man and his activities. Scovell was a great networker and used letters as the principal means to maintain connections with his diverse social, ex-military and field sports circles. Those connections could

example, D.M. Kregier, 'Lloyd George's Lucre: The National Liberal Fund', in *Chiefs without Indians: Asquith, Lloyd George and the Liberal Remnant*, ed. Krieger (Washington DC, 1982), 113–47.

8 Albert James Sylvester (1889–1989), principal private secretary to Lloyd George, 1923–45.

9 The archive is dedicated to the memory of the Reverend James Lawler.

10 Cameron Hazlehurst, Sally Whitehead and Christine Woodland, *A Guide to the Papers of British Cabinet Ministers 1900–1964* (Cambridge, 1996), 168, 242.

be, and were, used for political ends and as a two-way channel for patronage that could have political value. Most of that contextual material has been omitted, but its significance should not be lost sight of in terms of how Scovell operated within the political circles in which he was so very much a part. The papers within this volume are a representative sample, geared towards the overtly political issues of the day, of the material generated by Scovell which allows us to see inside the workings of a British political party in the early 1920s. Scovell's more personal correspondence, demonstrating his role in the network of relationships of patrons and clients that on a personal level effectively greased the wheels of British politics, has been kept to a bare minimum. A limited amount of additional material from outside the Scovell papers has been reproduced in order to contextualise the party-political issues that he wrestled with. Editing has been kept to a minimum and has been applied silently to the handful of cases where a word or apostrophe has been missed out. What we see in this volume is not the view from the top, or the view from the bottom; rather it allows us to see the critical juncture between the two and the kinds of activities (thinking, communications, research, forward planning) that was the lifeblood of British political parties in the first half of the twentieth century.

Yet how Scovell's papers were preserved remains something of a mystery. Scovell died without issue in South Africa, and of his siblings one died in infancy, his brother during the First World War and his sisters remained unmarried and without descendants. At some point in the early twenty-first century at least two blocks of his papers appear to have been placed on the open market by public auction; thus, in addition to the papers acquired by the Lloyd George Archive, dealing with his time as general secretary, papers dealing with his military career were acquired by a London book and paper ephemera dealer. A tranche of papers (as yet uncatalogued) dealing with some of his correspondence during the 1930s and 1940s can be found in a deposit of solicitor's papers in the Lincolnshire Record Office.[11] A predecessor to the firm that made the deposit had been owned by a member of the Scovell family, and it is likely that after his death the colonel's papers, by one means or another, passed into the solicitor's vault for safekeeping to be forgotten and passed down as one business succeeded another; the deposit to the Lincolnshire Record Office resulted from a routine and long overdue process of tidying the vault and removing redundant documents. After weeding, the surviving papers were given to the Record Office with none being placed on the market. The precise processes by which some of Scovell's papers did come onto the market remain obscure.

11 Lincolnshire Record Office, Walker's Rainey and Owen Collection. WRO additional/Col. G. J. S. Scovell Files/National Defence/1936–1945 (letters, newspaper cuttings, and miscellaneous papers): 1936–9/1–218 (2 folders); 1939–40/1–122; 1940/1–248; 1941/1–282 (2 folders); 1942/0–257 (2 folders); 1943/1–245 (2 folders); 1944/1–175 (2 folders); 1945/1–127.

Building a Party from Scratch: The Scovell Papers

Lieutenant-Colonel George Julian Selwyn Scovell CBE (15 April 1881–16 April 1948) was a somewhat unlikely man to head the organisation of the Coalition Liberal Party as its general secretary from 1919 to 1922. Coming from a military family, he was the son of Captain George Thomas Scovell of the 79th Highlanders.[12] He had four siblings and was educated at Haileybury and Sandhurst.[13] As a 2nd lieutenant in the Cameron Highlanders, which he had joined in 1900, he served in the South African war in 1901–2, thereafter continuing to rise through the ranks to lieutenant in 1908 and captain in 1912. From then until 1914 he served in Rhodesia as private secretary to the directors of the British South African Company, and after returning to the United Kingdom on the outbreak of war, he served on the general staff (Northern Command) at York from 1914 to 1916, during which he was appointed major in 1915, and rose to the post of assistant adjutant-general in the War Office from 1916 to 1917, and that of deputy director-general of recruiting in the ministry of National Service from then until 1918.

Promoted to lieutenant-colonel and given a CBE in 1919, Scovell retired from the army having already been asked by Captain Frederick Guest,[14] the Coalition Liberal chief whip, to 'take on the task of building up the organisation of the scattered Liberal adherents' of David Lloyd George.[15] Scovell might well have come from an old Liberal family, but it was his organisational abilities, sharpened in Westminster during the war, that had impressed Guest. The divisions in the Liberal Party which had opened up in 1916 with Lloyd George's coup against Herbert Asquith[16] had been cemented in 1918 in the 'coupon election', which saw 133 Lloyd George Liberals returned (with benefit of the coupon).[17] Conversely, just twenty-eight Asquith Liberals had taken their seats in the House of Commons in January 1919, with the party leader having himself been defeated in East Fife. The coupon election, with Lloyd George returned at the head of a Coalition dominated

12 *The Times*, 29 Apr. 1948, p. 3. George Scovell (b. 1837) died in 1923.

13 His mother Caroline (1848–87) died when he was a child. The other children, brought up by a governess, were Archibald Mathison (1884–1915), who served in the Seaforth Highlanders and died from tuberculosis in the sanatorium at Mundesley, Norfolk; Archille Mathilda (b.1884), who appears to have died in infancy; Caroline Georgina Katherine (1878–1944); and Ela Julia (1879–1956).

14 Guest (1875–1937), was Liberal MP for East Dorset 1910–22, Stroud 1923–4, Bristol North 1924–9 and Plymouth Drake 1931–7; treasurer of the household 1912–15, Coalition Liberal chief whip 1917–21, and secretary of state for air 1921–2.

15 LGA, Letter from Scovell to J.T. Davies, enclosed in one from Scovell to McCurdy, both dated 30 Oct. 1922.

16 Herbert Henry Asquith (1852–1928), 1st earl of Oxford and Asquith; Liberal MP East Fife 1886–1918, Paisley 1920–4; secretary of state for home affairs 1892–5, chancellor of the exchequer 1905–8, prime minister 1908–16, secretary of state for war 1914; leader of the Liberal Party 1908–26; ennobled 1925.

17 The coupon was an official endorsement in the form of a letter of recommendation by the Lloyd George government to indicate that the candidate was considered loyal to the coalition.

by the Conservatives, had brought a further worsening of relations between the two wings of the party. The split was apparent if not formalised in terms of separate party structures, and there was the possibility that some form of reunion might be affected. In the meantime, Lloyd George's followers within the party needed support, not least in terms of finance, publications and organisation. Guest, who had played an important role in negotiating the coupon with the Conservatives in 1918, lacked the imagination and the stomach for party building. As Kenneth Morgan argues: 'Guest was a genial playboy whose talents hardly lay in the realm of ideas … Guest's lengthy analyses of the political scene were unimaginative, stereotyped and always mindlessly optimistic'.[18] He was only too eager for someone to take on the rigors of building a party from below, which involved work, including in the constituencies which would take him away from the pleasurable lifestyle to which he had become accustomed.

For his part, Scovell, full of admiration for Lloyd George's 'wonderful services to progress and his country during the Great War', and especially because he needed a job, was only too happy to take up Guest's offer.[19] He was palpably relieved at leaving the army and accepting the initial challenge from 1 May 1919 of trying to draw together a network which could support Lloyd George's Liberal followers across the country.[20] In early June he wrote to a fellow officer in the Gordon Highlanders: 'I am thoroughly happy being at last a free man, and although fairly fully occupied have a certain amount of time in which to collect some vitality which at the time of the Armistice was at a very low ebb'.[21] Later that same month he asked a friend: 'Are you out of the Army yet? If not, why not? My experience of nearly two months now shows me that it is extraordinarily pleasant being out of it. One can treat brainless or sticky Generals as they ought to be treated, i.e., with silent contempt'.[22] The demands on his time remained considerable, however, and among his personal letters there is a considerable volume of correspondence with friends, former colleagues and acquaintances asking him for references or other forms of personal recommendation to secure positions following the post-war demobilisation.

A badly broken leg (his thigh bone was broken in five places) resulting from a fox hunting accident on Exmoor in October 1919 left Scovell in a nursing home for most of the remaining year.[23] The after-effects of the injury caused him ongoing difficulties for the next two years, restricting his participation in country pursuits and undoubtedly impacting his ability to do the job of general secretary of the party. To some extent, though, this did not matter. With Lloyd George and many senior party members reluctant to widen the breach in Liberal ranks, and with the

18 Morgan, 'Lloyd George's Stage Army', 233.

19 LGA, Scovell to J.T. Davies, 30 Oct. 1922.

20 LGA, Scovell to Brook's (St James), 27 Feb. 1923.

21 LGA, Scovell to Lieutenant-Colonel R.M. Dudgeon DSO, MC, 51st Battalion Gordon Highlanders, 12 June 1919.

22 LGA, Scovell to Major R.D. Fordyce, 23 June 1919.

23 LGA, Unknown (on behalf of Scovell) to Brigadier-General A. Chapman CB, CMG, CBE, Army and Navy Club, 8 Oct. 1919; Scovell to G.W. Chrystal (ministry of pensions), December 1919; Scovell to Lieutenant-Colonel J. Reid Hyde 10 Mar. 1920.

prime minister seemingly feeling his way in terms of the political future and the evolution of his relationship with the Conservatives, a 'stage army' was really all that he required, or desired, for the time being. As the political tide began to turn against Lloyd George during 1920, the demands on a slowly recovering Scovell (he would not be able to walk unaided until the middle of the year) began to change quite radically.[24] Lloyd George was keenly aware that he was the head of a Coalition Liberal group that did not exist as a separate party, and that beyond Westminster it cast more shadow than had genuine substance. To secure a long-term future, four options presented themselves: to secure a fusion between the different parts of the Coalition into a new party; to re-unify the Liberal Party with him as leader; to build the Coalition Liberals into a new party; or to defect to one of the other parties which might jump at the chance to secure the services of the 'man who won the war'. The option of fusion looked attractive and promising in 1919 as many Conservative MPs could see merit in the idea, and Andrew Bonar Law, the leader of the party, was prepared to go along with the proposal.[25] Nevertheless, in the constituencies there was some bitter opposition and in mid-1919 opposition to fusion began to crystallise around senior Conservatives such as Sir George Younger, the chairman of the party.[26] As David Close has demonstrated, Lloyd George's hopes for a fusion of the Conservatives and Coalition Liberals were finally dashed on 16 March 1920 when his Liberal ministers expressed grave misgivings.[27] The meeting in May 1920 of the National Liberal Federation demonstrated the full depth of animosity between the two wings of the Liberal Party with Coalition ministers being publicly attacked. It appeared as if there was no way forward into a new party of the centre right and no way back into a re-unified Liberal Party. Yet the development of either or both possibilities might be unlocked with the development of a separate Coalition Liberal Party. With a 'going concern' at his back, and underpinned by the powerful war chest which would be derived from the sale of public honours, the Lloyd George Liberals would no longer be seen as a one-man band. Lloyd George would have the collateral, in terms of organisation and finances, to pose sufficient threat to the Conservatives and the Asquithian Liberals that he might be able to negotiate his way either to a new centre party, or

24 At the end of June 1920 he reported, 'My leg is making splendid process, and I can now hobble about from room to room without any sticks': LGA, Scovell to Lieutenant-Colonel P. Mitford, 30 June 1920.

25 Andrew Bonar Law (1858–1923), Conservative MP for Glasgow Blackfriars and Hutchesontown 1900–6, Dulwich 1906–10, Bootle 1911–18 and Glasgow Central 1918–23; parliamentary secretary to the board of trade 1902–5, leader of the opposition 1911–15, secretary of state for the colonies 1915–16, chancellor of the exchequer 1916–19, leader of the House of Commons 1916–21, lord privy seal 1919–21, prime minister and leader of the House of Commons 1922–3, leader of the Conservative Party 1911–21 and 1922–3.

26 Sir George Younger (1851–1929), Viscount Leckie of Younger; Conservative MP Ayr Burghs 1906–22; chairman of the Conservative Party 1916–23, its treasurer 1923–9; ennobled 1923.

27 David Close, 'Conservatives and Coalition after the First World War', *JMH*, xlv (1973), 244.

a reunification of the Liberal Party with him as leader. Scovell, as evidenced in his papers, would play an important role in developing the party and in giving Lloyd George the collateral to shape his future and that of British politics – or so the 'Welsh Wizard' hoped.

With Asquith controlling most of the infrastructure of the Liberal Party (stepping down as prime minister in 1916 had not altered his status as party leader in control of its machinery and finances), Lloyd George needed to secure a powerbase down to constituency level to sustain himself and his adherents, at least in order to make fusion a more equal transaction in the eyes of some Conservatives. However, the form of that powerbase was to be problematic so far as Lloyd George was concerned; his hope of fusion was a distraction from the task of building up the party as a going and long-term concern. The idea that the party was being built up only for it to be negotiated away was a lingering worry in the minds of those tasked with the job. Fusion continued to draw a furious reaction from the right wing of the Conservative Party and continued to receive a lukewarm response from many of the prime minister's Liberal followers, some of whom had a genuine commitment to the party even if it was based on a dislike of the other parties and the personalities therein. The build-up of the Coalition Liberal Party was, in the circumstances, the only viable option to emerge from what Paul Adelman has described as political 'limbo', but Lloyd George had little desire to entrench the schism within British Liberalism.[28] He wanted to keep his political options open. The attitude of both the right of the Conservative Party and the Asquithian Liberals led him towards a separate Coalition Liberal Party which he seemed to hope would be more of a movement than a conventional party, rising above traditional political boundaries in the national (and his personal) interest. Thus, the Coalition Liberal Party was conceived with Scovell as one of its builders, but with a plan from an architect who was reluctant to build anything beyond a temporary structure that would alienate no potential future political partner.

This was a less than ideal position from which to approach the task of building a powerbase to support Coalition Liberal politicians in Westminster. The organisational effort required – to reach out to local constituency organisations loyal to Lloyd George, to create new local structures where Liberals aligned with Asquith, and to establish the regional and national bodies (personnel and procedures) to fight parliamentary elections – was considerable, as were the sums of money which needed to be spent in the process. There was no blueprint as to how this party was to be formed, for it mostly involved trying to build the fabric of the structure from whatever parts had broken away from the edifice of the old Liberal Party.

Publications offered one way forward to amass support, to encourage the formation of new constituency groups loyal to Lloyd George (where existing Liberal associations had not swung behind the prime minister) and, if nothing else, to create momentum by giving an appearance of a fast-developing party with a national presence. From October 1920 Scovell was involved in the production of a monthly *Lloyd George Liberal Magazine*, initially printing 30,000 copies a month

28 Paul Adelman, *The Decline of the Liberal Party 1910–31* (1981), 31.

(although publication eventually settled down to 20,000) to serve as a focus for the new party.[29] The cost was considerable, amounting to around £650 a month, a sum which was met from advertisements and gifts from supporters. As Cameron Hazlehurst has noted, the search for a format and a blend of material that would prove attractive to activists, potential voters and advertisers was to prove elusive. Reproductions of speeches, feature articles on particular political questions (with issues around the women's vote being particularly prominent) and constituency notes were among its standard fare. The magazine was subsequently coupled with the production of *Liberal Searchlight,* a four-page leaflet combining a mix of standard national features and material focussed on a particular constituency for distribution in that area. It was produced at the expense of the Coalition Liberal organisation in the constituencies and was intended to rival the Asquithian Liberal publication *Liberal Flashlight.*[30] While it made political sense as a handy campaign weapon, the printing of *Searchlight* also served as a way to make money for the central party. Advertising in the *Lloyd George Liberal Magazine* extolled the value of *Searchlight* to sitting members of Parliament and to prospective candidates as a means of finding answers to such vital questions as:

> How can I best get my views before the electors?
>
> How can I secure recruits for my Association?
>
> How can I provide regular and reliable information about the work of the Government?
>
> How can I keep in regular touch with my supporters?
>
> How can I best advertise meetings and other functions in my constituency?
>
> How can I most effectively reply to opposition?[31]

While publications provided a focal point and means to develop the party at the national, regional and constituency levels, other structures were constituted to the same end. For example, the Eighty Club had been established as a London gentleman's club for Liberals, and at different times both Asquith and Lloyd George had held senior honorary positions within it. After the split within the Liberal Party the club remained a bastion of Asquithianism, but in December 1920 thirty-five members broke away to form the pro-Lloyd George 1920 Club with rooms at 2 Whitehall Court, and within a year the new club's membership had grown to 863. Significantly, in contrast to the National Liberal Club which was next door, the 1920 Club was open to women members.[32]

29 Parliamentary Archives, Lloyd George Papers, F/168/2/16, p. 32, Annual Report of the Coalition Liberal organisation, 1920. See also Cameron Hazlehurst, 'Introduction' to *British Political Sources: Series 2: Twentieth Century Political Periodicals: The Lloyd George Liberal Magazine 1920–1923*, vol. 1 (Oct. 1920–Mar. 1921) (Brighton, 1973), p. xi.

30 'The Liberal Searchlight', *Lloyd George Liberal Magazine*, Nov. 1921, vol. 2 (no. 2), 118.

31 'Problems for MPs and Candidates', *Lloyd George Liberal Magazine*, Dec. 1921, vol. 2 (no. 3), 287.

32 '1920 Club Notes', *Lloyd George Liberal Magazine*, Jan. 1922, vol. 2 (no. 4), 330.

At almost every turn in the emergence and development of the structures of the Coalition Liberal Party the same problem was evident throughout, namely the great reluctance and sadness to break finally with the historic roots of the Liberal Party. Lloyd George did not envision a conventional party base, but his followers could not think beyond using the old Liberal Party as a template for the structures of the new. Rather than a failure of imagination this was evidence of a desire not to alienate traditional Liberal voters who might be prepared to vote for Lloyd George followers in the interests of keeping out Labour and containing the more reactionary parts of the Conservative Party. It did, however, mean that the party struggled to develop a truly separate identity and means to appeal to an electorate changed out of all recognition to that of pre-war Britain. In these circumstances making a particular appeal to the women's vote represented a potential means to steal a march on the other parties without widening the gulf with the Asquithian Liberals who might be persuaded to come over to Lloyd George. This the party certainly attempted to do, and in some of the developments within the party there can be glimpsed organic growth taking place and tentative steps towards a redefinition of post-war Liberalism. The Coalition Liberal Party might have come into being as Lloyd George's stage army but it did slowly start to take on a life of its own with future Liberal figures such as Archibald Sinclair (elected in 1922 as Coalition Liberal MP for Caithness and Sutherland)[33] rising within its ranks.

As he built up the contacts to provide a party base, Scovell provided a range of political intelligence to the chief whip Charles McCurdy, who took over from Guest in April 1921.[34] McCurdy, described by Kenneth Morgan as a 'more impressive figure' than his predecessor, had previously held significant departmental responsibility as minister of food control.[35] Very much a Coalitionist, he highlighted his commitment to the cause in a letter to Lloyd George on 21 April 1921.[36] McCurdy regarded the two-party system of the previous hundred years as having been marred by a sham politics in which division was emphasised over the realities of a much larger set of commonalities of approach and policy between the two parties.[37] For him, and part of the new ideas emerging within Coalition Liberal ranks, the age of the two-party system was over, and that a three party system, with greater collaboration between parties, was to be welcomed: Britain was moving towards an age of coalition. Indeed, in McCurdy's eyes it was almost a Christian duty to embrace co-operation as the basis of British politics; it would make explicit

33 Archibald Henry Macdonald Sinclair (1890–1970), 1st Viscount Thurso; Liberal MP for Caithness and Sutherland 1922–45; Liberal chief whip 1930–1, secretary of state for Scotland 1930–1, deputy leader of the Liberal Party 1931–5, leader of the Liberal Party 1935–45, secretary of state for air 1940–5; ennobled 1954.

34 C.A. McCurdy (1870–1941), Liberal MP for Northampton 1910–22; parliamentary secretary to the ministry of food control 1919–20, minister of food control 1920, Coalition Liberal chief whip 1921–2.

35 Morgan, 'Lloyd George's Stage Army', 234.

36 Parliamentary Archives, Lloyd George Papers, F/168/2/15, McCurdy to Lloyd George, 21 Apr. 1921.

37 See also C.A. McCurdy, 'Coalition, Caucus and Common Sense', *Fortnightly Review*, cix (Mar. 1921), 353–61.

the satisfactory working relationships between parties and politicians which were necessary for good government and progress. That being said, he understood that respect was essential for amicable working relations between parties. Guest's genial good humour had done much to offset Conservative concerns about the nature of the Coalition Liberal Party, but that was now wearing thin. The party would have to achieve genuine substance in organisation and performance to earn the grudging respect of those on the right of the Conservative Party. Given those views, McCurdy as chief whip for the Lloyd George Liberals would have played a significant role in framing the tasks facing the party and Scovell's job of assisting in its development.

Scovell's files demonstrate a steadily increasing workload (with a consequent increase in his salary during 1920–1 to £1,925) as he struggled to build the party.[38] This would, with McCurdy's views, have to be achieved without upsetting the good relations between the Conservative leadership and Lloyd George. In developing the party Scovell regarded himself as something of a talent scout sifting reports from local associations as to who might make a suitable candidate for a particular constituency at the next election. He was also keen to recruit competent agents and efficient staff for the offices of the Coalition Liberal Party at 25, Old Queen Street. A changing political context also made life difficult for him in his task of building up a Coalition Liberal Party. The downturn in the economy during 1920, the fight for Irish independence, public demands to reduce the tax burden, and a troubled international scene in which the threat of war was never far away, made for difficult politics. Those difficulties extended from the national level down to the constituencies, and by late 1921 Lloyd George was under no illusions that in Westminster many Conservatives wanted an end to the coalition. In the constituencies Conservatives appeared increasingly minded to ignore the spirit of the Coalition and to campaign against Coalition Liberals. Despite this, in late 1921 Austen Chamberlain, who had replaced Bonar Law as Conservative Party leader, tried to re-open the case for fusion or for other means whereby Conservatives and Coalition Liberals might once again go to the country together to secure a fresh mandate and to quell the rumblings in Conservative ranks.[39] The result was an even firmer rejection by the Conservative grass roots and much of the parliamentary party. Lloyd George's response was to talk about dissolution to threaten the Conservatives with the prospect of serious Labour gains. Chamberlain, aghast at Lloyd George's manoeuvrings, wrote to his sister Ida on 7 January to complain that 'Lloyd George put the fat in the fire with his talk of dissolution, so upsetting & perhaps permanently ruining my effort to join all that is reasonably progressive in the Unionist Party with what is sound & not too tied up in old party shibboleths in the Liberal Party'.[40]

38 LGA, Holt & Co. (Income Tax Department) to J. Robson, 14 July 1921.

39 Austen Chamberlain (1863–1937), Unionist MP East Worcestershire 1892–1914, West Birmingham 1914–37; postmaster-general 1902–3, chancellor of the exchequer 1903–5, 1919–21, secretary of state for India 1915–17, lord privy seal and leader of the House of Commons 1921–2, secretary of state for foreign affairs 1924–9, first lord of the Admiralty 1931.

40 Austen Chamberlain papers AC5/1/223, Austen Chamberlain to Ida Chamberlain, 7 Jan. 1922, reproduced in *The Austen Chamberlain Diary Letters: The Correspondence*

With clear warnings that the Coalition government might break up sooner rather than later in early 1922, Lloyd George decided to go further with the Coalition Liberal Party project. Following a meeting in London on 18 and 19 January it was agreed to set up a separate National Liberal Council, and within nine months around two hundred Coalition Liberal Constituency Associations had been built up with supporting regional councils. As Paul Adelman notes, the difficult task of building a party was supported by Lloyd George's private war chest established with the sale of honours, but the Coalition Liberal Party could not hope to rival parties rooted in decades of organic growth and history.[41] From the spring of 1922, as Scovell's files reveal, the new party was increasingly focussed on preparations to fight an election in the near future ostensibly as an independent party rather than as part of a coalition. In the meantime, Lloyd George played for time. In February he offered to step down as a deputation of 'diehards' visited Chamberlain to call for an end to the coalition. Chamberlain could see no reason to discard Lloyd George's services because a group of forty to fifty Conservative MPs were unhappy, especially because released from the coalition he might prove a devastatingly effective opponent.

The growing tensions between the Conservatives and Coalition Liberals further manifested themselves in growing difficulties for Scovell. During the summer his position came under increasing scrutiny from senior figures within his own party. While it is not possible to establish the cause with absolute certainty, a number of factors may have been involved. The Coalition Liberals were under severe pressure financially and politically, within the politics of Westminster with a hardening of opinion against Lloyd George on the Conservative backbenches, and in the form of poor showings in a series of by-elections.[42] Between 1918 and 1922 the Coalition Liberals contested twenty-five by-elections, losing nine (eight of them to Labour) and retaining the rest only thanks to Conservative support. Conservative 'diehards' pointed to the results and the anger at constituency level as local Conservative associations had to prop up Lloyd George's candidates. The string of losses exacerbated tensions in the coalition, inflaming the tide of 'diehardism' within the Conservative Party, and raising a range of difficult questions within the ranks of the Coalition Liberals. Those questions of grand strategy could be conveniently avoided by focussing on matters of party organisation.

The pressure of such scrutiny in turn generated an angry exchange between Scovell and the chief whip over the latter's expenditure in his Northampton constituency.[43] In the 1918 election the Labour candidate had received 10,735 votes (37.3% of the poll), and no doubt McCurdy reasoned that at a future election he might well lose, especially if the Conservatives fielded a candidate.[44] Scovell was

of Sir Austen Chamberlain with His Sisters Hilda and Ida, 1916–1937 (Camden Society, 5th series, v. 1995), 178.

41 Paul Adelman, *The Decline of the Liberal Party 1910–1931* (2nd edn. 1995), 32.

42 See, for example, document 63 below: 'Memorandum on Recent Bye-Elections and the Inferences to be Drawn from the Results' [undated but Apr. 1922].

43 LGA, Scovell to MacCurdy, 15 May 1922.

44 *Dictionary of Labour Biography, Vol. XI*, ed. Keith Gildart, David Howell and Neville Kirk (Basingstoke, 2003), 94.

less than diplomatic in his condemnation of 'the lavish all-in expenditure' which was the subject of considerable conversation within Liberal ranks 'far beyond the Midlands'.[45] He suggested that there was considerable resentment in other constituencies with activists questioning whether their fund-raising efforts were helping to support such profligacy by the Northampton constituency. McCurdy's response is unknown, but in July a committee was set up consisting of Sir Alfred Mond (minister of health),[46] Thomas Macnamara (minister of labour),[47]and Frederick Kellaway (postmaster general),[48] to examine the way that the Liberal organisation was functioning. On 31 July Scovell offered to resign should there be any question about his ability to 'steer the ship'.[49] The situation was somewhat altered that same day when details of the formation of the committee were published in the *Leicester Mercury*.[50] The news report suggested that there was dissatisfaction within the party at a perceived lack of progress in developing the organisation, and concern at growing friction between Conservatives and Coalition Liberals at the constituency level. Acutely aware that with matters out in the open a voluntary departure would be interpreted as acceptance of inadequacies on his part, Scovell retracted his resignation offer, arguing that he was not ready to accept blame for matters over which he was 'no more responsible than the office cat'.[51] The situation was less than ideal. With the Coalition Liberal Party gearing up for a probable election, to have the central office of the party convulsed by recrimination and intrigue was a less than auspicious way to prepare.

In fact, Scovell need not have worried. At some point over the summer (the relevant letter in the Lloyd George papers in the Parliamentary Archive is undated), Mond wrote to Lloyd George with the findings of the inquiry. Scovell was praised in the highest terms for his intelligence, energy and grasp of his work.[52] Since Scovell was better than anyone else in the office, Mond's letter advised that there should be no consideration of replacing him unless a substantially superior candidate was to be found. Instead, Mond suggested that the real difficulties lay with McCurdy, and advised that he be replaced as chief whip. Lloyd George's reaction to the findings is unclear, yet both McCurdy and Scovell remained in their posts. In all likelihood

45 LGA, Scovell to McCurdy, 15 May 1922.

46 Alfred Mond (1868–1930), 1st baron Melchett of Landford; Liberal MP Chester 1906–10, Swansea 1910–18, Swansea West 1918–23; MP for Carmarthen 1924–8, switching from the Liberals to the Conservatives in 1926; minister of health 1921–2; ennobled 1928.

47 Thomas Macnamara (1861–1931), Liberal MP Camberwell North 1900–18, Camberwell North West 1918–24; minister of labour 1920–2.

48 Frederick Kellaway (1870–1933), Liberal MP Bedford 1910–22; parliamentary secretary to the ministry of munitions 1916–20, secretary for overseas trade 1920–1, postmaster general 1921–2.

49 LGA, Scovell to McCurdy, 31 July 1922.

50 Cutting from the *Leicester Mercury*, 31 July 1922, forwarded by the Coalition Liberal office (Leicester) and enclosed in LGA, Scovell to McCurdy, 1 Aug. 1922.

51 LGA, Scovell to McCurdy, 1 Aug. 1922.

52 Parliamentary Archives, Lloyd George papers, LG/F/37/2/15, Sir Alfred Mond to Lloyd George, undated but summer 1922.

the internal office politics of the whip's department was overtaken by international politics and a resultant crisis in the politics of the Coalition government which would lead to Lloyd George's downfall in October. By September the coalition was deep in difficulties, with Scovell gearing the party towards a general election, as Lloyd George's near-eastern policy finally collapsed, leading to the prospect of war between Britain and a resurgent Turkey. In the midst of the crisis, with the cabinet prepared for war, more junior figures within the Conservative Party suspected that Lloyd George was about to use the renewal of conflict to stage another coupon election. The unexpected victory of an independent Conservative candidate in the Newport by-election on 18 October (a win over the Coalition Liberals) was sufficient to influence a meeting of Conservative MPs at the Carlton Club the following day. The meeting voted against the advice of the leader of the Conservative Party, Austen Chamberlain, and for a dissolution of the Coalition. Accepting the situation, Lloyd George went to the palace to offer his resignation, and on 25 October Bonar Law moved into Downing Street as leader of the Conservative Party and prime minister with an election immediately in prospect. This general election, which would be the acid test for the party which Scovell had done so much to build up, was now upon them; it was an election which would define the fortunes of the parties and establish many features of twentieth-century British elections.

Problems at Coalition Liberal Headquarters: A Move Against Scovell

Widespread unease at the potential fortunes of the Coalition Liberals in the lead up to the general election led to growing distrust of McCurdy and Scovell as the principal figures controlling the Coalition Liberal Party. This saw throughout the election the presence at the offices at 25, Old Queen Street of Alfred Cope, a career civil servant who had served in the ministry of pensions from 1919 to 1920,[53] and from then until 1922 had been under-secretary and clerk to the privy council of Ireland, in which capacity he played a significant role in negotiating the Anglo-Irish settlement with the leaders of Sinn Fein. Such brief career details conceal the fact that Cope was a close friend of senior Liberal politicians such as Alfred Mond, and a protégé of Lloyd George. From the contemporary diary of Thomas Jones, assistant secretary to the cabinet,[54] Cope emerges as a critical and shady figure acting as a go-between and messenger from the British government to Sinn Fein, as Lloyd George struggled to reach an accommodation with Irish nationalism.[55] It was Lloyd George who had sent him to Ireland in 1920 to open relations with Sinn Fein. In order to do this, it appears that Cope secured the dismissal of anti-Sinn Fein civil servants,[56] and also, it appears, revealed sensitive information to Sinn Fein leaders

53 Sir Alfred William Cope (1877–1954).

54 Thomas Jones (1870–1955), senior British civil servant, deputy secretary to the cabinet 1916–35.

55 See, for example, Thomas Jones, Diary 24 June, 13–17 Aug., 30 Oct., 12 Nov. 1921, in *Thomas Jones: Whitehall Diary*, vol. 3, ed. Keith Middlemas (1971), 79–81, 98–101, 150–1, 162–3.

56 *Ibid.*, 25, n. 2.

in order to build their trust.[57] On 23 October in London, as Lloyd George presided over the ruins of his administration, setting the date for an election on 18 November, a cabal of officials pressed him to replace Scovell with Cope as general secretary to the Coalition Liberal Party. Jones noted in his diary that part way through an extended meeting starting at 12.40 p.m. that day, 'Grigg and I tackled him [Lloyd George] on the importance of securing Cope to run his party machine at Queen Street. I said that Curtis,[58] Grigg,[59] and I were unanimous in our opinion of Cope's great powers of push and go'. Again, this seems remarkably bad timing in view of the election that was now upon them, and in view of Mond's earlier endorsement of Scovell as head of the office as a diligent, vigorous and efficient administrator and organiser. Even if Cope looked likely to be a significant improvement on Scovell as head of the office, making such a change at such a time reflected poor judgement; the potential learning curve for an incoming general secretary, sitting at the heart of a party network of national, regional and constituency connections was considerable to say the least. Lloyd George's response to the proposal to swap Scovell for Cope was therefore surprising: 'Very well', he said, 'I am for it. Tell J.T. Davies to tell McCurdy'.[60] The prime minister's decision was modified, probably as a result of protest from McCurdy that, on contractual grounds alone, Scovell could not be simply replaced at the drop of a hat. McCurdy also probably objected on the grounds that to dismiss the man who had played such a leading role in building up the Coalition Liberal Organisation, in the midst of the campaign, would inflict a blow to the morale of party workers and threaten chaos as Cope could struggle to come to terms with his new role and have trouble building good working relationships with key staff and candidates. Scovell would remain in his job with Cope effectively shadowing him. Perhaps in compensation to Cope for the failure immediately to secure the post of general secretary, he received a knighthood in the dissolution honours list.

The move against Scovell was not well received in the Coalition Liberal Organisation and the parliamentary party. Lloyd George's judgement was clearly open to question whatever the personal merits of Cope. The inquiry by Mond and others had established that Scovell was doing an acceptable job, and the timing could not have been worse. The episode does raise questions about Lloyd George's political sense in late 1921 through to late 1922: he had failed to manage both the growing restlessness amongst the ranks of Coalition Conservatives and the political crisis arising out of the Chanak Affair; now he was willing to endorse a cabal seeking personal advancement of a crony/fixer, to the detriment of the party that had been built to support the political futures of the parliamentary Coalition Liberals. Jones's

57 Geoffrey Sloan, 'Hide Seek and Negotiate: Alfred Cope and Counter Intelligence in Ireland 1919–1921', *Intelligence and National Security*, xxxiii (2018), 176–95.

58 Lionel Curtis (1872–1955), author, secretary to the Irish conference, colonial office advisor on Irish affairs.

59 Edward Grigg (1875–1955), 2nd baron Altrincham; journalist, private secretary to Lloyd George 1921–2, Liberal MP Oldham 1922–3, Conservative MP Altrincham 1933–45; ennobled 1945.

60 Thomas Jones, Diary 23 Oct. 1922, *Whitehall Diary*, vol. 1, ed. Keith Middlemas (1969), 217.

diary entry for 23 October 1922 paints a portrait of a prime minister, who had been in post since December 1916, behaving like he was tired and fully resigned to the situation – making jokes, reflecting on the past and potentially taking some unwise decisions at a moment of weakness.[61] Perhaps, though, Jones's impression was that Lloyd George's jollity was a sign not of tiredness but an expression of his certainty that the Conservatives could not gain a majority in their own right and that, sooner rather than later, they would be forced to make some new arrangement with the Coalition Liberal Party.

Either way the writing was nevertheless on the wall for Scovell, and the election was a stay of execution rather than a permanent reprieve. Remarkably, in the middle of the campaign the former chief whip Freddie Guest wrote to Scovell in a letter marked 'secret' to encourage him to contest one of the still available seats for the Lloyd George Liberals. Guest made his suspicions very clear: 'They mean to get rid of you'. Scovell circled the phrase in pencil. The approach had seemingly been agreed with Lloyd George:

> I am in a position to inform you that if you were, say tomorrow morning, to inform the Chief that it was your desire to jump at an opportunity of such a character and to name the place and at the same time assure him that the machine would function in spite of your absence, the request would receive immediate approval.[62]

Scovell was seemingly unwilling to quit his post in the middle of the general election, but he did heed Guest's warning, writing to McCurdy three days later to say that he would be standing down after the conclusion of the campaign.[63] As a backdrop to fighting an election this was not exactly a positive development.

The 1922 General Election Result and the Resignation of Scovell

The election results, when they came in on 15 and 16 November 1922, made grim reading for many in the ranks of the Lloyd George Liberals. Former ministers, leading lights in the party, such as Winston Churchill[64] in Dundee and Freddie Guest in Yeovil, lost their seats in a string of shocks. For historians and biographers, Lloyd George's behaviour in the election was marked by a distinct lack of vigour, suggesting either tiredness after years in government or that he was struggling to come to terms with loss of office and the transformed political realities

61 *Ibid.*, 23 Oct. 1922, pp. 216–17.

62 LGA, Guest to Scovell, 27 Oct. 1922.

63 LGA, Scovell to J.T. Davies, 30 Oct. 1922, enclosed in Scovell to McCurdy, 30 Oct. 1922. See also McCurdy to Scovell, 30 Oct. 1922.

64 Winston Churchill (1874–1965), Liberal MP for Oldham 1900–6, Manchester North West 1906–8, Dundee 1908–22, Conservative MP for Epping 1924–45, Woodford 1945–64; president of the board of trade 1908–10, home secretary 1910–11, first lord of the Admiralty 1911–15, chancellor of the duchy of Lancaster 1915, minister of munitions 1917–19, secretary of state for war 1919–21, secretary of state for air 1919–21, secretary of state for the colonies 1921–2, chancellor of the exchequer 1924–9, minister of defence 1940–5, 1951–2, prime minister 1940–5, leader of the opposition 1945–51, prime minister 1951–5.

of post-war Britain.[65] While the somewhat confused application of the coalition coupon in 1918, some local peculiarities of party label and a string of by-election losses for the Coalition Liberals during the 1919–22 parliament generate substantial issues when it comes to a truly precise accounting of the fortunes of that party in the 1922 general election vis-à-vis the 1918 contest, the general sense of it has been neatly summed up by Chris Cook and John Stevenson:

> In 1918, 138 Coalition Liberals had been returned. Only 60 survived the 1922 election. No fewer than 81 seats were lost, 21 of which had even lacked defenders. Whilst 57 seats were retained, only three new seats were won ... Only in its stronghold of rural North Wales was Coalition Liberalism able to survive unaided against Conservative and Labour attacks. The net result of 1922, as far as the Coalition Liberals were concerned was a disaster.[66]

The scale of that 'disaster', however, needs to be set against the positions of the parties in 1922 and the actual strategy Lloyd George pursued in that election.

There was simply never any prospect of the Coalition Liberal Party forming a government on its own, and this had never been Lloyd George's intention. The best that could be hoped for was that the Coalition Liberals would emerge as the junior partners in some new arrangement with another party under a new prime minister. A return to coalition government after the election seemed unlikely, at least in the minds of those whose opposition to Lloyd George had helped to pull it down, but it was a rather different case in the minds of the pro-coalition Conservatives. Bonar Law was not about to close the door to the possibility, and in any case, there were plenty of other 'arrangements', including a supply and confidence agreement, which could leave Lloyd George holding the balance of power in a House of Commons in which there were four potential parties of government. Coalition was detested by some within the Conservative Party, but it was only a minority that considered that the party, which had not won an election on its own since 1902, would be able to win a majority in the House of Commons in November 1922. Once the dust of Lloyd George's downfall had settled (and the outcome of the Carlton Club meeting came as a shock to many within the Conservative Party), stopping socialism from getting its hands on government was an even bigger priority than stopping Lloyd George. For both Lloyd George Liberals and for many Conservatives, an election to clear the air, and some new arrangement with Andrew Bonar Law as prime minister, seemed to be the most likely scenario for British politics following the end of the Coalition. Lloyd George knew that there would be a retreat in the fortunes of the Coalition Liberals from the artificial high-water mark of 1918, but he hoped that a defensive strategy would produce sufficient numbers of MPs to secure the arrangement with the Conservative Party. Some fifty to seventy seats looked likely to leave him holding the balance of power and ready to appeal to his old Conservative friends for co-operation in the interest of 'stopping socialism'. The outcome of the Carlton Club meeting could not erase lingering wartime sentiments in favour of cross-party working in the interest of

65 Michael Kinnear, *The Fall of Lloyd George: The Political Crisis of 1922* (1973), 155–6.
66 Cook and Stevenson, *A History of British Elections*, 127.

meeting a national threat, especially when that threat, be it the Kaiser's Germany, or Bolshevik Russian socialism, could be characterised as 'foreign'.

What successes the Coalition Liberals did have in the election were underpinned in many cases by the existence of anti-socialist pacts at the local and regional levels. Scottish and Lancashire Conservatives officially declared against any disruption to the local agreements which might let Labour in. Given the circumstances of an election in which Bonar Law, as Conservative leader, privately remained open to the possibility of post-poll co-operation, while in public denying any possibility of 'coalition', the perception that the Coalition Liberals might be prepared to unleash a slate of candidates helped to underpin these local truces and pacts. Conservative Central Office took refuge behind a public declaration supporting local parties in whatever local arrangements they might prefer, rather than risk a kind of mutually assured destruction between the two former partners in the coalition government.[67] Scovell had seemingly done a good enough job of building up the party for the threat of a larger number of Coalition Liberal candidates to be believed in Conservative Central Office. As evidenced by the Scovell papers, the diligent work done in constituencies suggests that there was some substance to the threat. It was not until the close of nominations on 4 November, and in spite of the actions of some diehard Conservatives, that the leaderships of both the Conservative and Coalition Liberal parties could be certain that their pantomime cold war, in which references to each other were largely mildly positive, would not turn hot. The number of Conservative versus Coalition Liberal contests was kept to a minimum. Securing fifty to seventy seats was Scovell's target, and that is what was delivered on election day; his predictions of the likely number of seats which the Coalition Liberals could win was borne out by the results. What went wrong for Lloyd George then, and what turned a defensive strategy into the deliverer of defeat, was the unexpectedly strong showing of the Conservatives, who were able to form a majority government with 344 seats in a House of Commons of 615 members, thereby shutting him out. In seats where Labour was the principal rival to sitting Coalition Liberal MPs the socialist threat proved unstoppable as the Labour Party began its process of breaking through to become the challenger to the Conservatives. For Lloyd George there would be no balance of power to hold, and the result was a major blow to the Coalition Liberal Party.

Lloyd George's strategy in the 1922 general election and Scovell's role in it can be evidenced by the apparent contradiction of the general secretary's satisfaction with its outcome. He and the party machine had delivered what they had been asked to achieve. On 23 November 1922 he wrote:

> Considering all things, I think we have done very well … I am not a complacent person, but I have heard nobody, except the ignorant and uninformed, animadvert in any way on the result. After all, we were without a policy, without a real and definite leader, we were limited in the scope of our organisation, and the real truth is that the country wanted a change.[68]

67 *Western Daily Press*, 28 Oct. 1922, p. 12.

68 LGA, Scovell to Gunn, 23 Nov. 1922.

The conditions under which he had been asked to work, and the sense of personal sleight that came with some of the shenanigans from the leadership, meant that Scovell was keen to walk away from Coalition Liberal headquarters as soon as the results were in. The day after the poll on 15 November he wrote to McCurdy to ask to be released since the election was over and the situation with Cope in the same office was 'absolutely impossible'.[69] He was released with effect from 1 December but did not depart quietly, writing to Lloyd George's secretary on 16 November to state that he was leaving because of the 'perpetual intrigues' against the Coalition Liberal organisation, the setting up of a secret inquiry and 'the complete lack of courtesy and tact displayed by the sudden foisting on the organisation of a totally unqualified stranger in the middle of the Election without warning, consultation or discussion or (as far as I know) rhyme or reason'.[70] Scovell's resignation brought forth a torrent of letters from Coalition Liberals he had worked with across the country, the tone of which suggests genuine concern at his departure.[71]

During the early part of 1923 Scovell watched from a distance the steady reduction of the Coalition Liberal organisation and the staff of 25, Old Queen Street by Cope (appointed secretary to the National Liberal Organisation with Scovell's departure).[72] He wrote on 25 February: 'I have now heard the news and nothing surprises me'.[73] He did, however, remain in contact with many of those with whom he had previously worked and showed concern as to their future employment, writing testimonials and recommendations in support of their job-seeking activities.[74] Indeed, on 14 February he had received a letter from Cope indicating that he was 'engaged on a general reduction of staff' and asking for his help with regard to finding employment for one of the female employees.[75] Scovell in return wrote to Cope urging him to increase the pay of one of the remaining members of staff to ensure that his knowledge and experience were not lost from the organisation.[76] With the retrenchment extending to the payments from the Lloyd George fund to some of the poorer Liberal MPs, Scovell was also ready to intervene with Cope to urge continuing financial support for some of them.[77]

Despite his disappointments, Scovell remained a committed Liberal and a Lloyd George loyalist, and at the 1923 general election he contested the Broxtowe seat for the recently re-united Liberals. With a Labour majority of just 317 votes more than the Liberal candidate obtained at the 1922 general election, in 1923 Broxtowe was regarded as a very winnable seat for the Liberals, but in the event Scovell came second as the national swing to the Liberals (0.9%) was eclipsed by a swing to

69 LGA, Scovell to McCurdy, 16 Nov. 1922.
70 LGA, Scovell to Stevenson, 15 Nov. 1922. See also, Stevenson to Scovell, 29 Nov. 1922.
71 See, for example, LGA, J.R. Want (honorary secretary London committee of National Liberal agents) to Scovell, 6 Feb. 1923.
72 Cope held the post until 1924, later going into the coal industry in South Wales.
73 LGA, Scovell to Grant, 15 Feb. 1923.
74 LGA, Dimbleby to Scovell, 13 Apr. 1923. See also Scovell to Brook's (St James), 27 Feb. 1923.
75 LGA, Cope to Scovell, 14 Feb. 1923.
76 LGA, Scovell to Cope, 23 Mar. 1923.
77 LGA, Scovell to Cope, 30 Jan. 1923.

Labour of 1%.[78] With his political ambitions ended, he travelled to South Africa to pursue a career in business (goldmining and related industries) where he became chairman of the Swaziland and General Gold Mining Company and several other mining firms, and he seems to have spent much of the 1920s travelling widely across the length and breadth of Africa in connection with his business projects. Yet by the mid-1930s, perhaps because of his health, Scovell could be found back in London, politically energised by the increasing threat of Nazi Germany. He used his existing political and military networks in support of national rearmament, with his correspondents including Churchill, the wife of Lord Halifax, the military thinker J. F. C. Fuller, historians, defence correspondents of major newspapers and old friends in the military including Ludlow Hewitt (who rose to the rank of Air Chief Marshall in 1937) and Lord Trenchard (the father of the Royal Air Force). Scovell networked extensively to express his concerns and those of others who agreed with him about the growing danger. And given his First World War service and political connections, he had some influence, including the ability to have old parliamentary friends ask questions in the House of Commons.

Scovell also seems to have devoured books, journal articles and newspaper reports to enable him to write with authority on the widest range of military matters. There is some evidence that this was in part driven by increasing physical incapacity, perhaps as a result of complications arising from his hunting accident in 1919. He became a mine of information and ideas, many of which in 1938 and 1939 were increasingly prescient, and with the outbreak of war his productivity as an ideas man and a networker increased to new levels; he was happy to supply his friends in parliament with a steady stream of letters, papers and press clippings. During the emergency caused by the fall of France in 1940 Scovell went into overdrive, making very solid suggestions on a range of issues from rebuilding the army to long-term reconstruction. On issue after issue, he was ready to comment: from the means to construct emergency runways and the obsolescence of the bolt action rifle, to the need to develop technologies to enable a cross-Channel invasion. Clement Attlee (deputy prime minister from 1942) and Brendan Bracken (Churchill's principal private secretary) routinely corresponded with him, although his productivity tailed off as the war situation stabilised and as peace approached. In 1945, as his thoughts turned to the development of the British Empire after the war, he published a pamphlet, *The Social and Economic Development of the British Colonies*, before dying at Port Elizabeth three years later.

After the First World War, Scovell, who had never married, lived a rather solitary life beyond his horses and a Norwegian elkhound named Thor, not to mention the sharing of a house in London from 1919 to 1922 with Ludlow Hewitt, a Royal Air Force officer.[79] Although he was a regular visitor to his physi-

78 Broxtowe 1923: George Spender (Labour), 13,219 votes (54.5%); George Scovell (Liberal) 11,049 votes (45.5%): Labour majority 2,170.

79 Edgar Ludlow-Hewitt (1886–1973), commissioned Royal Irish Rifles 1905, served with the Royal Flying Corps, and then the Royal Air Force (promoted air chief marshal 1937) until 1945.

cally infirm father living in retirement on the Sussex coast at Brighton until his death in 1923, he does not appear to have kept in frequent contact with his two surviving sisters.[80] Scovell may have had little in the way of family, but he did have a wide circle of friends. In a short obituary, Lord Trenchard[81] described him as 'always full of energy, always ready to help and take on difficult tasks which wanted doing, and he was a friend to many'.[82]

Conclusion

The short-lived political career of Colonel Scovell, the party which he served as general secretary and the archive which he left to posterity, provide us with a fascinating insight into modern British politics at a key point in its emergence. The 1922 general election was in some senses the first 'modern' British election and saw the Labour Party emerge as a potential party of government. The Conservative Party, meanwhile, won its first general election since 1900 and would go on to dominate British politics during the mid to late twentieth century. The divided forces of British Liberalism were reduced to a disappointed third force and this set the tone for the next hundred years. Just as much as it marked a beginning, the 1922 general election also marked the beginning of an end of the politics of the pre-democratic age as the ramifications of the 1918 Representation of the People Act and the wider repercussions of the First World War created an expanded electorate with a fresh set of concerns, calling for new approaches to politics and perhaps realigned political parties. Lloyd George firmly believed that anti-socialism versus socialism would be the future axis upon which British politics would turn, and in a sense the Coalition Liberal Party was a milestone on the road to a new progressive party in which Conservatism and Liberalism would be fused. For Lloyd George the Coalition Liberal Party as it developed after 1919 was the collateral element that he required to secure a centre right party between his adherents and the Conservatives, or to provide the means to reunify and reinvigorate the Liberal Party. The Coalition Liberal Party was a power base to secure his future in the short term, which could be negotiated away in some fresh arrangement, and the Scovell papers show this political strategy in operation. The party was, however, more than just a stage army lacking substance and ethos. For the generation that had gone through the First World War, including Scovell, 'co-operation', 'cross-party' working in the interests of nation and not of party, really meant something: a means of keeping faith with those who had not returned from the war in the interests of a better Britain. In addition, Lloyd George, like many within his own party and the Conservatives, was obsessed with the threat from radical

80 LGA, Scovell to Major Duncan Campbell, 2 Sept. 1920.

81 Hugh Montague Trenchard (1873–1956), entered the British Army 1893, head of the Royal Flying Corps 1915–18, chief of the air staff 1918, chief of staff of the Royal Air Force 1919, retired from military service 1929; commissioner of the Metropolitan Police Force 1931–5, chairman of the United Africa Company 1936–53; ennobled as Viscount Trenchard of Wolfeton 1936.

82 *The Times*, 5 May 1948, p. 7.

Labour ranging from unions to the revolutionary zealots of the Communist Party of Great Britain. Their revolution, their advance to socialism, could bring chaos, unrest, bloodshed and even civil war.

Lloyd George believed in his principles to the point that he took for granted the willingness of the rank and file of the Conservative Party to fall into line behind their party leadership and acquiesce in the emergence of a new party. It was only with some reluctance that he accepted the need to develop the Coalition Liberal Party to create a power base to provide constituency-level support to his Liberal adherents in Westminster in furtherance of the idea of fusion, and as a political insurance in case the ebb and flow of political change left him beached. To Lloyd George the party was a means to a movable end: an end that shifted and developed between 1920 and 1923. In 1922, and despite the efforts of Scovell and others to build the party, the 'stage army' was partially stood down in the interests of maintaining a truce with the Conservatives in the hope of continued coalition. In 1923 it was dissolved in the interest of Liberal re-union.

While Lloyd George's approach to the party was marked by extreme expediency, some Liberals genuinely believed in the Coalition Liberal project and a progressive, anti-socialist alliance as a means to extend the patriotic co-operation that had secured victory in the First World War. That same spirit could be glimpsed in some of the local deals struck at the time of the 1922 general election. Lloyd George's adherents were not simply careerists clinging to his coat-tails, and many Conservatives saw no good reason to overthrow good candidates in the aftermath of a war of shared national sacrifice and pooled resources in the interests of the nation. The Coalition Liberal Party was not brought and bought into creation by Lloyd George alone, no matter what the machinations of the 'Welsh Wizard' were, or the sums in his war chest from the sale of honours. The party needed activists, committed believers to carry out the basic organisational work at the constituency level. Scovell's papers point towards that activism and to a party that was developing at some pace from hesitant beginnings. To emerge from the fractured remains of the Liberal Party, and to be able to contest the 1922 general election and secure the return of over fifty members of parliament, was a remarkable achievement.

Whether the Coalition Liberals in 1922 would have done as well without the existence of local party pacts with the Conservative Party is open to question. Without those pacts the Coalition Liberal Party would have returned fewer members, but that was probably also true not only of the Conservative Party but also of the Asquithian Liberals. As Michael Kinnear identified, in 1922 'over 200 Liberal and Conservative candidates ran under the aegis of two or more parties', including 'prefixless Liberals', 'Constitutionalists', 'Conservatives with Liberal support' and 'Liberals with Conservative support'.[83] In the circumstances of 1922, and considering the strong possibilities of some form of renewed coalition or arrangement, some of these labels and local arrangements were vital to preventing a wider Labour breakthrough, but they also amounted to a hedging of bets by some candidates, just as the creation of the Coalition Liberal Party was an

83 Kinnear, *The Fall of Lloyd George*, 243.

insurance policy to safeguard Lloyd George's ambitions. In 1922 many had no wish to alienate sections of the electorate that might be persuaded to vote for them, and they had no wish potentially to exclude themselves from a role in whatever government might emerge from the election. So widespread were the local arrangements, and so loose were the party labels, that it really is difficult to think, except in the very broadest terms, of the 1922 contest as constituting a truly general election, carried out by truly national parties with centrally directed campaigns. Resolving the political landscape from the confusing mass of local arrangements and flag of convenience labels for many candidates took time after the election as members of parliament declared their allegiances by accepting party whips.

To some extent historians have failed to resolve the complexities of the election and that has fed through into its historical understandings. As the author of one work commented, 'The election results, devastating for the Liberals, speak for themselves'.[84] Scovell and others were pleased at the Coalition Liberal returns, but in the longer term the holding action of 1922 failed to deliver to Lloyd George the balance of power and appeared in retrospect to be a key milestone on the road to Liberal irrelevance. A seemingly confused election has resulted in a somewhat confused historiography, but with the Scovell papers we can go beyond the surface of explanations that the 1922 general election, and with it the cause of Coalition Liberalism, was 'a curious affair'. We can see that Lloyd George was much more than 'the ghost at the feast' after the Carlton Club meeting.[85] He was playing a high-stakes game that he expected to win with the Coalition Liberal Party being part of his collateral. From the Scovell papers we can glimpse the genuine substance of a party that was strong enough in 1922 that deals could be struck at the local and, de facto, at the national level to contain conflicts between Coalition Liberals and Conservatives. It was a party that had been built up with painstaking spadework by Scovell, McCurdy and others. The Coalition Liberal Party may have looked like a stage army in 1922, but it left the ex-prime minister waiting in the wings with what he firmly believed was going to be a surprise encore as the power broker in the new parliament. Bonar Law's surprise victory robbed Lloyd George of the dramatic re-entrance at the head of his Coalition movement that he so desperately craved and for which so many had worked so hard to achieve from 1920 to 1922. The Scovell papers give us insight into one of the most confused and confusing episodes of modern British political history.

84 Rosemary Rees, *Britain, 1890–1939* (2003), 121.
85 David Powell, *British Politics, 1910–35* (2004), 118–19.

Coalition Liberal Party Documents 1919–23[1]

1. *Memorandum in the Chief Whip's Office, 'The Social Democrats' [undated but circa 1919–20]*

During the last quarter of a century, Socialists in this country have been divided into three organisations:

The Social Democratic Federation,

The Independent Labour Party,

The Fabian Society.

The first-named has changed its name more than once. It started as the "Democratic Federation", which was formed by a number of Radical Clubs in London. In 1883, it declared for Socialism and altered its title to "Social Democratic Federation".[2] After twenty-eight years of activity, the S.D.F. took in some minor organisations and adopted the name "British Socialist Party". As it happened that a majority of the members of this B.S.P. declared at the annual Easter Conference, 1916, for a kind of internationalism that appeared unpatriotic to a minority, this minority broke off and became the "National Socialist Party". The original Social Democrats are now, therefore, subdivided into the B.S.P. (anti-war) and the N.S.P. (patriotic).

1 Unless otherwise stated the following documents are in the Lloyd George Archive.

2 The S.D.F. put forward a progressive programme of limiting the length of the working week, abolishing child labour, supporting measures of gender equality and championing the principle of secular education. Its early history was riven by faction and its involvement with public protests leading to disorder damaged its potential appeal, causing others to explore new opportunities to engage with the working classes and potential voters. Significantly, the S.D.F. identified the Liberal Party as a potent check to the progress of the left wing of British politics as it sought to ameliorate the worst features of the socio-economic status quo.

Official Organ.

In January 1884 the S.D.F. established an official weekly organ, *Justice*. This weekly has had the longest life of any Socialist periodical in the United Kingdom. For the greater part of its career of 35 years it was edited by Harry Quelch,[3] a working man who succeeded in educating himself until he could read more than one foreign language and had a fair understanding of economics. After his death several years ago, H.W. Lee[4] (secretary for a long period) became editor and is the editor to-day. *Justice* is printed by a company formed for the purpose. This company passed through financial crises and was re-organised in 1918 as the Twentieth Century Press (1912) Limited. Its address is 39a, Clerkenwell Green, E.C.1., and 160, Fleet Street, E.C.4. The paper appears on Thursdays; the price was 1d. but is now 2d. The chief writers for the paper are H.M. Hyndman,[5] H.W. Lee, E. Belfort Bax,[6] A.S. Headingley,[7] F.J. Gould,[8] and Mrs. Hyndman (Rose Travers Hyndman).[9] Headingley's real name is Adolphe Smith; his people came from Headingley, near Leeds, and he is an authority on questions of public health. When the secession took place in 1916, the patriotic minority managed to retain *Justice*, presumably because a majority of the shareholders in the printing company belonged to the patriotic section.

Mr. Hyndman.

Mr. Hyndman has been the recognised leader of the Social Democrats since the early eighties. He is now seventy-seven years old. His political views and tactics have been throughout of a violently aggressive type, and he told the present writer with gusto that when he asked a friend whether he regarded him as conceited the friend replied: "I should rather have said arrogant". This bullying temperament was mainly responsible for the formation of the Independent Labour Party in 1893. Keir Hardie and a number of others, largely Scotsmen, resented the dictatorial methods of Hyndman, and they attracted to themselves certain Socialists of the "brotherly" type, including some persons (High Church and others), who were repelled by the revolutionary spirit of the Hyndmanites. It is also the fact that Hyndman's preaching of the class war idea caused Socialists of the University type to form the Fabian Society in the early eighties.

It is interesting to recall that Hyndman played in the Sussex County Eleven[10] more than forty years ago, was a war correspondent for the *Pall Mall Gazette* in

3 Harry Quelch (1858–1913), Marxist, journalist and trade unionist.

4 Henry W. Lee (1865–1932), socialist and journalist.

5 Henry Mayers Hyndman (1842–1921), English writer and socialist (initially a Conservative) who played a leading role in popularising the works of Karl Marx.

6 Ernest Belfort Bax (1854–1926), barrister, journalist, advocate and historian.

7 Adolphe Smith Headingley (1846–1924), left-wing writer.

8 Frederick James Gould (1855–1938), teacher and secular humanist.

9 Rosalind Travers (1875–1923), married Henry Hyndman in 1914.

10 Hyndman's first-class career was confined to 13 matches (20 innings) in 1864–5, with a batting average of 16.26 and a top score of 62.

the Italian campaigns of 1866, and wrote the first English books on Socialism (of the modern variety) in 1881 – "England for All".[11] During the war he served on the Food Consumers' Council. He has been a constant contributor to the *Morning Post* on foreign questions, and in Gladstonian days was pro-Turk and anti-Russian, which gave him a status with *The Times* and the Conservative Press generally. He is remarkably well informed and was formerly a great diner-out (Lady St. Helier's, etc.) He knows Clemenceau and has written a book about him.[12] Hyndman's platform ability is very considerable; at times he approaches the orator, but he lacks judgment, and his fulminations though greeted with uproarious applause, read like fustian when printed. He is well equipped with facts about company promoting, American trusts, and financial scallywags. He has done a large amount of company promoting himself. Hyndman's father gave £150,000 to build churches in the East End, but he himself has been in financial difficulties – popularly attributed to his sacrifice for the people, but really due to the failure of some of the financial schemes with which he was connected.

Other Members of the Party.

Of the other Social Democrats, the most important are Lt. Col. Will Thorne, MP,[13] Dan Irving, MP,[14] and Ernest Belfort Bax and the Countess of Warwick.[15] Thorne has been in the House of Commons thirteen years. He was a latherer at a barbers' at six years of age. Since 1889, he has been paid secretary of the Gas Works Union (now called the National Union of General Workers). He is somewhat illiterate for a secretary. His popularity in this constituency (West Ham) has always been pronounced; he was Mayor of West Ham over two years ago. Irving only won a seat last December, but has been several times a Parliamentary candidate. Bax is a man of means. His books on Socialism are numerous and of an uncompromising type.

The B.S.P.

The patriotic B.S.P. has been dealt with first, because, although it is a sectionist minority, it is likely to count for more than the other section as long as it possesses Parliamentary representatives and the old-established *Justice* to say nothing of Hyndman's personal prestige. But the British Socialist Party occupies the old home of the Social Democratic Federation, Chandos Hall, 21 Maiden Lane, Strand, W.C. Its official organ is the Call (a new publication). The secretary of the B.S.P. is Albert Inkpin.[16]

11 H.M. Hyndman, *England for All* (1881).

12 H.M. Hyndman, *Clemenceau, the Man and His Time* (New York, 1919).

13 Will Thorne (1857–1946), Labour MP for West Ham South 1906–18 and Plaistow 1918–45.

14 David Daniel Irving (1854–1924), Labour MP for Burnley 1918–24.

15 Frances Evelyn Greville (1861–1938), countess of Warwick; British socialite.

16 Albert Inkpin (1884–1944), first general secretary of the Communist Party of Great Britain 1920–9.

Political Programme

The old S.D.F. had as its object the establishment of the collective ownership of the means of production, distribution and exchange. All these things were to be controlled by a democratic State. Labour was to be set free from the domination of capitalists and landlords. The programme included the election of all administrators by direct adult suffrage, the abolition of a standing army, and the establishment of a national citizen force. The administration of justice was to be free to all. Apart from its ultimate objects, the S.D.F. advocated a number of "palliatives" (to be adopted during the continuance of the present industrial system), such as the eight hours' day, state railways, the extension of post office banks to absorb all private banks, nationalisation of the land, and the abolition of the monarchy. With certain modifications and extensions that programme may be said to have continued to the present time. The secession of 1916 has made an important change in the emphasis placed on some of these proposals.

Attitude to Bolshevism

The B.S.P. is frankly sympathetic to Lenin and the N.S.P. is determinedly anti-Bolshevik. It is a little difficult to explain the antipathy of the N.S.P. to Bolshevism, in view of the strong line taken by the S.D.F. in past years. Quelch, the editor of *Justice*, said on one occasion that they were prepared to use all methods "from the bomb to the ballot-box". It may be the case that, had the B.S.P. and Ramsay Macdonald and the I.L.P. denounced Bolshevism, the N.S.P. would have defended it. But, as that theory may be unfair, another explanation may be discovered in the fact that some of the Social Revolutionary Party in Russia (rivals of Lenin) have influenced English friends. There is also the fact that the Bolsheviks have declared war to a certain extent on the educated classes as well as the trading middle classes, and some of the N.S.P. regard themselves as intellectuals. In any case the I.L.P. is more inconsistent in supporting Bolshevism, than the revolutionists of the British Socialist Party. The latter were always wild spirits, while the I.L.P. used to talk largely of fraternity as an alternative to the war of classes.

Conclusion.

This little monograph only refers to I.L.P. or the Fabian Society incidentally. It should be known, however, that many people identified with those two bodies or with certain other political associations have belonged to the S.D.F. at one time or another and left it – generally after a dispute about tactics. The list of those who have seceded from the S.D.F. include John Burns,[17] Mrs. Besant,[18] the poet William

17 John Elliot Burns (1858–1943), Liberal MP for Battersea 1892–1918; socialist and trade unionist.

18 Annie Besant, née Wood (1847–1933), socialist, theosophist, campaigner for women's rights and supporter of Irish and Indian nationalism.

Morris,[19] J.F. Green (now M.P for Leicester),[20] Tom Mann,[21] Ben Tillett, MP,[22] and Victor Fisher.[23]

2. *Scovell to W.T. Leach, 3 May 1919*

Like a good friend would you do me a favour? I have left the War Cabinet and come over here[24] and I find that I am without a telephone. The application has already been lodged with Mr. Pegden of the Contracts Branch, Dean Street, and it is now only a question of getting the connection made with the main line. The instruments are already in this office, so the job will not take long. Will you for the sake of Auld Lang Syne ask Mr. Pegden to hustle the men round to do the work as soon as possible.

For your information I think I had better let you know that this office is an extension of 12, Downing Street, but I do not want to go to Captain Guest to solicit the Post-Master General's help, because I feel that a letter to you will be quite successful.[25]

3. *Tom Barnshaw (Secretary and Agent, Crewe Liberal Association) to Scovell 2 June 1919*

Referring to the visit of Pte. Childs and myself to London and the interview we had with you on Monday, the 19th May, I should be glad to know if you have yet been able to put matters in train for the demobilisation of Pte. Childs. At the same time I should like to bring before your notice another case. This is the case of Pte. G.H. Nicklin, who wishes to be demobilised on compassionate grounds. I know the case well, and it appears to me to be a strong case. Enclosed papers have been handed to me by Pte. Nicklin, and I send them on to you as they give all the particulars. I should be obliged if you could go into the matter and let me know what can be done. You might please return the papers after perusal.

I should like to take this opportunity of enquiring whether you have at Headquarters capable women speakers, whom you could send down to this Constituency to address meetings of our various Women's Liberal Associations. Perhaps if you could spare a good lady speaker it might be possible to arrange meetings on several consecutive days, which would save travelling expenses.[26]

19 William Morris (1834–96), designer, poet and writer.

20 Joseph Frederick Green (1855–1932), National Democratic and Labour Party MP for Leicester West 1918–32.

21 Thomas Mann (1856–1941), communist and trade unionist.

22 Ben Tillett (1860–1943), Labour MP for Salford North 1917–24 and 1929–31; socialist and trade unionist.

23 Frederick Victor Fisher (1870–1954), socialist and activist in the National Democratic and Labour Party; unsuccessfully stood for the party in the Stourbridge constituency in 1918.

24 To 25, Old Queen Street, SW1.

25 Scovell's telephone was installed on 9 May: LGA, W.T. Leach to Scovell, 10 May 1919.

26 LGA, Scovell to Barnshaw, 3 June 1919, indicated that the two cases mentioned were subject to normal demobilisation procedures, and that he had forwarded the request

4. *Scovell to Lieutenant General T.E. Clarke*[27] *at the War Office, 28 June 1919*

As a taxpayer and as one of the many who are being bombarded by appeals to take up War Bonds, I would beg of you to have enquiries made into the following matter:-

On Saturday, June 21st, a strong military band of the Cavalry, I think, was playing at the Wellington Polo Ground (Berkshire). On the conclusion of their performance this band returned to their Barracks, presumably Aldershot, some 10 miles distant, in two capacious Government motor lorries. Those of us who witnessed their departure are naturally anxious to know:

1. Whether a fair charge on a proper cost basis for taking this band to and from its destination was made by the appropriate authorities on behalf of the public purse against those responsible for engaging the band,

Or

2. Whether the public are to be put to the cost of transporting musicians to a place where enjoyment was given to a mere handful of people, players and spectators, who judging by the motor cars and ponies present could well afford to pay the full charges.

I would also like to remind you that a Railway Station is within a stone's throw of the Polo Ground.

In view of the increasingly strong feeling which exists throughout the length and breadth of this land on the extravagance of the public services I feel to approach you direct will save your time and mine.[28]

5. *Scovell to G.W. Chrystal*[29] *(Ministry of National Service & Reconstruction), 17 July 1919*

First of all, I must congratulate you most warmly on your new appointment. I was delighted when I saw it because I felt that although you have got a great work in front of you I believe you have the experience that will assist in pulling the chestnuts out of the fire.

I enclose herewith a copy of a report which I have had from the North, and if I may do so and if it will be any kindness to you I will gladly pass you on documents of a similar nature which come to hand. I have just returned from the North and

---

for a woman speaker to Miss Hogan, the chief women's organiser in Lancashire and Cheshire.

27 Lieutenant-General Sir Travers Edwards Clarke (1871–1962), served in the British army in the South African War and First World War; quartermaster general to the armies in France 1917–21.

28 In response Scovell was given a detailed answer to his points and assured that, as a result, it was considered that 'the position was now satisfactory': LGA, General T.E. Clarke to Scovell, 28 July 1919.

29 Sir George William Chrystal (1880–1944), civil servant and writer.

I am more impressed than ever with the fact that if we wish to stabilise things in this Country the greatest possible attention must be paid to a vigorous administration of (1) Housing, (2) Pensions, (3) questions connected with profiteering, not only in food but in the ordinary commodities of life from blankets to socks, from kitchen utensils to hair-brushes, and so on.

6. *Francis Vernon Willey*[30] *To Scovell, 27 July 1919*

Events of the last 10 days in connection with the coal situation seem to have intensified the need for taking stock of the general Labour position. The picture I get in connection with import, storage, and distribution of wool seems to be fairly representative of very many commodities. Briefly it is this, while we made arrangements for big supplies of raw material to be imported, while stocks actually in the country are bigger than ever before, the demand for cloth is greater than ever, and we have more, rather than less, machinery than before the War, the production from the machines is substantially less. We find congestion at the ports, in the warehouses, on the docks, all made worse by the decreased consumption by the machines. The whole thing, of course, springs from firstly, reduction of hours actually worked. The national loss is tremendous and by not producing manufactures we are losing the advantage of exports.

There is perhaps not an unnatural belief current among all sections of the population that there is an inexhaustible well of national wealth, from which greater ease in every form can be drawn. We are living in a world of dreams. Pay for hours not worked (out-of-work donation) payment by the Government (E.P.D.)[31] subsidised railway rates, subsidised bread, etc., etc. All these necessitate more borrowing by the Government, increased currency, higher commodity values, and increased cost of living, and with the Exchange going steadily against us, this cost of living is going to go steadily up. Perhaps a rather pessimistic picture, but one which every thinking person is well aware of, although he may try to put it out of his mind. My point is this, why not instead of having a Committee of the House of Commons to examine the causes of profiteering, etc., get more quickly to the root of the matter.

Here is my suggestion. Why does not the P.M. make an earnest and serious speech to the House of Commons and tell every MP to go into his constituency forthwith and carry the message to his constituents. Have it as widely circulated as possible by every auxiliary means and make a real effort for a National Campaign of Propaganda to bring the situation home to the workers. This would do much more than petty wrangling at Westminster. Such a campaign, if properly organised, would do an immense amount of good, and I know well enough that your imaginative brain and inexhaustible energy could very soon lay the lines and direct the means of carrying out.

30 Francis Willey (1884–1982), 2nd baron Barnaby; Conservative MP for Bradford South 1918–22; succeeded his father in 1929.

31 Excess Profits Duty, introduced in 1915 to tax excessive business profits.

7. *Commander J.B. Adams[32] (Ministry of Labour) to Scovell, 28 July 1919*

Herewith some more tripe for you which shows that things were distinctly on the mend until the coal crisis caused another set-back.

8. *Scovell Personal Letter to Commander J.B. Adams, 28 July 1919*

Very many thanks indeed for your letter of the 28th inst. The figures you give me are most interesting, although as a matter of fact I have been kept in close touch with Labour matters by reason of the fact that I have now in my employ some of your old officers who have given me the statistics out of their hands.

As soon as I know whether I am standing on my head or on my feet I must get you to come and lunch with me.

9. *Scovell Personal Letter to Lieutenant Colonel Gordon, 5 August 1919*

I was awfully sorry to have missed you when you came here to say goodbye. I had no idea that you were off so soon to your farm and I cannot tell you how much I envy you. If I come out to South Africa again, I shall be sure to look you up and I shall not forget your kind offer and give recommendations to anybody whom I know to pay you a visit.

Despite the universal pessimism in this country and all our apparent difficulties I believe things are moving along slowly towards a settlement. I do not think anyone can gauge the real feeling of the country from a somewhat neurotic press. Experience has taught me in the past that "Julyitis" is a kind of neurotic fever which comes over people working in London at high pressure during the month of July. Not that I wish to minimise for one moment the enormity of the tasks yet to be accomplished and the change of heart and temperament that are lacking in many of the reactionaries of all classes in this country. I think our main difficulties lie in the direction of housing and profiteering. Any reduction in the cost of living will come as a Godsend. But every nation so far has signally failed to exercise any control in this direction and at the present moment I believe this country has the cheapest living by a long way.

When one reads history from 1815 to 1819 one realises what a long way we have yet to go before things will be thoroughly settled and our nerves, energy and sense of proportion to be restored. Generals still want to command a million men; Admirals are anxious to handle fleets of 50 units; Ministers are still anxious to have Government Departments of 10,000 strong; and the average humble individual wants to go and enjoy himself. In these circumstances how can anyone expect to reduce the cost of living or bring our exports up to their pre-war level. You will probably hear in a few weeks a great deal of agitation in regard to the trade policy

32 Commander Jameson Boyd Adams (1880–1962), Royal Naval Reserve officer, polar explorer and civil servant.

of this country. Three months ago I was an ardent supporter of Free Trade – now I have an open mind on the whole question of Tariffs: and I believe this country is in now exactly the same position as any of our Overseas possessions as regards nascent industries. Personally, I doubt very much whether we shall ever be able to get back to the 1914 system of Free Trade. I write all this so that you should not be thoroughly disheartened when you read the English press in a few weeks' time. Patience and a sense of proportion are required more than anything else.

Some day I shall write out and ask you to find me a cottage on the Cape Peninsula, if possible half-way up the mountain, when I can look down on the world below and laugh.

10. *C.R. Dudgeon*[33] *(for G. Dudgeon, Cargen Holm, Dumfries) to Scovell, 4 September 1919*

Just a line to let you know that my young cousin, Hyslop-Maxwell, got into Sandhurst alright, very many thanks for what you did on his behalf. We are looking forward to seeing you here any day now, & I do hope you have been able to fix a visit to us, into your plans.

By-the-bye ten ex-Service men in Dumfries & District are getting up a Garden Fete, at the end of this month, for the purpose of raising funds to allow grants being given to hard cases among the dependents of men who have fallen. The Committee who are organising this Fete, are very anxious to get Winston Churchill to open it. If this could be arranged & if Churchill would address a demonstration in the evening of the same day as the fete, in the town of Dumfries, in furtherance of the Public & Private Economy Campaign, I feel certain it would do a very great deal to strengthen the Government's cause in the South of Scotland. The Committee above mentioned have asked me to try & get Churchill down for this affair & if you can help me in the matter, I should be most truly grateful.

11. *Walter Myers to Scovell, 9 October 1919*

I only heard of your mishap[34] to-day and hasten to express my deepest sympathy. It is a great misfortune that you should be down on your back at this period where sane organisation and wise discrimination are so much needed. Myself, I shall feel your absence keenly as during our co-operation I have learnt to value your sympathy and interest, feeling that our points of view were not divergent. As soon as you are out of the thickest part of the wood I hope you will let me run down for a few hours for a little chat. Anything I can do in the meantime do not hesitate to indicate, either direct or through Jackson.

33 C.R. Dudgeon would go on to contest Galloway (Kirkcudbrightshire and Wigtownshire) in 1922, beating the Conservative candidate by 1,849 votes; he would hold the seat in 1923 but lose it in 1924. Re-elected in 1929 with 13,461 votes, in 1931 he stood for the same seat for Oswald Mosley's New Party, coming last with 986 votes.

34 A riding accident on Exmoor in which Scovell broke his leg.

I saw Guest to-day and he seemed in a cheerful mood. The strike's settlement has unquestionably provided fresh capital for the L.G. firm, which was beginning to lose some of its customers. The middle class have re-rallied wonderfully and businessmen are ceasing to shake their heads. At the same time the miners may unsettle things again in a little while. It was a tactical blunder to speak of "anarchists" and to claim credit for improvising anti-strike machinery as far back as February. We live in a world of suspicion; not to excite it is difficult; to fan it is sheer folly.

I am wondering whether your condition will stand a letter so long. Myself, I am full of new energy.

Every good wish.

Sincerely yours,

Wallis Myers

Colonel Scovell.

P.S. I am seeing Mrs. Boyd Dawson[35] on Monday.

12. *Unnamed to Lieutenant Colonel H.A.S. Prior, 10 October 1919*

In the absence of Colonel Scovell, I have to acknowledge the receipt of your letter of the 8th inst. You will be sorry to learn that the Colonel met with an accident whilst out riding on Saturday last, and sustained a broken thigh. In consequences he is confined to a nursing home at which he will probably be detained for at least two months. I am forwarding your letter on to Colonel Scovell at Minehead as he will no doubt be interested to learn the result of your application to the Board of Agriculture.

13. *Memorandum 'Formation of a Centre Party' by Russell Davis, sent to Chief Whip by Scovell, 10 April 1920*

1. The formation of an Association to be formed for the purpose of promoting co-operation between different political groups.

If this is successful it will form the nucleus of the new party. Its function will be to do in the constituencies what the new members groups seem to do in the House with this advantage, that it does not permanently associate itself with Coalition a state of things which is incapable of permanence. If it is not successful, the association will just cease to function and the position will be no more than it is at present. The movement appears to give the most practical opportunity of splitting the Associations of both independent Conservative and of independent Liberal.

2. I would suggest its title should be The "Centre" Political Association. "Centre" because I believe that in the end the new party with a national policy will come to be known as the centre party. National would exclude Scotland to say nothing

35 Social activist then serving on the executive of the Fabian Society.

of Wales – and Centre has a recognised meaning in politics as standing for the common weal between reaction and revolution.

3. In my opinion it is a sine qua non that the political leadership of the Association should be determined beforehand and find expression in the list of Vice Presidents – I suggest the following in order of merit.

1. Lloyd George.
2. Balfour, Churchill, Birkenhead, Barnes.
3. Crewe, Chamberlain, Bonar Law, Mond, Roberts.
4. E. Wood, Horne, Kellaway, Macnamara.
5. Certain representative men and women who are not in Parliament and who should be selected as representing localities and political groups and particular interests.

4. The association would be organised on the unusual lines of a political association on a Constituency basis and with Area Offices in the big centres and the movement might well originate in Manchester.

5. Executive power would be at first vested in a nominated provisional Committee who would carry on until developments justified a permanent constitution.

6. Officially you should have nothing to do with it – your control would be safeguarded by the fact that you nominated the Committee.

7. The formation of the Association would be announced in a circular letter signed by the provisional Committee – which after giving the names of those who had consented to act as President and Vice Presidents and dealing with certain details of how to join, etc. would have some such tosh as the following:

> "It must be obvious to all thinking men and women that the great need of to-day is for co-operation between the various political groups. The international position, the problems which present themselves at home can only be successfully tackled if men of goodwill draw together in the spirit of Imperial unity to work for the common weal. There are not wanting at the present time signs of disintegrating forces which must lessen the prestige of Britain in the eyes of the Nations, weaken the hands of Imperial Government, and render more difficult the task of carrying through in a constitutional manner and with due regard to the financial situation the reforms which the Democratic spirit of the day rightly demands. This Association has been formed for the purpose of affording a rallying point to all men and women of good will, whatever their particular political label may be, who desire unity rather than disruption, national peace rather than party strife, and constructive progress rather than destructive criticism. It has taken the name of "Centre" because it will seek to encourage that middle policy which shuns the extremism of reaction or revolution, and which, while recognising to the full, Imperial responsibility, is in close and sympathetic touch with Democratic ideals. Should it become necessary the Association will not hesitate to put forward its own candidates but it may be hoped that its mere existence if sufficiently supported will obviate such

necessity by creating so strong a demand for co-operation that existing political parties will be unable to resist it."

8. You will observe that I have not suggested a President – and I am in some difficulty over this. My feeling on the whole is that the first President should be if possible a prominent individual not too closely associated with existing parties – e.g. a man like Lord Weir[36] or Lord Inchape.[37] I mention these as examples of the type of man with expressing any opinion as to the suitability of these particular individuals.

14. *Extract from a Letter from Colonel G. Gunn (Addressed to Colonel Scovell), 14 April 1920*[38]

On Monday evening I attended a meeting of the West Edinburgh Liberal Association when Vivian Philipps[39] (Asquith's P.S.)[40] delivered an address. The refrain of his song was the necessity for 'clean politics' and the total lack of principle shown by the P.M. and the Coalitionists; the waste of money on the Russian business; the unsettled world outlook; the Irish mess; the alienation of the American people; Government waste and extravagance – in short, all the evils from which we suffer are due to the unprincipled P.M. and his followers! The meeting was well attended and enthusiastic, with no opposition. I gathered that V. Philipps is to be invited to become the Liberal candidate for West Edinburgh.

A short way off in the Usher Hall, at the same hour, a Sinn Fein deputation from Ireland, which included Griffith[41] (acting as President of the Irish Republic), John McNeil,[42] and others, were abusing the tyrannical 'English' Government with full Irish fervour. The trouble in Ireland apparently is entirely due to the atrocious conduct of the 'English' Government. There was a full house and all the Irish people of Edinburgh seemed to have been collected together for the occasion. On the platform were several young priests. The Irish republican flag was in evidence

36 William Douglas Weir (1877–1959), 1st Viscount Weir; businessman and administrator.

37 James Lyle Mackay (1852–1932), 1st earl of Inchape; businessman and colonial administrator.

38 Copies sent to Sir William Sutherland, Captain Guest and others. Gilbert Gunn (1866–1940), was a Scottish soldier who rose from the rank of private to achieve that of colonel in March 1918.

39 Vivian Philipps (1870–1955), Liberal MP for Edinburgh West 1922–4; teacher and lawyer.

40 Private secretary.

41 Arthur Joseph Griffith (1871–1922), founder of Sinn Féin, Sinn Féin MP for Tyrone North West and East Cavan 1918–22 and for Fermanagh and Tyrone in the Northern Ireland parliament 1921–2; minister of home affairs 1919–21, minister of foreign affairs 1921–2, president of Dáil Éireann 1922; deputy leader of Sinn Féin 1905–11 and 1917–22, leader of Sinn Féin 1911–17.

42 John McNeil (1867–1945), Sinn Féin MP for Londonderry City 1918–22 and for Londonderry in the Northern Ireland parliament 1921–5; teachta dála for Clare 1923–7, minister for finance 1919, minister for industries 1919–21, ceann comhairle of Dáil Éireann 1921–2, minister of education 1922–5.

on the platform and elsewhere, while girls were selling and distributing Sinn Fein literature among the audience. While I was present there was not a single note of opposition. I had not seen any notice that the meeting was to take place and I only discovered accidentally what was on while waiting for my wife who was at the Carl Rosa Operatic performance in the next building (Lyceum Theatre).

These meetings indicate what is going on in our midst. The local politicians, Wedgwood Benn,[43] Hogge,[44] and Pringle,[45] are an unscrupulous lot who will stop at nothing to achieve their object. At present they are doing all the attacking, and I would say that a strong counter-attack should not be delayed too long. The platform party on Monday night appeared to me to consist of the old Tory type of Scottish Liberal – just the sort who had learnt nothing from the War, or War conditions.

15. *The Times report of a Meeting of the General Committee of the National Liberal Federation, 7 May 1920*

Liberal Split Widened: Uproar at Leamington: Ministers Refused a Hearing.

The annual meeting of the General Committee of the National Liberal Federation was held at the Town Hall, Leamington, yesterday afternoon, under the presidency of Sir George Lunn.[46] When Dr. Addison[47] and other Ministers took their seats on the platform they were greeted with cries of "Rats". They were followed by Sir Donald Maclean, MP,[48] who was loudly cheered. The President expressed sympathy with the Prime Minister and the Chief Liberal Whip (Captain F.E. Guest) in their illness, and offered a welcome to the large numbers of Liberal

43 William Wedgwood Benn (1877–1960), 1st Viscount Stansgate; Liberal MP for St George's (Tower Hamlets) 1906–18 and Leith 1918–27, Labour MP for Aberdeen North 1928–31 and Manchester Gorton 1937–42; secretary of state for India 1929–31, secretary of state for air 1945–6; ennobled 1942.

44 James Hogge (1873–1928), Liberal MP for Edinburgh East 1912–23; social researcher and politician.

45 William Henderson Pringle (1877–1967), lawyer, civil servant, educator and Liberal politician who unsuccessfully contested three seats for the Liberals in the general elections of 1922, 1923 and 1924.

46 Sir George Lunn (1861–1939), Liberal politician, mayor of Newcastle 1915–18 and chair and president of the National Liberal Federation 1918–20.

47 Christopher Addison (1869–1951), 1st Viscount Addison; Liberal MP for Shoreditch 1910–22, Labour MP for Swindon 1929–31 and 1934–5, member of the House of Lords 1937–51; minister of munitions 1916–17, minister of reconstruction 1917–19, president of the local government board 1919, minister of health 1919–21, minister without portfolio 1921, parliamentary secretary to the ministry of agriculture and fisheries 1929–30, minister of agriculture 1930–1, secretary of state for dominion affairs 1945–7, secretary of state for commonwealth relations 1947, paymaster general 1947–8, lord keeper of the privy seal 1947–51, lord president of the council 1951, leader of the House of Lords 1945–51.

48 Donald Maclean (1864–1932), Liberal MP for Bath 1906–10, Peebles and South Midlothian 1910–22, North Cornwall 1929–32; leader of the opposition 1918–20, president of the Liberal Party 1923–6, president of the board of education 1931–2.

members present. Their presence, he said, was a gratifying sign of the desire of Liberal members of all shades of opinion to get into touch with realities. (Cheers.) People came to Leamington to get a tonic they needed. He moved the election of Mr. Arthur Brampton,[49] president of the Birmingham Liberal Association, as chairman of the committee for the ensuing year. This was seconded by Mr. John Massie,[50] and carried.

The main interest of the meeting centred in the discussion on the resolution passed by the Executive Committee on the subject of the independence of the Liberal Party and its organisation. The resolution, which has already appeared in *The Times*, reaffirmed confidence in Mr. Asquith as leader of the Liberal Party. It declined the invitation of the Prime Minister to enter into "closer cooperation" with the Conservative Party on the grounds that the wartime necessity for a coalition of political parties no longer existed, that its continuance was impossible except at the sacrifice of principle, and was calculated to mislead the electors, and that to promote an unreal alliance between Liberals and Conservatives for the alleged purpose of fighting Socialism was certain to aggravate and precipitate class warfare, to which true Liberalism must always be opposed. The Executive Committee urged affiliated associations to maintain the independence of the party and the efficiency of their organisations, and warned Liberals, especially in constituencies represented by Coalition Liberals, against proposals to suspend or disband the party organisation and make an alliance with the Conservative Party, a course which could only result in handing those constituencies over to Toryism or Labour. The resolution submitted by the General Committee emphasized the latter portions of the Executive Committee's resolution, and pledged the delegates to use their utmost efforts to maintain the independence and efficiency of the organisations they represented.

"An Ambiguous Position".

Mr. Brampton, in moving the resolution, said its aim was to clarify a position, which was ambiguous, bewildering, and dangerous to Liberalism. Mr. Lloyd George urged Liberals to cooperate closely with Toryism. This meant that the differences between Liberalism and Toryism were so unimportant that they might be brushed aside in face of the serious problems of reconstruction. If any man thought that, he might be honest, but he was not a Liberal. (Cheers.) The problems of reconstruction were the problems they wanted to see settled on Liberal, and not on Tory, lines. The troubles that weighed heavily on the world could never be removed by Toryism. They were the fruits of Toryism. Given time, the greater party would absorb the lesser, and so they feared it would be in this case. The experiment was tried by Liberal-Unionists in 1886, and they in Birmingham watched it at close quarters. Birmingham, once the citadel of Liberalism, had for 36 years been the impregnable stronghold of Toryism. They were warned that by passing this resolution they would drive good Liberals out of the party. By their continued

49 Arthur Brampton (1864–1955), businessman and Liberal politician, chair of the National Liberal Federation 1920–31 and its president 1930–3.

50 John Massie (1842–1925), Liberal MP for Cricklade 1906–10; academic and politician.

association with Toryism Mr. Lloyd George and his followers had already driven tens of thousands of good Liberals out of the party into the ranks of Labour. They could trifle with the situation no longer.

Mr. Brampton was repeatedly interrupted by Coalition delegates, who greeted his references to Toryism with a shout of, "We are not dealing with Toryism". Mr. George Peel,[51] seconding the resolution, alluded to the description of Mr. Lloyd George having "crossed the Rubicon," and said all he was waiting for was his luggage. In regard to the proposal to have a Liberal National Democratic Party, he said that party was neither Liberal, National, Democratic, nor a party, and they would not have it. The President said that the North Hammersmith Liberal Association desired to withdraw their amendments to insert a proviso urging the Associations to effect a reconciliation in their constituencies between all sections of Liberalism. In order that the withdrawal of the amendment might not be misrepresented, he said that the Executive had decided to move it, because they did long for reconciliation between all sections of the Liberal Party. The amendment was carried.

Dr. Addison Heckled.

The newly-elected chairman then took charge of the meeting, and in calling on Dr. Addison, Minister of Health, said that the proposed reference back of the resolution was out of order, and Dr. Addison must therefore speak for or against the amendment. Dr Addison spoke amid an almost continuous crossfire of taunts and interruptions and the counter-demonstrations of his own supporters. He expressed deep regret that the chairman had decided that a motion of that kind had to be decided in a discussion of 51 minutes duration, and that it was thought that some of them, who were life-long Liberals – (cheers and cries of "Rats.") – were more anxious to catch their trains than to consider the future of the Liberal Party; also that a speaker had thought fit to describe them before the Liberals of the country as "luggage". The resolution meant a sentence of excommunication against life-long Liberals. (Shouts of "Turncoats," and "What about Spen Valley".) Let them get away from the temper of some people in the meeting and look at the real state of affairs in the world. In India, in Egypt, in Ireland, they had some of the most difficult problems of government and maintenance of liberty and protection of our fellow-citizens. (A delegate – "You are not the people to deal with it".)

References by Dr. Addison to the state of Europe were met by shouts of "Houses," to which the right hon. gentleman replied by asking if there was anyone in the audience so stupid as to think that it was in anyone's power to make up for the great world shortage all in a moment. This is not a time, Dr. Addison continued, when every difficulty that besets us, when every danger that stands in our way, is to be made the subject of party clack and clatter. I say with every confidence that any set of men who sought to conduct the government of this country on those principles would be repudiated by the country. If this Coalition were to cease every man here knows that you would have to replace it by another. Are we, because we are Liberals – (derisive cheer, and "We are as good as you are") – to entertain those views to be shut out, as it were? There were cries of "Yes," and further interruption,

51 George Peel (1869–1956), Liberal MP for Spalding 1917–18.

during which Dr. Addison turned to the chairman, and observed, "I claim a fair hearing. You had it yourself."

The Government Record

Dr. Addison went on to say that no decision of that meeting would alter their allegiance to their principles. They valued Liberal organisations, but they loved their country more. In more intervals of shouting, Dr. Addison claimed that the Government had abolished conscription, and they had conferred on India, under great difficulties, the greatest measure of self-government which any white race had conferred on its dependencies. Were these things a betrayal of Liberalism? He continued:– "We have spent millions – (loud cheers) – in training men to make up for the disabilities of their wounds". Another delegate shouted "Houses," and Dr. Addison asked whether he was to understand by that ignorant jeer that this meeting objected to that. As to housing, the first 50,000 acres for the purpose of houses had been acquired at a less price than they were obtained in 1913–14. Was the establishment of the Ministry of Health an illiberal thing? We had made more progress than any other nation, and had now under construction and nearing completion nearly three times as many houses as the Liberal Administration from 1906 to 1914. Dr. Addison's final appeal to the meeting not to indulge in proscription of their fellow-Liberals was met by the report, "You did".

Mrs Walter Runciman,[52] chairman of the Women's National Liberal Federation, supporting the motion, said she agreed with Dr. Addison that the world was full of trouble, but she believed the best solution was to be found in Liberalism. It was a ridiculous pretence to say that the Coalition could adequately meet the situation and that party strife could be avoided. I have just been in a battle, said Mrs. Runciman, and I never saw a more magnificent Tory array. I don't quarrel with Conservatives fighting Liberals if they are sincere, but in the last election they were reinforced by Coalition Liberals, who said they had not sacrificed their principles, but who readily sacrificed Liberal candidates. (Cheers)

Dr. Macnamara's Defence

Dr. Macnamara, Minister of Labour, on rising to oppose the resolution, was greeted with much hissing. A delegate rose and demanded to know in what capacity Dr. Macnamara was speaking. I understand that he was adopted by a Liberal Association, said the delegate, but by a Tory organisation, and we want to know in what capacity he appears? The Chairman said invitations were extended to all who were nominal Liberals. Dr. Macnamara made a defence of his position. The President, he remarked, said he longed for reconciliation. (Uproar and cries of "Go on Mac".) Well, as conciliators, you beat the band, said Dr. Macnamara. I used to learn at the Federation meeting that measures, and not men, was a cardinal faith with this assembly. (Loud cheers) If to-morrow the present Coalition disappeared – (uproar) – do you think the historic Liberal Party could form a Government? Why, you would have at once to espouse the thing you profess to loathe. Dr.

52 Hilda Runciman (1869–1956), Viscountess Runciman of Doxford; Liberal MP for St Ives 1928–9; president of the women's National Liberal Federation 1919–21.

Macnamara was greeted with much opposition when he referred to the Radical Prime Minister. By pursuing the course they sought to adopt they would make the Liberal Party not historic but prehistoric, he shouted, amid deafening cries of disapprobation. Mr. F. Thornborough, a Newcastle delegate and chairman of the Executive of the National League of Young Liberals, said they would have listened to Dr. Macnamara if he could have explained to them his action in Spen Valley, where he went to assassinate Sir John Simon.[53] Dr. Macnamara had taught them the words "proscription" and "excommunication". Young Liberals would have nothing to do with this Coalition.

A Scene of Disorder

A scene of disorder followed the rising of Mr. Kellaway, MP, Secretary to the Department of Overseas Trade, and resulted in the eventual withdrawal of the Coalition Ministers and their supporters. Mr Kellaway's opening words were: "I was fighting the Liberal cause when some of those who are making these interruptions were taking refuge in a tabernacle to assassinate Sir Henry Campbell-Bannerman".[54] There were noisy demands for a withdrawal, to which Mr. Kellaway replied:– "I have not the slightest intention of withdrawing". Coalition members of Parliament shouted, "Don't withdraw, you are quite right". A delegate said that if Mr. Kellaway would withdraw his falsehood this meeting would hear him. "Having made no statement which was not absolutely true, I do not intend to withdraw", said Mr. Kellaway. The meeting continued in an uproarious mood, and Mr. McCurdy, MP, Food Controller, who was seated near Mr. Kellaway, rose on a point of order and asked whether, in estimating the five minutes allowed to Liberal Ministers on their defence, the time occupied by the audience was included or excluded. Dr. Macnamara remarked sarcastically, "Included, of course". The Chairman said the principle on which they worked was set while he was speaking. His time included all the interruptions.

The Chairman then called on Mr. G.R. Thorne, MP,[55] to speak and the Coalitionists yelled for Mr. Kellaway, who rose again several times. Sir Gordon Hewart, the Attorney General,[56] also rose, but was waved aside by the Chairman, who was assailed by Coalition cries of "Sit down, jellyfish". The Chairman accused Mr.

53 John Simon (1873–1954), 1st Viscount Simon; Liberal MP for Walthamstow 1906–18 and Spen Valley 1922–40; solicitor-general 1910–13, attorney-general 1913–15, home secretary 1915–16 and 1935–7, chancellor of the exchequer 1937–40, lord high chancellor 1940–5; ennobled 1940.

54 Sir Henry Campbell-Bannerman (1836–1908), Liberal MP for Stirling Burghs 1868–1908; chief secretary for Ireland 1884–5, secretary of state for war 1892–5 and 1886, leader of the opposition 1899–1905, leader of the Liberal Party 1899–1908, prime minister 1905–8.

55 George Rennie Thorne (1853–1934), Liberal MP for Wolverhampton East 1908–29; Liberal chief whip 1919–23.

56 Sir Gordon Hewart (1870–1943), 1st Viscount Hewart; Liberal MP for Leicester 1913–18 and Leicester East 1918–22; solicitor general 1916–19, attorney general 1919–22; ennobled 1922, he served as lord chief justice of England 1922–40.

Kellaway of defying the chair. Sir Gordon Hewart protested against including interruptions in a speaker's time, when there was a concerted and prolonged endeavour to shout the speaker down. We have very little fair play here to-day, he added, and I do hope. Mr. Kellaway again rose, and the Chairman asked whether it would meet the wish of the meeting if they cut out all speakers except Sir Gordon Hewart and Sir Donald Maclean. Mr McCurdy put, as a point of order, that the chairman had previously ruled that no resolution might be put to the meeting of which notice had not been given. Sir Gordon Hewart said he had realized that the meeting could shout louder than they could speak, and was willing and anxious to vote on the resolution without hearing any argument at all. As a protest against the concerted unfairness and insult with which we have been received here, I decline to speak, he concluded.

Coalition Delegates' Withdrawal

Sir Gordon Hewart then walked off the platform, followed by his colleagues, and their supporters, who numbered 57 members of Parliament and about 20 delegates … amid derisive cheers. The cheers of the retiring body could be heard outside the building, but were drowned when Sir Donald Maclean MP rose to speak. "I regret that the Coalition Liberals have seen fit to leave the meeting", he said, "but the incident which gave rise to it reflected no credit on the speaker, because he said what was really a very offensive thing. I think the audience were wrong. It would have been very much better if they had listened to him". Sir Donald Maclean went on to say that the real issue before Liberalism was whether it was to remain a fighting, beneficial force in our national life. There could be no doubt at all that "closer cooperation and fusion" meant the death of the Liberal Party. The records of the divisions in the House of Commons showed that those who had remained true to Liberalism were the independent Liberals, and it was because of the fact that this had risen in the determination to say that the time had come for straight politics and no compromise. What had the majority at Sunderland got to do with it? Principles were not a question of numbers. The resolution was carried with four dissentients.

The Manchester resolution, calling for a reformation of the economic and industrial policy of the Liberal Party, in order to meet the needs of the present day, and requesting the new executive to proceed with the drafting of a policy for submission to the next annual meeting, was moved by Mr. W. Doyle. Lord Emmott,[57] who supported the motion, said he would like to see a Liberal leader come forward with a policy which takes the line of profit-sharing and co-partnership. He thought the words in the resolution referring to the nationalisation of certain monopoly services were not very wise. He did not think they could tell him a single so-called monopoly service which he could not show was not a monopoly at all. The resolution was carried, as were also others, one asking for a vigorous and constructive programme, a second opposing the reactionary proposals of the

57 Alfred Emmott (1858–1926), 1st baron Emmott; Liberal MP for Oldham 1892–1911; deputy speaker of the House of Commons 1906–11; under-secretary of state for the colonies 1911–14, first commissioner of works 1914–15; elevated to the peerage 1911.

Minister of Education in regard to the Cowper-Temple clause, and a third called on the Government to stop the wholesale arrest of persons on suspicion in Ireland and protesting against the detention of untried persons in prisons.

Mr. W. Runciman,[58] proposing a vote of thanks to the chairman, said the air had been cleared. A great deal of humbug had been experienced during the last 18 months, but that had been brought to a dramatic conclusion that day.

The Coalitionists held an impromptu meeting on the steps of the Town Hall. Sir Gordon Hewart said that was the first time in his life – and he hoped it would be the last – when occasion should arise to leave his fellow-Liberals as a necessary protest against the unfair and insulting procedure of the delegates. He was followed by the singing of the National Anthem and loud cheering.

16. *Resolutions of the General Committee of the National Liberal Federation held at Leamington Spa, 7 May 1920*[59]

The Independence of the Liberal Party and its Organisation Moved by the Chairman of the General Committee, seconded by The Hon. George Peel (Vice-President of the Rugby Division Liberal Association), and *resolved*:

"That this General Committee of the National Liberal Federation at its first meeting since the declaration of the result of the Paisley bye-election,[60] welcomes Mr. Asquith's return to the House of Commons and reaffirms its unabated confidence in him as Leader of the Liberal Party. It declines the invitation extended to Liberals by the Prime Minister to enter into 'closer co-operation' with the Conservative Party, believing –

(a) That the war-time necessity for a Coalition of political parties no longer exists.

(b) That the continuance of such a Coalition is impossible except at the sacrifice of principle, is calculated to mislead the electors, and is therefore contrary to the National interest.

(c) That to promote an unreal alliance between Liberals and Conservatives for the alleged purpose of fighting Socialism is certain to aggravate and precipitate class warfare, to which true Liberalism must always be opposed.

The Executive Committee urges the Affiliated Liberal Associations to employ every effort to effect a reconciliation in their Constituencies between all sections of

58 Sir Walter Runciman (1870–1949), Viscount Runciman of Doxford; Liberal MP for Oldham 1899–1900, Dewsbury 1902–18, Swansea West 1924–9, St Ives 1929–37; president of the board of education 1908–11, president of the board of agriculture 1911–14, president of the board of trade 1911–14, lord president of the council 1938–9; ennobled 1937.

59 *Proceedings in Connection with the Thirty-Seventh Annual Meeting of the National Liberal Federation, Nov. 25th and 26th, 1920* (1921), 27–31.

60 The modern spelling is by-election; bye-election, the older spelling, was routinely in use in the 1920s.

Liberalism and to maintain the independence of the historic Liberal Party and the efficiency of their Organisations, and warns Liberals everywhere, but especially in the constituencies represented to-day by Coalition Liberals, to be on their guard against insidious proposals to suspend or disband their Party organisation, and to force them into alliance with the Conservative Party by whatever name it may be called – a course which, if followed, can in the long run only result in handling over those constituencies either to Toryism or to Labour.

The General Committee desires to emphasise the request and the warning of the Executive Committee to the Affiliated Associations as expressed in the last paragraph of the foregoing Resolution, and delegates now present pledge themselves to use their utmost efforts to maintain the independence and efficiency of the Liberal Organisations which they represent."

The Following Resolutions were adopted on the motion of Affiliated Associations:

An Economic and Industrial Policy for the Liberal Party

From the Manchester Liberal Federation:

"The General Committee is of opinion that the time has come when the economic and industrial policy of the Liberal Party should be reformulated to meet the needs of the present day. While there is much in common between the policies of the Liberal and Labour Parties on such questions as Free Trade, Home Rule, Foreign Policy, Devolution, Land Reform, Women's Questions, and the Nationalisation of certain Monopoly services, the Liberal Party is of opinion that the policy of the nationalisation of all forms of industry would be disastrous to the interests of all classes in the country. The Committee recognises that such questions as unemployment, the existing control of industry and distribution of its rewards, are causing increasing unrest and dissatisfaction with the present industrial system. With a view to the early redress of grievances and inequalities, this Committee requests the newly elected Executive to proceed immediately with the drafting of an industrial policy, stating the Liberal Party's alternatives to communism, and making it perfectly clear that the Liberal Party's alternatives to communism, or part in a class war, and trusts that the Executive will submit its proposals to the Council at the Annual General Meeting."

A Liberal Programme

From the London Junior Liberal Federation:

"That the General Committee of the National Liberal Federation urges:

1. The urgent necessity for defining with as much detail as practicable a fighting and constructive programme for the Liberal Party.

2. That in view of the immediate need of educating the electorate it is essential to the future of the Party that such policy be given the widest possible publicity by a vigorous campaign."

The Reactionary Proposals of the Minister of Education

From the South Paddington Liberal Association:

"That this Committee adheres to the Cowper-Temple clause and declares its unqualified opposition to the reactionary proposals of the Minister of Education."

Government of Ireland

From the South Paddington Liberal Association:

"That this Committee calls upon the Government to stop the wholesale arrest of persons upon suspicion in Ireland and protests against the detention of untried persons in prisons."

In communicating the report of these proceedings to the Chairman, which was carried by acclamation.

In communicating the report of these proceedings to the Affiliated Liberal Association the Officers of the Federation felt it necessary to issue with it the following explanatory letter in order to correct statements made in a portion of the Press and by certain members of the Government and other Coalition Liberal members of Parliament respecting the cause of the disturbance during the discussion of the Resolution on the Independence of the Liberal Party:

[Copy]

Dear Sir, In accordance with practice, we enclose a copy of the Resolutions passed at the Annual Meeting of the General Committee which was being held at Leamington on Friday, May 7th. We beg to direct your special attention to the Resolution affirming the Independence of the Liberal Party and its Organisation, and declining the Prime Minister's invitation to enter into "closer co-operation" with the Conservative Party.

Previous to this Resolution being put to the meeting, the Coalition Liberal members of Parliament, with one or two exceptions, left the hall, and about twenty delegates joined them; the total number who thus withdrew being seventy-seven. When the Resolution was put to the meeting there were five hundred delegates present, and it was carried with four dissentients.

It is to be regretted that the Coalition Liberal members of Parliament were not given a quiet hearing, but the responsibility for this rests on their own shoulders. Their conduct from the outset was provocative in the extreme. From the beginning of the meeting they challenged the ruling of the Chairman, and noisily objected to the necessary time-limit for all speakers which the chair announced would have to be enforced in order that the voice on the main Resolution could be taken before the majority of the delegates would be compelled to leave for their trains. It was plain that the opponents of the principal Resolution intended either to talk that Resolution out or prevent a full vote being taken, and these tactics reached a climax when one of their leaders (a member of the Government) insulted the whole body of delegates, ignored the vote of the meeting that he be no longer heard, and persistently defied in which defiance he was encouraged by no less a person than the Attorney-General.

These provocative demonstrations, however, had their real origin prior to Leamington. They were the culmination of a series of acts in the constituencies, which were well within the knowledge of the delegates present at the meeting; these acts including the incursion of Coalition Liberal members of Parliament into bye-elections to oppose Liberal candidates adopted by the free choice of the Liberal Associations, as at Spen Valley; the sending of emissaries into constituencies represented by Coalition Liberals to promote "closer co-operation" with the Conservative Party in those constituencies and thus to bring about the suspension or silence of the local Liberal Association.

The decision come to at Leamington by the General Committee of the National Liberal Federation, at one of the largest and most representative meetings of that Committee ever held, must obviously be followed up by action in the constituent bodies which comprise the Federation, viz., its affiliated Associations. We desire to learn whether any, and, if so, which of our Liberal Associations disagree with the Resolution. Accordingly, we invite the Liberal Association of every constituency to meet at the earliest possible date to consider the Resolutions passed at Leamington, and more particularly the Resolution to which this letter principally relates. Wherever the Resolution is adopted, the next thing will be to see that, by propaganda and by other means, it is made effective in the constituency. In some areas represented by Coalition Liberal members of Parliament it is possible that the Resolution may not be adopted, and it will then remain for the Liberals in those constituencies who are not prepared for "fusion" or "closer co-operation" with the Conservative Party to determine what steps they will take to preserve the independence of Liberalism. The responsibility resting on the Free Liberals of those constituencies cannot be over-estimated. It is to them in particular that the warning contained in the latter part of our Resolution is directed.

Following on the decision come to at Leamington, our business is to maintain the independence of Liberalism, to strengthen our national and local organisation, and to free ourselves of entangling alliances.

The working of the coupon at the last General Election gave the country a Tory House of Commons. The closer co-operation now advocated could only result in perpetuating this state of affairs, inasmuch as it comes a crime for any Liberal, Coalition or Free, to stand for a seat now represented by a Tory. In effect the Prime Minister asks all Liberals to enter into a state of lasting bondage to the Conservative party. Leamington answered that invitation with a decided negative. It rests now with the Liberal Associations and the Liberal rank and file to see to it that, whatever the immediate consequences may be, Liberalism shall neither barter away its freedom nor surrender its principles.

– We are, Yours faithfully,

George Lunn (President), Arthur Brampton (Chairman of Committee), Frank Wright (Treasurer), John Massie (Chairman of Finance Committee), Robt A. Hudson (Secretary), Frank Barter (Assistant Secretary).

P.S. We particularly request that we may be informed (by letter addressed to the Secretaries) immediately your Association takes any action on the subject of this letter.

42, Parliament Street,

London, S.W.1

22 May, 1920.

The response to the invitation to the Affiliated Associations to meet and to consider the Resolution to which the foregoing letter principally relates, was very satisfactory. All the District Liberal Associations met and adopted the Resolution. In seven cases the Resolution was considered but either not submitted for adoption or decision was deferred, and only two Associations intimated their disagreement with the Resolution.

17. *Scovell Memo to the Chief Whip, 'Forest of Dean', 11 May 1920*

I spent the weekend in the Forest of Dean, and had long talks with Colonel Morgan-Jones (brother of Sir E. Jones), interviewed Colonel Kerr, the Chairman of the Provisional Skeleton Coalition Committee, and also did a rapid tour of the Constituency.

The following summarise in brief form my conclusions:

1. For various reasons of a personal and public nature – too many to enumerate in detail here – I am of the opinion that the result of the General Election (when Sir H. Webb went under) is no real criterion of the state of the political pulse of the Forest of Dean.

2. With regard to existing organisations:

   (a) Unionist Party – Nil.

   (b) Liberal Party – Moribund, but apart from the unpopularity of Jordan (Sir Charles Dilke's[61] old agent, and Webb's too), has possibilities of revival.

   (c) Labour Party – Static.

3. There is a possibility that the constituency Labour member, Wignall,[62] who is a docker, may be replaced by a miner's representative. Wignall seems to be respected but his temperance views do not tally with those of the Miners.

61 Charles Dilke (1843–1911), Liberal MP for Chelsea 1868–86 and Forest of Dean 1892–1911; president of the local government board 1882–5, his reputation was ruined by a public scandal in 1885–6, but in 1889 the Forest of Dean Liberal Association approached him to stand as their candidate. Despite returning to the House of Commons in 1892, the political career of a man once touted as a future leader of the Liberals never revived.

62 James Wignall (1856–1925), appointed secretary of the Swansea branch of the docker's union, later president of the union 1905–8; Labour MP for Forest of Dean 1918–25.

4. The constituency under redistribution seems evenly divided between Industry and Agriculture.

5. The salient factor, in my opinion, is the unknown strength of the Asquithians. I am inclined to the view that we run little or no chance of their torpedoing us if we launch a candidate, but to make doubly sure I have instructed Mr Wood – our Chief Agent in these parts – to go round the constituency once again, this week if possible, and sound all prominent Coalition Liberals who have come out into the open. He will report to me direct as soon as he has done this.

6. Having made certain on this point I think the next step should be the appointment of an Agent of our own who must incidentally be a "live wire". I have instructed Mr Wood to sound Jordan, who has private means and is at the moment acting as Local Food Controller, whether he would be prepared to assist us in a purely advisory capacity at an annual retaining fee. As he receives no money for any political activities which he undertakes at the present juncture, this, I hope, will minimise any chance of an Abingdon Street torpedo. Concurrently with the taking of these steps, we will have to consider the nobbling of the local newspaper. Colonel Morgan-Jones is acting as a sounding-board in this respect.

7. Despite the anxiety of the local people to have a candidate in the field now, I advocate very strongly that this should be delayed until we have got our Agent well in the saddle and have collected some funds and got the Liberals and Conservatives pulling well together. To this end we shall have to be prepared to put down some money until such time as local subscribers see that we mean business and come forward and help.

8. The type of candidate required seems to me to be a well gifted youngish man with plenty of grit – neither a "carpet-bagger" nor a profiteer, and if possible, endowed with some private means and a strong sense of humour.

9. It will take many years before the electorate forgets the exceptional personality of Sir Charles Dilke and the assiduous way in which he courted and wooed the constituency. A new man has, therefore, a hard task before him, and after due reflection I cannot recommend any candidate at the moment who would fit the bill.

18. *Scovell to Freddie Guest, 'Tour of Cardiff, Bristol, and Forest of Dean', 13 May 1920*

I forward herewith an account of the short tour I made last week of Cardiff, Bristol, and the Forest of Dean.

Cardiff: I spent Friday, the 7th inst., in our office at Cardiff, dealing principally with the question of the re-organisation of Wales into three Areas – each independent of the other – as follows:

North Wales (Office at Bangor): 8 Constituencies: Mr. L. Edwards in charge, assisted by Mrs Price White and Miss MP Williams.

Mid Wales: (Office at Swansea): 11 Constituencies: Mr Joseph Jones in charge, assisted by Miss Philipps.

South Wales: (Office at Cardiff): 14 Constituencies: Mr Llewelyn in charge, assisted by Miss Herbison temporarily, and another woman who is yet to be appointed.

In view of the re-organisation, I made arrangements to dispense with the services of, and find other suitable employment for, Mr Morgan, the clerk who has hitherto been dealing (under Mr Llewelyn) with the administration of all our Offices and personnel in Wales. I also interviewed Mr Treharne, the Liberal Agent in Monmouthshire who is practically starving as the Liberal Association is almost entirely out of funds. As he is a good man and absolutely with us and has lately been employed on bye-election work I gave Mr Llewelyn instructions to employ him temporarily as his assistant until such time as a post of paid Agent can be found for him. I also went very carefully into the various qualifications of our Women's Staff in Wales and decided to dispense with the services of Miss Roberts of Wrexham and Miss Jones of Aberystwyth, neither of whom I consider pull sufficient weight for our purpose and who are now hardly up to the enhanced standard that we are aiming at when selecting our Women's Staff. I also had a long talk with Mr Davies, the sub-Editor of the South Wales Daily News,[63] who has been of the greatest assistance to us and has a very keen political mind. He informed me that in his opinion the two great questions in Wales to-day are "High prices" and "Housing" – plus the great question of Temperance, and he emphasised more than once how strongly he felt on the vital importance of this question being tackled by the Prime Minister in real radical fashion as early as possible. He told me that a great deal of disappointment had been expressed over the throwing out of the Private Bill on this subject in the House of Commons a week or two ago.

Bristol: I reached Bristol late on Friday night, the 7th inst., and spent most of the next day in the Bristol office. Unfortunately, Mr. Millman, our head there, was ill and I could not see him. I was enabled, however, to interview some 8 or 10 Women Organisers who have just concluded in a very strenuous Speaker's Course lasting about 10 days which had been organised by Miss Gordon and Miss Pressley Smith and which had been very successful. Speaker's Class at Swansea (Women): I also made arrangements for a similar class to be held at Swansea as there are several local women there who are anxious to receive instruction, and there are several of our own staff who need more practice in view of the speaking campaign in the Autumn. Most of the Women Organisers I met there seemed well up to standard, but I am warned on all sides that more education in purely political questions of the day is urgently needed. Speaker's "Parliament": In this connection, I have every intention of recommending to you at a later date that we should hold a Parliament of all our Speakers – men and women – early in October, lasting about a fortnight, as I am seeing more clearly every day that this is urgently necessary.

63 *The South Wales Daily News* was regarded as a Liberal leaning newspaper, while *The South Wales Daily Post* was considered Conservative.

Forest of Dean: On Saturday evening, the 8th inst., I arrived at Newnham in the Forest of Dean, and after dinner interviewed Colonel Morgan-Jones (Sir Edgar Jones' brother) who is in business in the Forest. On Sunday morning, in company with Colonel Jones I motored round the Forest and got a bird's-eye view of the various aspects of Sir Charles Dilke's old seat – at present held by Wignall the Labour member. On Sunday afternoon I interviewed the Chairman of the Coalition Committee (which consists of six Liberals and six Conservatives and has just been formed) on the subject of our putting up a candidate. I subsequently had two further interviews with Colonel Morgan-Jones and fully discussed the matter with him. On Monday morning, Mr Wood (our Agent for that part of Gloucestershire and neighbourhood) had breakfast with me and I went very fully into things with him and Colonel Jones. I am persuaded from what I heard that we have a very good chance of winning back this seat if we reduce all chances of an Asquithian torpedo to a minimum, and if we can find the right type of candidate for such an extremely difficult constituency. I gave Mr Wood instructions to again go round the constituency and explore the Asquithian strength there and to report to me as early as possible. Despite the insistence of the Chairman of the Coalition Committee I am in favour of organising this constituency before finding a candidate, and on my return to London I found a letter from Colonel Jones saying that it was quite impossible for him on financial grounds to consider being our candidate – although he is obviously the right type – but that he would undertake to organise the constituency for us. In the meantime, I am laying the whole matter before the Whips' Thursday meeting and awaiting the report from Mr Wood with respect to the remaining strength of the Asquithian element. I was amazed to note the strength of the imprint of Sir Charles Dilke's personality in this constituency wherever I went. It is obvious that politically it is a very highly educated constituency and to be successful our candidate will have to be a young energetic man of fine fighting qualities.

19. *Scovell to Guest, 'Visit to Leeds', 29 May 1920*

I have to report that I visited Leeds on Tuesday the 25th inst., where I met in confidence:

Mr. L.J. Grant – Northern Group

Mr. R. Dickson – Yorkshire Area,

Mr. T.J. Fletcher – North Eastern Area,

Mr. F. Monks.

We had a continuous sitting of six-and-a-half hours, and explored the whole position of some ninety constituencies in Yorkshire, Durham, Northumberland, etc. Mr. Monks dealt with the status and efficiency of all Liberal Agents in those constituencies.

Labour Seats: I came away convinced that we have good chances of recapturing many Labour seats in Yorkshire and the North-Eastern Area, provided Coalition Committees are set up as soon as possible: This is proceeding.

Liberal Seats held by Unionists: There are also a large number of obviously Liberal seats now held by Unionists which the latter should be persuaded to deliver up to us before the next General Election.

Staff: I found our staff in this part of England quite inadequate to meet the strain of present conditions and in-so-far as lay in my power I took steps to remedy this, but it can only be done over a period of time as the necessary trained personnel is not yet forthcoming.

Liberal Agents: It was ascertained that there are very few Liberal Agents of any use at all in these two Areas; most of them are old men past their day, and the few competent ones seem to be either part-timers or else independent Liberal. I can see perfectly well we shall have to train on a number of younger men for these posts before a General Election.

Constituency Information: I issued various instructions with regard to the speeding up of investigations in certain constituencies.

Advisory Committees: I also informed Mr Grant that he should push on with the actual formation of Advisory Committees, the personnel for which he has already submitted to London.

Street Orators: After dinner, accompanied by Messrs Grant and Fletcher, I listened to the Communist street orators outside the Town Hall at Leeds. I came away with the impression that their efforts were to the benefit of the Coalition. They merely spouted hot air, and the only people who listened seemed to be the curious rather than the seeker after real knowledge.

I returned to London by the breakfast train on Wednesday morning, the 26th inst.

General: The general impression I gained from this meeting was that the same steps that I took at Leeds will have to be repeated at all Group offices as soon as possible.

Mr. F. Monks: The presence of Mr Monks was of the greatest benefit, and together we cleared up all sorts of outstanding difficulties and questions.

20. *Guest to Scovell, 'Visit to Leeds and Area Advisory Committees', 3 June 1920*

I read with great interest the report of your visit to Leeds. I think it has been most useful. Now that the ice is broken I want to go full steam ahead with the immediate formation of the Area Advisory Committees. I shall try to arrange for the P.M. to visit them all this autumn. I should not hesitate to advertise their formation. The Area Whip should attend their inaugural meeting.

21. *Scovell to Guest, 'Area Advisory Committees', 4 June 1920*

Thanks for yours of June 3rd. Here are a few details which may interest you:–

Monks: Just when we want him here, he has been forced by his daughter's very serious illness to remain at home up in Lancashire. This is a severe handicap at the present time.

Grant: Grant's father having suddenly died he has been called away to Invernesshire. This is also a serious handicap as it will devolve on him being the only son to settle up things at home. This is very unfortunate at the present juncture.

Liberal Agents: I have managed to get hold of at present some eight Liberal Agents who have hitherto been in the pocket of the Wee Frees.[64] This is a useful reinforcement and I hope to find more as time goes by.

Advisory Committees: I am doing everything possible to push on with the formation of Advisory Committees, but I think from a practical point of view you will find in the end that Coalition Liberal Committees in the constituencies are much more important.

Speakers: We are generally increasing our Speakers Panel and two men have been placed on the Retaining Fee basis during the past week.

Committees: I am setting up two standing committees at once, viz:

(a) A Kinema Committee, consisting of seven, White and one or two others with Erskine-Orr as Secretary.

(b) A Speakers Committee, to go into the whole question of the Autumn campaign the Speakers Parliament in October, etc., with Erskine Orr as Secretary.

(c) The Agents Committee, consisting of Thompson, Monks and Wood with Erskine Orr as Secretary. This Committee for reasons which I have already stated has not yet been able to meet.

Mr Aronson has come as a great Godsend and is rapidly picking up all the frayed ends and getting things onto a proper basis.

I do hope you will soon be back with us and that your progress is being well maintained.

22. *Sir William Sutherland[65] to Guest, 'Seats in Scotland', 4 June 1920*

Thanks for your letter of yesterday. I have spent a good deal of time on this matter since taking up the Scottish duties and can give you a good deal of information now. As you are aware, because of the illness of my predecessor and other things, our

64 The term 'Wee Free' was an epithet commonly applied to the anti-Coalitionists of the Liberal Party.

65 William Sutherland (1880–1949), Liberal MP for Argyllshire 1918–23; colliery owner, Liberal politician, Lloyd George confidant, and civil servant, chancellor of the duchy of Lancaster 1922.

organisation in Scotland, when I took over, was deficient. I am getting it improved; and had the satisfaction only yesterday, and after two months negotiations, of signing on Mr. Gibb as our representative in Glasgow and the West of Scotland. Mr. Gibb is the best official in the Liberal machine in Scotland and this is undoubtedly a catch for us. Our previous man in that area was worse than useless – Hutchinson was his name. He did not get on with any of the West of Scotland Liberals, and all our friends there, strongly pressed for his removal. He was doing us no good at all in the area. We are getting the organisation improved. When Gibb gets going properly he should be a very powerful assistant to us in the West of Scotland where he is widely known and respected among Liberals; and it is in the Western Area that many of the difficulties, you refer to, occur.

Glasgow, Lanarkshire, Edinburgh, are our worst cases. Their representation in:

	Co. Unionists	Co. Libs	Wee Frees	Labour
Glasgow	10	3	–	2
Lanarkshire	4	1	–	2
Edinburgh	3	–	1	1
Total	17	4	1	5

Liberals in these Areas are much dissatisfied with their share in the representation.

Consider Glasgow first:

Of its 15 Seats, I do not imagine any person would raise objections about the following:

Coalition Unionists.	Coalition Liberals.
Bonar Law (Central)	Pratt (Cathcart)[66]
Horne (Hillhead)[67]	MacCallum Scott (Bridgeton)[68]
Gilmour (Pollok)[69]	Sir R. Balfour (Partick)[70]
Mackinder	(Camlachie)[71]

66 John William Pratt (1873–1952), Liberal MP for Linlithgowshire 1913–18 and Glasgow Cathcart 1918–22; parliamentary secretary to the ministry of health for Scotland 1918–22.

67 Robert Stevenson Horne (1871–1940), 1st Viscount Horne of Slamannan; Conservative MP for Glasgow Hillhead 1918–37; minister of labour 1919–20, president of the board of trade 1920–1, chancellor of the exchequer 1921–2; businessman and advocate.

68 Alexander MacCallum Scott (1874–1928), Liberal MP for Glasgow Bridgeton 1918–22; private secretary to Winston Churchill. In 1924 he sent a letter of support to Labour candidates not standing against Liberals, and joined the Labour Party in 1927, then being adopted as a parliamentary candidate.

69 John Gilmour (1876–1940), Conservative MP for East Renfrewshire 1910–18 and Glasgow St Rollox 1918–40; junior lord of the treasury 1921–2, home secretary 1932–5.

70 Robert Balfour (1844–1929), Liberal MP for Partick 1906–18 and Glasgow Partick 1918–22.

71 Halford John Mackinder (1861–1947), Conservative MP for Glasgow Camlachie 1910–22; geographer.

Of the remaining 8 two are Labour:

Barnes Co. Lib. (Gorbals)[72]

Neill MacLean I.L.P. (Govan)[73]

The I.L.P. have a man (the Rev. Charles Hengham) whom they talk of running against Barnes and, of course, if Barnes remains Coalition he will be opposed by the I.L.P. I have a note made to discuss the position with Barnes. Apart from the exceptional position of Barnes we should be disposed to claim this Seat for Lib. Coalition. MacLean in Govan has been working hard and my idea is to try to get D.T. Holmes to contest it as a Coalition Liberal. We want a democratic Coalition Liberal here.

The remaining six Seats are considered by Glasgow Liberals to be Liberal Seats, they are:

1. Mitchell-Thomson (Maryhill)[74]
2. J.M. Macleod (Kelvingrove)[75]
3. Vivian Henderson (Tradeston)[76]
4. Macquisten (Springburn)[77]
5. G. Murray (St. Rollox)[78]
6. Admiral Adair (Shettleston)[79]

It is in regard to these that the question of a deal arises and there is some difficulty in claiming definitely that they all are in fact Liberal Seats, owing to the great charges in areas brought in by the Re-distribution Bill. I take them one by one:

72 George Nicoll Barnes (1859–1940), Labour MP for Glasgow Blackfriars and Hutcheson Town 1906–18 and Glasgow Gorbals 1918–22; leader of the Labour Party 1910–11, minister of pensions 1916–17, minister without portfolio 1917–20; socialist and trade unionist.

73 Neil McLean (1875–1953), Independent Labour Party (and then Labour Party) MP for Glasgow Govan 1918–50; socialist and conscientious objector during the First World War.

74 William Mitchell-Thomson (1877–1938), 1st baron Selsdon; Conservative MP for North West Lanarkshire 1906–10, Irish Unionist MP for North Down 1910–18, Conservative MP for Glasgow Maryhill 1918–22 and South Croydon 1923–32; postmaster-general 1924–9, chaired the television committee 1934–5 and the television advisory committee 1935–8; ennobled 1932.

75 Sir John Mackintosh Macleod (1857–1934), Conservative MP for Glasgow Central 1915–18 and Glasgow Kelvingrove 1918–22; accountant.

76 Vivian Leonard Henderson (1884–1965), Conservative MP for Glasgow Tradeston 1918–22, Bootle 1924–9 and Chelmsford 1931–5; soldier.

77 Frederick Alexander Mcquisten (1870–1940), Conservative MP for Glasgow Springburn 1918–22 and Argyllshire 1924–40; lawyer.

78 Gideon Oliphant Murray (1877–1951), 2nd Viscount Elibank; Conservative MP for Glasgow St Rollox 1918–22; after breaking with Lloyd George over Ireland in 1922, succeeded to the viscountcy on the death of his father in 1927; colonial administrator.

79 Thomas Benjamin Stratton Adair (1861–1928), Conservative MP for Glasgow Shettlestone 1918–22; naval officer.

1. Mitchell Thomson should hold his Seat. He is Under-Secretary in the Food Ministry. Is popular in his seat and has paid a good deal of attention to it. He is little different from any ordinary Liberal in politics. I should propose leaving this seat as it is, for the present consideration.

2. Macleod's seat is pretty certain to be claimed by the Unionist side. Macleod comes of a highly respected family and is personally popular in Glasgow; but my information is that he is losing ground in his Constituency. This seat takes in a considerable section of West End Glasgow and the Unionists have considerable claims on it. Of course, there are many working-class people in it, as well but, at the moment, I should be disposed to leave it to the other side.

3, 4, 5, 6.

Strong claims for vigorous Liberal candidates for these more working-class Districts.

In 3. Vivian Henderson is a very nice fellow who has been attentive to his seat and is fairly popular, though not a strong candidate.

In 4. Macquisten doubtful, but strong Coalition Lib. should hold the Seat. Of course, Macquisten is a type by himself who establishes a certain position by his own peculiarities.

In 5 and 6. Present members very weak and we should have strong Coalition Liberals for them. I have a definite scheme for getting suitable candidates and negotiating with the Unionists about these Seats. So far have been much impeded by the entire futility of our so-called organisation in Glasgow; but with the substitution of Gibb for Hutchinson, we should get a proper beginning made.

In Edinburgh.

Liberals consider they should have four out of the five seats. However, Ford is now established in North Edinburgh (he won the recent Bye-Election from Runciman) and assuming he continues, this gives the Unionists South Edinburgh (C. Murray) and North Edinburgh (P. Ford). I have discussed the remaining three seats often with the Edinburgh Unionists and can, I believe, manage to get from them (subject to something being done for Jameson the sitting member) West Edinburgh. It is really a Liberal seat.

Hogge sits for East Edinburgh. His present opponent is a N.D.P. man, but not good enough. I want a strong Coalition Liberal here. Central Edinburgh is held by Labour – William Graham.[80] I have a scheme in hand to try to get him for Coalition. Failing that, I shall put up a good democratic Coalition Liberal. I consider it a Liberal seat also.

Lanarkshire.

The four Unionist members are:

Nelson (Motherwell)[81]

80 William Graham (1887–1932), Labour MP for Edinburgh Central 1918–31; financial secretary to the treasury 1924, president of the board of trade 1929–31.

81 Robert Frederick William Nelson (1988–1932), Conservative MP for Motherwell 1918–22; businessman.

Elliot (Lanark)[82]

McLaren (Northern)[83]

Buchanan (Coatbridge)[84]

These Lanarkshire seats have a long Liberal tradition; but the growth of Labour has made some difference.

Nelson in Motherwell is a very democratic Conservative. He is very popular, an excellent fellow, a respected and popular employer, a keen supporter of local football clubs and other local sporting institutions. He is Managing Director of Hurst, Nelson & Co., large Locomotive Builders, is young and attends well to his Constituency. Elliot is also popular, locally, and like Nelson is much more Radical than many so-called Liberals. He, too, would be hard to displace. He is an extremely good fellow, a keen politician and his father (a local auctioneer) is the best known, most popular and most highly respected man in the Constituency. He can hold the seat. North Lanark (McLaren's Seat) should be held by a Coalition Liberal. There is a strong Liberal tradition here and McLaren is not a strong candidate. He was a Home Office inspector. Coatbridge (Buchanan) has a strong Labour element and Labour expects to win it. I have these two seats under consideration at present. About North Lanark, I think there is no doubt. We must have a Liberal here. It has always to be remembered that, in such industrial and mining districts as Motherwell, Coatbridge, Bothwell (Labour at present) the nominal politics of the candidate are not always the best determining factor. This was shown in the Bye-Election in Bothwell when the Libs. put up Provost Moffat the best known and respected Liberal in the locality only to have him soundly beaten by Labour. The personality, etc., of the candidate counts, particularly in these mining and iron-works localities in Lanarkshire just as in Yorkshire and elsewhere. The Unionists, for example, are working hard at present in the Bothwell Division (Labour at present) and as the Liberals lost it in the by-election, and Labour is strong here, it may be best, in the end, to leave it to the Unionists. At present, I think, for example we should fight Hamilton. The N.D.P. want it, but I doubt if they can win it. A good Coalition Liberal would, I think, do better. At present it is Labour.

The other outstanding cases of seats in Scotland at present held by Unionists, which the Liberals think they should have are:

East Fife (Sprot). Sprot[85] beat Asquith in 1918, but it is not generally believed that he will hold the seat. Libs. think they should have a Coalition Liberal here.

82 Walter Elliot (1988–58), Conservative MP for Lanark 1918–23, Glasgow Kelvingrove 1924–45 and 1950–8, Combined Scottish Universities 1946–50; financial secretary to the treasury 1931–2, minister of agriculture 1932–6, secretary of state for Scotland 1936–8, minister of health 1938–40.

83 Robert McLaren (1856–1940), Conservative MP for North Lanarkshire 1918–22.

84 Arthur Louis Hamilton Buchanan (1866–1925), Conservative MP for Coatbridge 1918–22; soldier.

85 Alexander Sprot (1853–1929), Conservative MP for East Fife 1918–22 and North Lanarkshire 1924–9; former soldier.

Forfar (Shaw). James Falconer[86] has been adopted as Wee Free candidate. Seat is a Liberal seat. Not expected that Shaw will hold it.

Midlothian North (Sir John D. Hope).[87] A Liberal seat and Hope not expected to hold it.

Dumfries (Major W. Murray). Same thing here. Murray beat Gulland; but seat has been Liberal otherwise since 1885 and though Murray is an extremely nice fellow and a very attentive and hard-working member, he has a big job in front of him to hold Seat.

Aberdeen 2 Seats. At present represented one Labour candidate (Rose) and one Unionist (F.C. Thomson); is regarded by Liberals as an essentially Liberal city and prior to the 1918 Election, regularly returned two Liberal members.

North Aberdeen (Rose, Labour).[88] Ought to be Coalition Liberal and I have this under consideration at present.

South Aberdeen (F.C. Thomson, Unionist).[89] Is an Advocate in Edinburgh; who acts in the House as Parliamentary Private Secretary to Horne. He is a good fellow and very attentive to his Constituency and by no means, a pronounced Conservative. He is keen about his Seat and anxious to hold it.

Dundee. The Coalition Liberals will have to oppose Wilkie[90] (Labour), I take it.

Linlithgow (Kidd). Alex Ure[91] held this seat a long time as a Liberal and after him Pratt held it till 1918. The Liberals think they should have it.

The above gives the information you want as regards Scotland; but it should not be circulated to the Cabinet Committee or to the other branch of the Coalition at present. It is for your private information. I don't think the Cabinet Committee should go beyond a general expression of their opinion that the Liberal Coalition should have many more seats in Scotland, at the present time. I shall shortly, I hope, make up some of the past neglect of organisation there has been in Scotland. The matter to be successful, must depend to a great extent on local negotiations and take into account the peculiarities of each constituency and also the personalities of particular candidates. This is more so, generally, in the industrial and mining areas. In the counties the old party label counts for more, it is true.

86 James Falconer (1856–1931), Liberal MP for Forfarshire 1909–18 and 1922–4.

87 John D. Hope (1860–1949), Liberal MP for Fife West 1900–10, Haddingtonshire 1911–18 and Berwick and Haddington 1918–22.

88 Frank Rose (1857–1928), Labour MP for Aberdeen North 1918–28.

89 Frederick Charles Thomson (1875–1935), Conservative MP for Aberdeen South 1918–35.

90 Alexander Wilkie (1850–1928), Labour MP for Dundee 1906–22.

91 Alexader Ure (1853–1928), 1st baron Strathclyde; Liberal MP for Linlithgowshire 1895–1913; solicitor general for Scotland 1905–9; ennobled 1914.

23. *Scovell to Acting Chief Whip, 'The Need for Women in Parliament', 25 June 1920*

I attach hereto a communication I have received from Miss Pickering which, I think, deserves very close consideration. Mrs Ogilvie Gordon and myself have had more than one discussion on this matter and it is with a view "to caution" that I recommend that in the first instance a meeting be arranged between the Coalition Whips – Liberal, Unionist, and N.D.P. – and a representative group of this special committee, at which nothing more is done than "letting off steam" on the part of the latter. I cannot believe any harm can possibly be done by such a course. On the other hand I feel sure you will not be at all anxious to see the launching of "a female torpedo" into some of the Coalition Constituencies at the last minute before a General Election.

(signed) G.J. Scovell

Enc. Mabel K. Pickering to Scovell, 'The Need for Women in Parliament', 22 June 1920

I should like to draw your attention to a definite movement on the part of the National Council of Women and the National Union of Societies for Equal Citizenship, to work up a strong backing for women candidates in the Next Parliamentary election. The special committee that is carrying on the work is composed of representatives from the executives of these two societies. The members of the committee all actively take part in the work; they are gathering women voters very assiduously into their own or other women societies which deal with political matters on non-party lines, and are speaking at meetings here and there through the country for the purpose of impressing upon women voters the urgency of their duty to be looking out suitable women candidates and securing popular support for them in their respective localities.

The following are some of the more influential members of the Committee:

Chairman: Mrs. Ogilvie Gordon,[92] (Coalition Liberal)

Hon. Sec. Miss Rosamond Smith, (Coalition Unionist)

Miss Helen Fraser,[93] (Coalition Liberal)

Miss Eleanor Rathbone,[94] (independent Liberal adopted Liverpool – E. Toxteth – Town Councillor)

92 Maria Matilda Gordon, née Ogilvie (1864–1939), Liberal activist and geologist. In 1922 she was selected as Lloyd George Liberal candidate for Canterbury, but withdrew before the poll; contested Hastings as a Liberal in 1923, coming second.

93 Helen Fraser (1881–1979), suffragist and educator, Lloyd George Liberal candidate for Glasgow Govan in 1922, coming second, and Liberal candidate for Hamilton in 1923, coming second.

94 Eleanor Rathbone (1872–1946), independent MP for Combined English Universities 1929–46.

Mrs. H.A.L. Fisher,[95] (Wife of the President of the Board of Education)

Miss Macadam, (Lecturer on Social & Economic Subjects, University Extension Board, London University; able; probably extreme Liberal).

Mrs. How-Martyn,[96] (L.C.C. ran as independent candidate, Hendon, 1918).

Mrs. Corbett Ashby,[97] (Asquithian Liberal, adopted for Richmond).

Miss Bertha Mason,[98] (Coalition Liberal).

See also Annexure (A).

There are several others, who, although not members of the Committee are in close touch with it and intend to stand, e.g.

Mrs. Gotto, (Coalition Unionist).

Mrs. Oliver Strachey,[99] (Coalition, without label)

Miss Chrystal Macmillan,[100] (At present travelling abroad for suffrage purposes).

Mrs. Stocks, (Extreme Socialist views).

Excepting Mrs. Corbett Ashby, this Group of women is not in any sense Asquithian and it is well worth an effort to win some of them. I wish very much that you would bring this matter of women candidates for Parliament before the Coalition whips, and would urge them to make some approach to this particular Committee. They might put it that they are anxious to give opportunities to women to contest certain of the parliamentary seats at any future election and wish to be preparing the way for the selection of women candidates in such constituencies. They might also add that having heard of the work of this Committee they thought it would be helpful if an interview could be arranged at an early date between any or all of the members of their Committee and the Coalition Whips themselves. In laying this matter before the Whips will you kindly point out that if no approach is made from their side the attitude that will be taken by these women is that they are bound to fend for themselves. They will, of course, point out to the public that Labour has put forward women candidates and that Asquithian Liberals have been active in this direction but that the Coalition parties have done nothing. Lady

95 Lettice Fisher, née Ilbert (1875–1956), founded in 1918 the National Council for the Unmarried Mother and her Child. Wife of Herbert Albert Laurens Fisher (1865–1940), Liberal MP for Sheffield Hallam 1916–18 and Combined English Universities 1918–26; president of the board of education 1916–22; historian and educator.

96 Edith How-Martyn (1875–1954), suffragist who had unsuccessfully contested Hendon as an independent in 1918.

97 Margaret Irene Corbett Ashby (1882–1981), unsuccessfully contested Birmingham Ladywood 1918, Richmond Surrey 1922 and 1923, Watford 1924, Hendon 1929, Hemel Hempstead 1935 and 1937 for the Liberals and Bury St Edmunds 1944 as an independent Liberal; suffragist.

98 Bertha Mason (1855–1939), suffragist and Liberal activist.

99 Rachel Pearsall Conn Strachey, née Costelloe (1887–1940), unsuccessfully contested Brentford and Chiswick in 1918, 1922 and 1923 as an independent; suffragist.

100 Jessie Chrystal Macmillan (1872–1937), unsuccessfully contested Edinburgh North for the Liberals 1935; suffragist and lawyer.

Astor's[101] case is considered as quite exceptional and was never regarded as a sign that the party was anxious to have a woman member.

In regard to finance, I understand the Committee has a sufficient fund for carrying on the preliminary propagandist work and as time goes on they expect to attract donations from men and women supporters.

There is no question that a spirit of resentment towards the Coalition Government is developing among active-minded women because of the way in which they are ignoring the capabilities of women for parliamentary work, and if this movement is allowed to develop while there is a growing disaffection towards the Government on other grounds, the result would be that a number of these women who are pecuniarily in a position to do so, will come forward as independent candidates even if their chance is slight, and will create a women's demonstration against the attitude of the political parties which have kept women at a distance.

As may be seen from Annexure (B) the list of adopted women candidates contains Labour, independent Liberal, Asquithian Liberal, but no Coalition candidates. If an approach were made by the Coalition Whips to this committee of women it would at least have the advantage of making it impossible for the women to say that no[102] approach had been made from the side of the Coalition. I imagine it would be well for both Liberal and Unionist Coalition Whips to do this and probably do it jointly.

(Signed) Mabel K. Pickering.

Annexure A

The Need for Women in Parliament.

(The National Council of Women & National Union of Societies for Equal Citizenship).

Chairman. Mrs. Ogilvie Gordon, D.Sc., Ph.D., White Lodge, 34 Abbey Rd., N.W.8. (Coal. Lib.)

Hon. Sec. Miss Rosamond Smith, 12 Eaton Place, S.W.1. (Coal. Un.)

Hon. Treas. Miss Helen Fraser, 191, Cromwell Road, S.W.5. (Coal. Lib.)

Secretary. Miss D. Robinson, 62, Oxford Street, W.1.

National Union for Equal Citizenship Representatives.

Miss E.F. Rathbone, T.C., J.P., White Gables, Mossley Hill, Liverpool. Pres. (Extreme Lib.)

Mrs. H.A.L. Fisher, Thursley, Godalming, Surrey (Wife of Pres. of Bd. of Education).

Miss Macadam, 50, Romney Street, Westminster S.W.1. Hon. Sec. (Extreme Lib.)

Mrs. How Martyn, 38, Hogarth Hill, N.W.

Mrs. Hubback, 62, Oxford Street, W.1. Parl. & Information Secretary.

101 Nancy Witcher Astor (1879–1964), Viscountess Astor; Conservative MP for Plymouth Sutton 1918–45.

102 Emphasis in the original.

National Council of Women Representatives.

Lady Cowan, 215, Ashley Gardens, S.W.1.

Miss A. Garrett, 2, Gower Street, W.C.1.

Mrs. Corbett Ashby, 33, Upper Richmond Road, Putney, S.W.15

Mrs. Ralph Durand, "Allens", Plaxtol, Kent.

Miss Green, Parliament Mansions, Victoria St., S.W.1. Sec.

Miss Bertha Mason, 6 Hans Place, S.W.1. (Coal. Lib.)

Note.

This Committee organised and held a meeting in the Queen's Hall on 12th Feb. 1920, at which the Prime Minister was to have spoken, but owing to international business was prevented. Mrs. Lloyd George was present and read a letter from him. Sir Hamar Greenwood, MP was also deputed by him to make a speech.

Among other speakers were:

The Viscountess Astor, MP

Sir Donald Maclean, MP

Mr. Robert Toothill, MP, C.B.E.[103]

Chair. Mrs. Ogilvie Gordon.

The object of this meeting was to arouse public interest in the need for the return of more women to Parliament.

Annexure (B).

List of Adopted Women Candidates.

Mrs. Moody, Liberal, Hanley.

Mrs. Phillip Snowden,[104] Labour, Leicester.

Mrs. Scott Gatty, independent Liberal, Huntingdon.

Lady Warwick, Labour, E. Walthamstow.

Miss E.F. Rathbone, independent Liberal, Liverpool (E. Toxteth).

Mrs. Corbett Ashby, Asquithian Liberal, Richmond.

Mrs. Billson, Free Liberal, Shrewsbury.

Miss Mary Macarthur, Labour, Stourbridge.

103 Robert Toothill (1850–1934), Labour MP for Bolton 1914–22.

104 Wife of Phillip Snowden (1864–1937), 1st Viscount Snowden; Labour MP for Blackburn 1906–18 and Colne Valley 1918–31; chancellor of the exchequer 1924 and 1929–31, lord privy seal 1931–2; chair of the Independent Labour Party 1903–6 and 1917–20, its treasurer 1920–2; ennobled 1931.

24. *Scovell to Guest, 'Norfolk', 9 July 1920*

I have sent you across this morning a report received from Mrs Parish giving the results of her efforts in Norwich. I think we owe her a great debt of gratitude for all pains and trouble and I have telegraphed her our thanks. The following extract from her letter to me may interest you:–

"I hasten to convey to you my report of the meeting of the North Norfolk Liberal Council held today at Lowestoft. The presence of so many delegates from all corners of the division had an excellent effect upon the meeting, and both the agent and the Hon. Sec. were much gratified at the result. I think you will agree that it only shows how necessary it is for personal calls and to offer mode of transport to busy men and women who reside at a distance. This was done to-day, and I venture to suggest must be done again whenever the date is fixed for the meeting of the Council. The Liberal women complain that after working hard for years to keep the Liberal Club, it was sold, and to-day they have no place in which to meet or hold meetings – but I am hoping to arrange for the hire of a room in the premises owned by the Girl Guides in Lowestoft. This news has greatly encouraged the women, and a good number were present at to-day's meeting."

25. *Guest to Thompson, 'Thornbury', 15 September 1920*

It appears probable that Fussell knows more about the position in Thornbury than anybody else and also that the Tory opposition has been somewhat exaggerated. I have decided to stick to Fussell, at any rate until after the Unionist Meeting on the 30th of September and have written to Colonel Sanders to this effect. I have also asked Sanders to ask his local folk to accept the Fussell Nomination. Willshire therefore should not be seen until after that date when we will re-discuss the situation.

26. *Guest to Scovell, 'Colonel Fox', 22 October 1920*

You will have heard of a certain Colonel Fox who towards the end of the war commanded a Battalion of Scots Guards. He is a remarkable street orator and can face and control any audience, however rough. I think he could be trained to use his capabilities for political purposes. In the opinion of those who have heard him he should be well worth £700 or £800 a year to us if we can afford it. At the moment he is seeking a small Governorship but I believe for the sum I have mentioned he would much prefer to stay in England. Will you please consider this and see him? You may remember him as the man who escaped from a German prison.[105]

105 Marginal comment by Scovell confirmed that the matter was discussed between the two of them at the House of Commons. Scovell agreed to see what might be found for him.

27. Scovell to Guest, 'The National Democratic Party', 11 November 1920

In anticipation of your seeing Mr Macleod of the National Democratic Party, I have thought it advisable in the light of our conversation of last week-end to put down a few points for your consideration:

1. From conversations I gather that the N.D.P. are faced with a crisis which will involve any one of the following alternatives in respect to "closer co-operation":

(a) With the Coalition Liberals;

(b) With the Unionist Party – without loss of prestige and abandonment of all principles and personal antipathies, this hardly seems possible;

(c) With the Dudley-Docker Group: This would involve a lock, stock and barrel sale to a Capitalist Group, and could only be the refuge of a bankrupt concern;

(d) With the Nationalist Party: For reasons which I gave you any such step would involve eventually absorption into the Unionist ranks;

(e) With the Wee Frees:

(f) With the Labour Party:

I don't think we need to comment on (e) or (f) – both alternatives are too remote for obvious reasons.

2. A further course for the N.D.P. to pursue were they so inclined, would be to reduce their staff to the minimum, obtain a subsidy (on terms) for their paper, and to carry on a kind of Guerilla War on the flanks of all the Constitutional Parties leading to endless difficulties. This would really amount to political blackmail.

3. If you decide in principle to continue negotiations I would suggest that special stress should be laid on the following:

(a) Frankness in respect to their Parliamentary representatives – This I happen to know is not at present contemplated.

(b) The financial aspect should be dealt with on a basis of:–

(i) Seats at present held in Great Britain;

(ii) Potential seats – say not to exceed 10;

(iii) Concentration of effort on the above seats as distinct from the present system of dispersal and inconsequence;

(iv) X number of pounds monthly at a rate of say £60 per month for a seat now held and £50 per month for a potential seat in Great Britain.

(c) You or your representative to have complete control of all negotiations and arrangements in connection with Sanctuary Chambers or with their head Provincial representatives.

(d) Complete control of policy in any way affecting the N.D.P. within and without the House of Commons.

(e) Closer co-operation not only in principle but in fact – in London as well as the provinces and so on.

4. I have purposely not asked Mr Macleod to table his organisation or schedule his personnel in detail, nor have I obtained from him any exact statement showing what he considers to be:

(a) Seats at present now held;

(b) Seats which may be termed potential.

I have thought it advisable to defer doing this until you have seen him and agreed the main principles.

5. From information I have to hand there seems no question that apart from their connection with the comrades of the Great War in certain parts of the country, the N.D.P. have influence, eg. Sheffield. In other parts, eg. South Wales, it is regarded as a moribund body. On the other hand, we have to bear in mind that the members of its group in Parliament have continually given us whole-hearted support, especially in the early and most difficult days of Coalition Liberalism. On this score alone we ought not to venture, I think, to turn down their approaches without for our part doing our utmost to arrive at an agreement satisfactory to both parties.

6. If any decision is arrived at which involves some form of subsidy, I advocate a black-and-white agreement, subject to a fairly lengthy time limit, say twelve months.

7. I further recommend that within certain well-defined limits they should be masters of their own house.

28. *Scovell to Guest, 'Reorganisation in Wales', 23 November 1920*[106]

1. In accordance with your wishes I now submit for your consideration my proposals for the reorganisation of our affairs in Wales, which I can safely say will lead to great things. They are only placed before you as a consequence of the changes which have taken place in the Executive of the Welsh National Liberal Council, as a result of the Llandudno meeting.

2. On the basis of the first eight months of 1920 we are now spending on political organisation in Wales, the following amounts per annum:

		£
(a) Grant to Welsh National Liberal Council	say	700.
(b) South Wales Office	say	2,800.
(c) Mid Wales Office	say	1,600.
(d) North Wales Office	say	1,800.
		6,900.

106 Marked 'Secret'.

3. On the present basis the costs of Welsh organisation (as enumerated above) are out of all proportion to the total number of seats held in Wales.

The seats in Wales are at present represented as follows:

Coalition Liberal	19.
Labour	10.
Unionist	4.
Independent	2.
N.D.P	1.
	36.

The average cost per seat per annum held by us is therefore £363, if all Seats are taken into account, the cost per seat works out at £190. per seat per annum.

4. In view of the altered position in the affairs of the W.N.L.C., and after discussions I have had with Mr. Salathiel, I have to make the following recommendations:

(a) That on the 31st December, 1920, the whole of our organisation in Wales should cease to function, and that as from the 1st January, 1921, the whole staff should be dissolved.

(b) That as from the New Year the functions hitherto undertaken by our officials in Wales should be performed by the Executive of the W.N.L.C.

(c) That the annual grant made to that body by this office (at present £700. p.a.) be increased say to £200. per month, or £2,400 per year – or if you prefer it £250. per month or £3,000 per year.

(d) That in the event of the W.N.L.C. finding it necessary to augment their existing staff in order to carry out this new work, they should be asked to give priority in selection to our existing staff, and I recommend that it be made part of the bargain with them that the following two officials be taken on by them on whatever terms they care to arrange:

Mrs. Price White (Bangor), who has done excellent work for us during the past two years, but who for domestic reasons cannot become a mobile member of our provincial staff.

Mr. Treharne (Cardiff) ex Liberal Agent of many years standing, who could in time be absorbed as a Constituency Agent in South Wales.

(e) The remainder of the staff be retrenched on generous lines, or if suitable and vacancies admit, be absorbed into the English or Scottish portion of the machine.

5. From conversations I have had with Mr. Salathiel, I gather that more good could be done by subsidising Liberal Agents in the Constituencies for work in connection with this organisation than by employing whole time officials who are not Constituency Agents, and who are considered locally as being what we may term political "super-spies". We are employing the former system to a certain extent in Lancashire, with, I think, fair success, and it is certainly much cheaper than employing whole time male officials with substantial salaries.

6. The only two officials whose services I am not at all anxious to lose from this organisation, are:–

(a) Mr Joseph Jones – Mid Wales.

(b) Miss Owen – South Wales.

If the W.N.L.A. does not require their services I think I should be asked to find places for them.

7. A List of the staffs of the Welsh Areas showing salaries and date of first joining the organisation is appended for your information.

29. *Scovell to Guest, 'Party Finances', 20 December 1920*

Very Secret Indeed

Chief Whip.

1. I feel it is my duty to let you know that another heavy overdraft at the Bank is in sight.

2. You will remember that you paid off the last overdraft on October 21st. This covered the increased expenditure from July.

3. Before I proceed to details I should remind you that although my monthly cheque is £7,000 or £84,000 per year, the expenditure for some time has been closer on £9,000 per month, and I suggest for your consideration that this is the amount that should be paid into my Account monthly from the 1st January, 1921: if you include the N.D.P. this will make it £10,000 per month.

4. I think I should also mention that the pressure on my time limits that which I can devote to economy, but while the demands on our resources become greater and greater there are certain features in the situation which I may describe as the "silver lining". These are stated in a separate paragraph below.

5. To return to the overdraft, the following exceptional payments have been made during the month of November and December:

6.

		(Approx) £
Wallis Myers' Outstanding Accounts		1278
Pettit Case (via Messrs Bircham & Co)		2000
Publicity Dept (Sept A/cs)		2190
Ditto (Oct A/cs)		3253
(Note: As I have previously explained to you the Last two items largely concern the "stocking of the Shop")		
Final settlement,	Mr Dickson	200
Ditto	Mr Mitchell	60
Ditto	Mr Arenson	250

Ditto	Mr Wherry Anderson	288
Ditto	Mr Corbett	25
Ditto	Mr Barter	40
	Brought Forward	9584
Final settlement,	Mr Turner	75
Expenditure,	Mr Kellaway's Constituency	114
Ditto	Mr Purchase's Constituency	20
Ditto	Mr Glanville's Constituency	108
Ditto	Oxford University N.R. Club	113
Downing Street Motor A/cs		572
(Note: This includes special charge of £121 for 600 gallons of petrol re. coal strike. Much of the remaining expenditure represents improvements to cars and non-recurring expenditure Generally)		
Central Office: Non-recurring expenditure		350
(Note: £100 to £150 more will complete non-recurring expenditure under this head: this includes fire alarms, shelving, repairs and renovations to furniture, alteration of lighting etc)		
Total of Extraordinary expenditure		£10,936

7. In considering this overdraft and as will be seen from the above explanation I feel I should lay emphasis on the fact that this has largely been caused by the very large payments on behalf of the Publicity Dept amounting in all to approximately £6,700. In addition to this we have the special payment to Messrs Bircham and Co., of £2,000, making a total of £8,700.

8. I think also I ought to make it clear to you that during the current year we are carrying in part or in whole so to speak no less than fifteen constituencies.

9. A further point which has to be borne in mind is that in the past month we have had to pay very heavy fees and expenses of speakers. The annual report will, however, give a clearer indication of what has been effected in this respect.

10. The Welsh reorganisation proposals which would have affected great economy have unfortunately fallen through.

Reports Towards Economy

11. I now give you the "silver lining" for what it is worth:

(a) All our London Offices have been disposed of with the exception of 38 Lower Belgrave Street which will soon be settled.

(b) During the past two months the number of resignations in the Staff in Men only number 10, and 3 or 4 more are expected. Of the Women Staff 4 or 5 further resignations are in course of submission. I am hoping to avoid replacing the majority of these members of the Staff.

(c) In two or three cases agents are beginning to find houses in their new locations, thus relieving us of payment of subsistence allowance owing to being separated from their families.

(d) As candidates come into the field it is hoped that the expense of our paying constituency Agents will diminish. For instance, in London if our plans mature as we think they will we shall save about £1,000 per annum on existing expenditures.

(e) I propose to re-consider retaining fees to speakers at an early date.

(f) I have now arranged that practically all supplies are bought on a wholesale or trade price basis.

(g) I have every reason to expect early in the New Year substantial help in respect to our Yorkshire and North East coast organisation.

(h) In the Publicity Dept we have as yet had no credits for trade sales or advertisements which now must amount to a considerable sum: on the other hand we have had approximately £1,600 in subscriptions.

(i) Economies are daily being affected in every possible direction, but lack of time and opportunity prevent me from effecting the same in as short a space of time as I should like.

Final Remarks

12. Early in February I hope to submit to you a complete Abstract of Expenditure for the year 1920.

13. Speaking for myself it is only after reading the Annual Report of work accomplished that one has any conception of what has been effected. Were it not for this I think I should despair to run an administration of this kind in these days of high prices is a thankless task largely perhaps because one is not in a position to see definite results either in the form of a dividend or any other concrete advantage.

30. *Guest to Scovell, 'Christmas Greetings', 24 December 1920*

Just a line on Christmas Eve to wish you a happy Christmas and to ask you to convey a similar message to Thompson and to your staff. You must not think that because I have not been able to see you very regularly that I have not appreciated the incessant work that you have devoted to the cause. The fact that I have been able to go sometimes for weeks without seeing you is the surest proof of the confidence that I have in your steady attention to business and in your efficiency to control a very difficult machine. I expect to go abroad on the 29th for two or three weeks and I hope you will do likewise. I am, however, counting upon you to arrange for a sufficient number of heads of departments to be ready to assist Mr. Ward during my absence. Please let me have a note indicating who will be there during that period.

31. *Scovell to Guest, 'Munitions Scandal', 11 February 1921*

I am somewhat anxious about a certain matter which Captain Loseby,[107] under the seal of confidence, drew my attention to last Saturday afternoon. I was so impressed with his statements that as you were not at Downing Street on Monday morning I went at once to Mr. E.R. Davies, who was acting for Mr. J.T. Davies, and mentioned the matter to him. The facts are roughly as follows:

Captain Loseby has in his possession, or available definite proofs of the charges which are formulated in the document attached hereto. Certain powers and influences are behind him which make it unavoidable that these charges are thrashed out to their final conclusion. It appears that he has already had several interviews with Lord Inverforth[108] and Mr. J.D. Hope, and the only satisfaction he has got – despite an "ultimatum" – is the offer of a departmental enquiry. He affirms that this will not be satisfactory as the charges are too serious and involve negligence and irregularity in respect to the very large sums indeed of public money. In brief he demands the setting up of an extra-departmental tribunal. His "ultimatum" expires to-night, and I understand that his request is not going to be granted. Mr E.R. Davies, to whom I explained the matter, (I was not at the time in possession of the charges formulated against the Ministry of Munitions) said he would speak to the Prime Minister about it, but as he (Davies) has left for Cardigan I am a little nervous in case the matter has been overlooked; the more so as I understand only this very morning Lord Inverforth gave no indication that he was going to do more than hold a departmental enquiry. In view of the political advantage that might be taken of the formulation of such charges in the House of Commons, it seems to me that you might care to suggest to the Prime Minister that he should insist on the Committee being an extra-departmental one.

Capt. Loseby assures me that he cannot and will not stay his hand no matter what pressure is put on him, and only came to me as being so closely connected with the political machine to explain that he has done everything possible before bringing the matter up in the House. I understand too that even if Captain Loseby were to back out of raising the matter in Parliament, the powers and influences behind him would not hesitate to lay the matter before the Opposition. This, presumably, would then make matters worse from a political point of view.

Charges Against the Ministry of Munitions.

1. That large sums of money, to which they are not entitled, have been and are being paid to contractors owing mainly to three causes:

(a) The culpable negligence of the Liquidation Committee, consisting of Messrs. Sutton, Hewitt and Barber.

107 Charles Loseby (1881–1970), National Democratic Party MP for Bradford East 1918–22; soldier and lawyer.

108 Andrew Weir (1865–1955), 1st baron Inverforth; surveyor general of supplies 1917–19, minister of munitions 1919–21; shipowner; ennobled 1919.

(b) The payment of contractors claims without adequate investigation.

(c) The failure to take into account before such final settlement of debts owing by such contractors of which the department has records, notably for loans, material supplied on repayment and free issues.

2. That in order to defeat a true and proper audit, orders were given by Mr Sutton of the above Committee to the heads of Ledger Departments, consisting of some thirty persons, to destroy all working papers, or such papers as would help Exchequer and Audit to do their duty, thereby rendering the detection of fraud or wasteful negligence more difficult.

3. That after Mr. Sutton had openly acknowledged in the presence of Lord Inverforth, and other high officials of the Ministry, including his immediate head, that he had given instructions that working papers were to be concealed in such a way that Exchequer and Audit were not to have access to them, he was retained in his then responsible position and given further and still more responsible work in the matter of disbursing public money.

32. *Scovell to Guest, 'Reaction to the Promotion of Hewart', 19 February 1921*

As you will see by the attached copy of the *Daily Chronicle* of 17th February, consternation was caused in our ranks by the publication of the promotion of Sir Gordon Hewart. This is specially exasperating having regard to the fact that:

(a) In the case of Kircaldy the secret has been well kept and we ought to score accordingly;

(b) In the case of Leicester the situation there has always been extremely complicated. The Annual Meeting of the Association is due in a few days' time and our friends there feel they have been let down by this premature announcement.

I would beg of you most earnestly to have exhaustive enquiries made into the whole matter. The announcement appears to us to come from the pen of Mr Nicolson. One would naturally expect a friendly organ to be more circumspect.

33. *Scovell to Guest, The Need to Engage Supporters, 23 February 1921*

I think it very advisable now that Councils are formed or are being formed, that during the next two or three months some opportunity should be afforded the Prime Minister of meeting his (Coalition Liberal) principal supporters in London and the Provinces at some central place like the Central Hall, Westminster. The Albert Hall is, I believe, distasteful to him as its acoustic qualities are so bad. I think you will agree that unless something of this kind is done we shall not be able to pull these Councils together and keep them enthused for long. On the other hand if we were in a position to allot a substantial number of tickets to his most influential supporters of all creeds and classes in each area in the provinces, we should at least have given our friends an opportunity of seeing and hearing him whether they were in a position to come to London or not. In this connection it seems to me that the great thing, if it is possible, is to give people ample notice in view of the heavy travelling expenses involved.

34. *'Rules of the 1920 Club' included in Colin Coote*[109] *to Scovell, 4 March 1921*

Name: The name of the Club shall be the "1920 Club".

Object: The object of the Club shall be the maintenance and promotion by Coalition Liberals of the principles of national unity and co-operation in the new situation which has arisen after the War:

(a) By providing speakers for political meetings, workers at elections and assistance in local organisation; and

(b) By constituting a centre for political discussion and social intercourse.

Membership: British subjects proposed and seconded by members of the Club, who, in the opinion of the Committee are likely by reason of their political ability and general fitness to further the objects of the Club, may be elected members. The subscription for members under 30 shall be 10/6 per annum; the subscription for members over 30 shall be a minimum of £1. 1. 0. per annum.

Associated Clubs: Any club which in the opinion of the Committee of this Club is satisfactorily constituted with the object of promoting the Coalition cause may be associated with this Club, upon such terms and conditions as may be mutually agreed upon.

Elections: The members of the Committee, other than those representing Associated Clubs, shall from time to time be elected by the members of the Club. Until the adoption of a definitive constitution, the Provisional Committee, together with the Vice-President, shall be the Committee of the Club. The election of all Officers and members shall be in the hands of the Committee.

Headquarters: The offices of the Club shall be at: 4, Wilfred Street, Buckingham Gate.

Property of the Club: All property of the Club shall be vested in the Treasurer for the time being.

Constitution: The adoption of a definitive Constitution shall be referred to the Committee for report in the course of 1921.

35. *Guest to Scovell, 'Change of Chief Whip', 4 April 1921*

Before I take up the new work which I have been called upon to undertake, I feel I must write and ask you to convey to all members of our staff, both in the Central

109 Colin Reith Coote DSO (1893–1979), Liberal MP for Wisbech 1917–18 and Isle of Ely 1918–22; journalist on *The Times* 1922–42 and editor of *The Daily Telegraph* 1942–64.

Office and in the Provinces, my deep appreciation of their untiring labours and their unfailing loyalty to me during the strenuous and anxious times we have been through. For all they have accomplished I am more than grateful and in bidding the organisation farewell I feel I am handing over to my successor a devoted band of workers who will, in a very short space of time, merit his gratitude in the same way, or even more so, than they have earned mine.

36. *Scovell to McCurdy, 'Constitutional Labour Party', 14 April 1921*

I have been warned that a gentleman called Alderman Naylor, J.P. is on the prowl trying to get funds for a Constitutional Labour Party. I am told that while he is very plausible he is a person whom one should keep at bay at all costs. I hear too that he is endeavouring to see the P.M. You may be glad to know this.

37. *Memorandum by McCurdy, 'The Principles of the Coalition', 21 April 1921*[110]

I should like the general principles upon which we appeal to the country to support the present Coalition Government to be carefully re-considered. It was quite natural in the first days of the Armistice, and obviously true, to say that the special wartime need which had called parties to a truce during the war had not ended by the signing of an Armistice agreement. It was not then therefore necessary to consider any deeper or more fundamental reasons for the maintenance of Coalition Government. As the war recedes further into the past, we have to consider what are the permanent principles which should govern politics in this country, and consider them, of course, in the light of the experience gained in the war.

The first thing that strikes me is the fact that since the war the Labour Party has definitely emerged into such a position of political strength that it can no longer be ignored, or treated as the humble handmaid of one or another of the political parties which in times past took turns to rule the State. In future there must be at least three distinct political parties, and thus the old party system which was essential in times past, the two party system, has come definitely to an end. What are we to put in its place? Two alternatives lie before us, first, that each of the three parties shall struggle for such a preponderance of votes as will make it possible to govern the country regardless of the political wishes and opinions of the minority. That was what took place under the two-party system, but it was tempered by the fact that the two great parties, Whig and Tory, Liberal and Conservative, had very much in common – in fact the points on which they agreed at all times really far out-numbered the points on which they differed. And on the points on which they differed, they did, in practice, come to compromise and agreement, whatever party was in power, with the opposition.

110 Parliamentary Archives, Lloyd George Papers LG/F/168/2/19.

It was by compromise and agreement, by a Coalition arrangement made beyond the Speaker's Chair, that the Liberal Franchise measure of 1885 became law, and as regards all the great reforms of our political history, the Repeal of the Corn Laws, the Reform Bill of 1832, Catholic Emancipation, the liberation of the slave, it could not be said of one of them that they were carried by a Party – every one was carried by a Coalition, under which one party was nominally in power. It relied for the necessary majority upon the votes of its political opponents.

There has been a great deal of sham and hypocrisy about party politics for the last hundred years; each party tries to make the public believe that the other party were worthless or evil minded people, and that their principles were wide as the poles asunder from the principles of their opponents, whereas in truth and in fact, as soon as they got into Parliament each party was always willing to co-operate with their opponents, knowing well that without such co-operation no real progress in law making or administration would be possible. During the war all this pretence was swept away from the time being. The two parties openly agreed that they would help one another, co-operate with one another for the effective prosecution of the war. That of course implied that when Liberals and Conservatives, meeting in the same Government, found that they were holding different opinions on points of policy it would be their duty to try their utmost to reconcile differences and to come to some compromise or agreement for the good of the country. It seems to me that in so doing they were not only adopting a procedure most likely to result in progress, so far as the work of Parliament and Government was concerned, but they were obeying a much higher law of morality than could be found in the working of the party system.

I think we ought frankly to lay stress for the future more and more upon the plain facts first, now that we have at least three parties in the State we never shall get practical government and practical reforms without some compromise, some agreement and some form of coalition between members of public political parties, whether they like it or not. Secondly, that this is not only inevitable, but it is not in the least to be regretted, because compromise and agreement are not evil and wicked things, as those imbued with the extreme partisan spirit would have us believe, but are simply an exemplification of Christian doctrine, as applied to politics. The articles which I have written for *The Fortnightly Review* recently and for the forthcoming *Contemporary Review* may be referred to as further explaining the views which I have in mind. I should be very glad if I could get one or two articles written by men of independent judgment, dealing with the problem from this point of view.

38. *Lloyd George Gives Thanks on the National Emergency, 4 July 1921*

I have much pleasure in personally thanking you and in conveying to you the thanks of my colleagues, for the services you have rendered during the recent national emergency. The readiness which you and others have shown in coming forward to defend the public was an effectual guarantee for the maintenance of law and order, and for the preservation of the people from threatened privation and misery; it will be remembered with gratitude by all sections of the community. I trust that no further demand will have to be made on your services. If, however, a fresh necessity should arise, I feel sure you will respond with no less public spirit and zeal than you have shown during the past crisis.

39. *Scovell to Miss West, '25 Queen Street Staff', 6 July 1921*

In accordance with instructions, I am sending you over for the Chief's information a list of officials working in the Central Office whom I think he would like to interview from time to time. As regards the timetable he mentioned, on further consideration I suggest that as the Chief's engagements are bound to be subject to fluctuation, you merely send over to the General Secretary, say twenty four hours in advance, a slip giving the names of those he wishes to see and the time of appointment.

On my return from Harrogate – and if experience shows that a more regular programme would be desirable – we can easily arrange it.

G.S. Scovell

Suggested List of Officials to be Interviewed by Mr McCurdy:

Mr L.J. Gooding	– Head of Publications Branch.
Mr G.W. Thompson	– Chief Agent.
Miss Pickering	– Chief Woman Organiser.
Mr. G.W. Gough (Senr)	– Special Branch.
Mrs Gallichan	– Head of Records & Information Branch.
Mr J.T. Stevenson	– Editor, L.G.L. Magazine & Popular View
Mr F.J.G. Dimbleby	– Press Agency Work
Mr A.C. White	– do. do.
Mr Wilkinson Sherren	– do. do.
Mr H.J. Price	– London Area Head
Miss C.M. Gordon	– do. do.
Mr. W.W. Champnes	– Supervisory Head of Home and Eastern Counties Area.
Miss Rowlands	– Home Counties Head
Mrs Beach	– do. do. (Women)

40. *Scovell to McCurdy, 'Lobby Pass', 22 July 1921*

The suggestion has been made from your office that I should hand over my highly prized Lobby Pass so that Dimbleby should have it. That Dimbleby must have such a pass is perfectly clear, but that Miss West's name should be on the Lobby List and that I should surrender my privilege in preference to hers cannot, I think, be in the best interests of the Organisation. The fact of my being on the Lobby List allows me to move about freely all over the House – from Ministers' Rooms to the Dining Room, along the passage to your room and the Whips' Room. Surely such a privilege is not required by Miss West, who I presume, merely requires a pass to take her direct to your room in the House? Looking at it purely from a business point of view, it seems to me that if I am asked to surrender my privilege, Thompson should take my place. Experience has shown me that it is pure waste of time to go down to the Whip's room and wait there for members to come to me. Moreover, the Whips' room is a very unsuitable place in which to conduct any peculiar kind of business, and so if you in your wisdom decree that my name is to come off the Lobby List, then I say one good turn deserves another in that under no circumstances whatever am I called to the House of Commons, but all my business with members is done at No. 25 or No. 12, and nowhere else, and that will be an understood thing by all parties.

You will, I feel sure, realize I have no wish to make difficulties, but the fact of my name being on the Lobby List was due to a long agitation that I had with your predecessor in Office: but I am quite ready to fall in with your convenience in the matter – subject to the one proviso I have mentioned above. I am desperately sorry you could not manage to get here this weekend. I had your rooms and all your baths arranged, and have been busily engaged trying to get our Chairman in the North to come over to meet you. However, it cannot be helped.

I hope to be back the middle of next week. My time up here,[111] however, has not by any means been altogether wasted.

Yours sincerely,

G.S.S.

P.S. If by any chance Miss West sees the foregoing I hope she will not take umbrage at anything I have written. As you know I yield to no-one in admiration of her abilities and anxiety to cause all-round co-operation.

41. *J.W. Clarke, Coalition Liberal Organisation (Midlands Group) to Scovell, 'Independent Trade Union Councils', 18 August 1921*

At the invitation of Mr. McCurdy I attended a small luncheon party at the House of Commons yesterday, which included amongst others Mr. Roberts, MP late Food Controller. The object of the luncheon was to afford the opportunity of discussing the question of the desirability of setting up independent Trade Unionists Councils in the various Constituencies. The absence of Mr. McCurdy tended to curtail a fuller discussion of this subject as there seemed a doubt in the minds of those present as to what the attitude and proposals of the Government were in regard to the questions, nevertheless, the conference was unanimous.

111 It is not clear where 'here' refers to.

Firstly, that there were very many Trade Unionists in this Country in almost every trade who resented the actions of the extremists in both national and local Trade Unions, and that in all probability these men and women will welcome an opportunity to combine together to make their influence and opinion of effect from time to time. Secondly, it was the general opinion of this conference that the reason these men already referred to have not up to the present asserted themselves as a protest against extremists was because up to the present no lead had been given to them by way of encouragement to take action by any of the leading independent Labour men of this Country. Thirdly, it was agreed that the most effectual way to organize these men upon independent Trade Union lines would be for the independent Labour members of Parliament and other leading Labour men to start the ball rolling, by initiating the movement from London and more particularly from Parliament, it was decided that several of us that were present should begin to make secret inquiries in the Constituencies that we are acquainted with, as to the likelihoods of this scheme succeeding if started.

I should take it as a favour if you would hand these conclusions on to either Mr. McCurdy or to Mr. Parker, MP who I believe is interested in this movement, as the meeting requested me to do this.

42. *Scovell to McCurdy, 'Organisational Difficulties', 27 August 1921*

To report that I saw Mr. T. Britten on August 26th and gave him the present you directed, plus a box of cigars. He dilated for hours on the shortcomings of Clarke both as an organiser and as a man. To sum up his points:

(a) Clarke runs his show like a Tsar of all the Russians.

(b) Clarke selects office bearers eg. Jones who T.B. thinks hopeless, a man of straw and without influence or savoir faire.

(c) Clarke's ideas of organisation are limited to the factory.

(d) Clarke brings fierce opposition on himself by the bitterness of his (or his friends) correspondence in the local Press.

I confess I rather took to old Britten. Incidentally the latter spoke in the highest terms of Mr. Irvine and he now bears no ill will to Mr. Gurney. We left the best of friends and he comes in to see me again in November or December.

43. *Election Forecast by Scovell, 'Candidates', 20 October 1921*

The attached forecast is based on the assumption that the General Election will take place under normal conditions, and at a time most favourable to the Government, as a Coalition Government. If the election, however, were based on a national issue such as the Irish question or World disarmament the forecast may be said to be slightly underestimated. One salient fact emerges from this forecast. There can be no confidence about our retaining seats that we hold unless the present members take a bold and definite line in support of the Prime Minister, and either carry on themselves an intensive organisation of the constituency or allow us to do so. We have been very much hampered in our work by certain members desiring to avoid friction with their old Liberal Associations, which, in a majority of cases, are as bodies neither representative nor trustworthy. Our experience is that in constituencies where a clean out has taken place, and active organisation has been engaged in, eg. Northampton and Bolton, we have established our claim to be the real Liberal Party, and the old Associations have shrivelled up.

Summary of Forecast for England & Wales

No. of Co. Lib. & NDP seats won at General Election	No. that can be held or won	No. that are doubtful	No. that will be lost
122	81	33	8
No. of new seats which are to be contested by Coalition Liberal candidates.			
29	3	19	7
...	...	...	...
151	84	52	15

Negotiations with the Unionist Party locally or in London, at present in progress, may result in the allocation of four or five seats in the North of England on which we have not reckoned.

Scotland.

No forecast has been submitted on Scottish seats, as it was felt that you might prefer to discuss the matter direct with Sir William Sutherland.

Summary of Election Forecast by Areas

[See p. 77].

The following seats were won by Co. Libs at the G.E. but will not be contested by Co. Libs at the next election:– The Wrekin, Spen Valley, Norfolk South, Duddeston. In the summary contained in the Memorandum these seats are included in columns 1 and [–][112] making the totals 122 and 8 respectively. [See p. 78].

112 Text unreadable.

<u>Summary of Election Forecast by Areas</u>

Area	Co Lib and NDP Seats won at General Election	Seats which can be held	Doubtful	Certain Losses	New Seats To be contested by Co. Libs	Seats which can be won	Doubtful	Certain Losses
North Western	10	9	–	1	3	–	2	1
Yorkshire	20	16	2	2	5	1	4	–
North Eastern	11	6	4	1	3	–	3	–
South Midlands	9	4	5	–	3	–	3	–
West Midlands	4	2	2	–	3	–	3	–
Home Counties	13	6	7	–	1	1	–	–
Eastern Counties	8	7	1	–	–	–	–	–
London	12	9	3	–	1	–	1	–
Western	9	7	2	–	2	–	2	–
North Wales	8	8	–	–	1	–	1	–
Mid Wales	9	6	3	–	2	–	–	2
South Wales	5	1	4	–	5	1	–	4
Total	118*	81	33	4*	29	3	19	7

Summary of Election Forecast by Areas

Area	Constituency	Co. Liberal sitting member	Seat can be held	Seat Doubtful	Certain Loss	Remarks
NW	Blackburn	Sir Henry Norman	x			Provided member will really move in respect to setting up a new organisation at once.
	Bolton	Capt. Wm. Edge	x			
	Crewe	Sir Jos Davies	x			Provided member continues to give plenty of attention to seat.
	Middleton & Prestwich	Sir Ryland Adkins	x			Provided member will allow us to organise this seat early.
	Mossley	A. Hopkinson			x	Labour will win. Nothing we can do will help him.
	Northern Universities	H.A.L. Fisher	x			
	Stockport	Harry Fildes	x			
	Stratford	Sir Thos. Robinson	x			
	Heywood & Radcliffe	W. Halls (Lab.)	x			If Col. England stands again.
	Westhoughton	R.J. Davies (Lab.)			x	Hopeless with or without organisation.
	Leigh	P.W. Raffan (Ind. Lib.)			x	Even if an agreed candidate is selected.
	Platting (Manchester)	J.R. Clynes (Lab.)			x	
	Oldham	Sir W.M. Barton (Ind. Lib.)	x			Provided a good candidate is placed in the field soon.
Yorks	Barnsley	Sir J. Walton			x	Member's neglect has made this seat hopeless.

Batley & Morley	Gerald France		x		
Bradford, E.	Capt. C.S. Loseby	x			
Buckrose	Capt. A. Moreing	x			
Halifax	Rt. Hon. J.M. Whitley	x			
Huddersfield	Sir C. Sykes	x			
Leeds, C.	R. Armitage	x			All Leeds seats hang on Unionist support and much depends on whether sitting members will allow us to set up a new organisation.
Leeds, N.	Major A.C. Farquharson	x			
Leeds, S.	Sir. W. Middle-brook	x			
Leeds, W.	J. Murray	x			
Attercliffe (Sheffield)	T.W. Casey		x		
Brightside (Sheffield)	Sir T. Walters	x			Provided member allows active organisation to proceed on definite Co. Lib. lines.
Hillsborough (Sheffield)	A. Neal	x			
Park. (Sheffield)	Lt. Col. Stephenson				
Colne Valley	F.W. Mallalieu			x	Unionists to object to present member who is faced with Philip Snowden as Labour candidate.
Doncaster	E. Nicholson	x			Provided member will work things up.
Don Valley	J. Walton	x			

Area	Constituency	Co. Liberal sitting member	Seat can be held	Seat Doubtful	Certain Loss	Remarks
	Pontefract	W. Forrest	x			
	Pudsey & Otley	A.R. Barrand	x			
	Shipley	H.N. Rae	x			
	Hull S.W.	Major Entwistle (Ind. Lib.)		x		
	Hemsworth	J. Guest (Lab.)			x	
	Normanton	F. Hall (Lab.)			x	
	Penistone	W. Gillis (Lab.)		x		Our organisation is aiming at keeping Pringle out.[113]
	Sowerby	Major R. Barker (NFDSS)[114]	x			Provided full Unionist support is ob-tained.
	NE Carlisle	W.T. Carr	x			
	Jarrow	Major G. Palmer		x		Labour will win unless Coalition forces pull together.
	Newcastle W.	Rt. Hon. E. Shortt (retiring)		x		much depends on personality and energy of candidates.
	Berwick	Sir F.D. Blake (retiring)		x		
	Wansbeck	R. Mason	x			
	North Shields	J. Havelock Wilson	x			

113 William Mather Pringle (1874–1928), Liberal MP for North West Lanarkshire 1910–18 and Penistone 1922–4.

114 Robert Hewitt Barker (1887–1961), independent Unionist MP for Sowerby 1918–22, elected with support of the National Federation of Discharged Sailors and Soldiers.

	Stockton	Capt. J.B. Watson	x			Provided candidate gives careful attention to organisation.
	Sunderland	Sir Hamar Greenwood	x			
	Blaydon	Major W. Waring	x			
	Wallsend	M. Simm			x	Unless Coalition forces come together.
	Bishop Auckland	B.C. Spoor (Lab.)	x			
	Middlesboro’	W.W. Thompson (Ind. Lib.)		x		Much depends on selection of candidate.
	Spennymoor	S. Galbraith (Ind. Lib.)		x		
	Newcastle E.	Major H. Barnes		x		Much depends on selection of candidate.
East Mids.	Belper	J.G. Hancock	x			
	Clay Cross	T.T. Broad		x		
	Ilkeston	Major Gen. J.E.B.	x			
	Derbyshire S.	H. Gregory		x		
	Leicester E.	Sir G. Hewart	x			
	Leicester W.	J.F. Green		x		
	Bosworth	Hon. H.D. McLaren		x		Only doubtful if local Unionists queer the pitch.
	Loughborough	Major Oscar Guest		x		Only doubtful as long as present member remains.
	Northampton	Rt. Hon. C.A. McCurdy	x			

Area	Constituency	Co. Liberal sitting member	Seat can be held	Seat Doubtful	Certain Loss	Remarks
	Wellingborough	W.R. Smith		x		If candidate improves and energises his organisation seat might be won.
	Broxtowe	G.A. Spencer (Lab.)		x		Much depends on persona of candidate.
	Mansfield	E. Carter (Lab.)		x		ditto
	Cannock	J. Parker	x			
	Lichfield	Sir G. Warner		x		All depends on willingness of sitting member to allow to organise seat.
	Hanley	J.A. Seddon		x		
	Stoke	Lt. Col. J. Ward	x			
	Wolverhampton East	G.R. Thorne (Ind. Lib.)		x		
	Newcastle Under Lyme	Col. J.C. Wedg-wood (Lab.)		x		
	Burslem	S. Finney (Lab.)		x		Largely depends on candidate.
	Bedford	Rt. Hon. Kellaway	x			
	Luton	C. Harmsworth	x			
	Buckingham	Capt. G.W.E. Bowyer	x			
	East Ham N.	Sir J. Bethell		x		Great need for action on part of member.
	Romford	Capt. A.E. Martin	x			
	Banbury	Sir Rhys Williams Bt.	x			

Southampton	Maj. Gen. Sir. I. Philipps/			x	Unless sitting members really set to work and organise.
	W. Dudley Ward		x		
West Ham S.	Glen Edwards		x		
Walthamstow W.	C. Jesson		x		
Saffron Walden	Sir C. Beck (Ind.) (Retiring)		x		Depends on candidate and co-operation of coalition forces.
Dartford	J. Mills (Lab.)	x			
Leyton, East	C.L. Malone (Com.)		x		
Portsmouth, C.	Sir T. Bramsdon	x			If Co. Lib. allowed to run an agreed candidate.
Cambridge County	Rt. Hon. E.S. Montagu	x			
Isle of Ely	Capt. C. Coote	x			
Norfolk, S.W.	Sir H. Winfrey	x			
Lowestoft	Sir B. Beauchamp (Retiring)	x			
Sudbury	S.G. Howard	x			Provided candidate really works.
Norwich	G.H. Roberts	x			Provided whole hearted support of Unionists is forthcoming.
	Com. E. Hilton Young[115]	x			

115 Edward Hilton Young (1879–1960), 1st baron Kennet of the Dene; Liberal MP for Norwich 1915–23 and 1924–6, Conservative MP for Norwich 1926–9 and Sevenoaks 1929–35; parliamentary secretary to the board of education 1919–21, financial secretary to the treasury 1921–2, minister of health 1931–5; ennobled 1954.

Area	Constituency	Co. Liberal sitting member	Seat can be held	Seat Doubtful	Certain Loss	Remarks
	Rye	A. Lyle Samuel		x		Unless Coalition forces can combine and a good candidate found.
	Battersea, N.	R. Morris		x		Unless a new strong candidate is Forthcoming.
	Bethnal Green N.E.	Sir E. Cornwall		x		Unless member reorganises.
	Camberwell N.W.	Rt. Hon. T.J. Macnamara	x			
	Peckham	Sir A. Richardson		x		Unless member really works.
	Hackney	W.J.U. Woolcock (Retiring)	x			
	Kennington	H.G. Purchase	x			
	Poplar S.	Sir A. Yeo	x			Provided unemployment trouble gets Over.
	Shoreditch	Dr. C. Addison	x			
	Southwark, C.	J.D. Gilbert	x			
	Southwark, N.	E.A. Strauss	x			
	Southwark, S.E.	Com. J.A. Dawes (Retiring)	x			Provided candidate takes a strong line.
	Limehouse (Stepney)	Sir W. Pearce	x			
	Bermondsey, W.	H.J. Glanville (L)	x			
	Bristol, E.	G. Britton (Retiring)		x		Unless a really strong candidate is (Retiring) forthcoming.
	Bristol, N.	E.S. Gange (Retiring)	x			

Bristol, S.	Sir W. Howell Davies	x			
Cornwall, N.	Sir C. Croydon Marks	x			
St.Ives.	Sir C. Cory		x		Unless member obtains fullest co-operation of all Coalition forces.
Barnstaple	Capt. J.T. Tudor Rees	x			
Dorset, E.	Rt. Hon. Capt. F.E. Guest	x			
Stroud	Sir J. Aston Lister	x			
Camborne	F.D. Acland (Ind. Lib.)		x		Unless candidate really puts his back into it.
Forest of Dean	J. Wignall (Lab.)	x			Much depends on brilliance of candidate.
Thornbury	A. (Ind. Lib.)	x			
Carnarvon Boroughs	Rt. Hon. D. Lloyd George	x			
Carnarvonshire	Major C.E. Breese	x			
Denbigh	Sir D.S. Davies (Retiring)	x			
Wrexham	Sir R.J. Thomas (Retiring)	x			
Flintshire	Col. T.H. Parry	x			
Merionethshire	Haydn Jones	x			
Montgomeryshire	Major E. Davies	x			
University	Rt. Hon. J.N. Louis	x			

Area	Constituency	Co. Liberal sitting member	Seat can be held	Seat Doubtful	Certain Loss	Remarks
	Anglesey	Brig-Gen. Sir O. Thomas (Lab.)		x		
	Brecon and Radnor	S. Robinson	x			
	Cardiganshire	Capt. E. Evans	x			
	Carmarthen	J. Hinds	x			
	Llanelli	J. Towyn Jones	x			
	Aberavon	Major. J. Edwards		x		
	Neath	J. Hugh Edwards	x			
	Pembrokeshire	Sir E. Jones Bt.	x			
	Swansea E.	D. Matthews	x			
	Swansea W.	Sir Alfred Mond Bt.	x			
	Gower	J. Williams (Lab.)			x	
	Ogmore	V. Hartshorn (Lab.)			x	
	Cardiff, E.,	Sir Wm. Seager	x			
	Pontypridd	T.A. Lewis		x		
	Aberdare	C.B. Stanton		x		
	Merthyr	Sir E. Jones		x		
	Newport	L. Haslam		x		
	Caerphilly	Morgan Jones (Lab.)		x		
	Abertillery	G. Barker (Lab.)			x	

	Bedwellty	C. Edwards (Lab.)		x
	Rhondda, W.	W. John (Lab.)		x
	Pontypool	T. Griffiths (Lab.)	x	
Scot	Aberdeen & Kincar-dine, E.	Sir W.H. Cowman		
	Kincardine & Western	Lt. Col. Hon. A.C. Murray		
	Banffshire	Sir. C.C. Barrie		
	Berwick & Haddington	J.D. Hope		
	Caithness & Sutherland	Sir R.L. Harmsworth		
	Dundee	Rt. Hon. Winston Churchill		
	Dunfermline Burghs	J. Wallace		
	Inverness	Rt. Hon. T.B. Morison		
	Ross & Cromarty	Rt. Hon. J. Macpherson		
	Morray & Nairn	Sir A. Williamson		
	Orkney & Shetland	Sir M. Smith		
	Kinross & Western	J. Gardiner		
	Perth	W. Young		
	Universities	D.M. Cowan		
	Roxburgh & Selkirk	Rt. Hon. H. Munro		
	Montrose Burghs	J. Long Sturrock		

Area	Constituency	Co. Liberal sitting member	Seat can be held	Seat Doubtful	Certain Loss	Remarks
	Stirling & Falkirk	Rt. Hon. J.R.M. Macdonald				
	Argyllshire	Sir W.M. Suther-land				
	Ayr & Bute	Hon. A. Shaw				
	Galloway	Major G. McMick-ing				
	Bridgeton	A. MacCallum Scott				
	Cathcart	J.W. Pratt				
	Partick	Sir Robt. Balfour Bt.				
	Rutherglen	A.K. Rodger				
	Renfrewshire E.	J. Johnstone				
	Renfrewshire W.	Col. J.W. Greig				
	Dumbarton Burghs	John Taylor				

44. *McCurdy to Scovell, 'Candidates', 26 October 1921*[116]

Hearing you are going to attend the Executive Committee Meeting of the London Area Council tomorrow, I submit a few notes for your personal consideration:

1. We hold 12 seats and are responsible for 13 candidatures. I suggest we remain directly responsible to you in all respects for the Organisation, and working up of these seats, of course welcoming any advice or help the Executive Committee care to give.

2. We have, outside the above, some 20, varying in strength of membership from 12–200, Committees or Associations in Seats held by Unionists. I suggest the funds of the Council under the direct responsibility of the Executive Committee be devoted to stimulating these bodies by paying for propaganda, meetings, socials, and organisers to increase their strength and influence.

3. If the Executive Committee wish in the near future to obtain increased Liberal representation in London, I suggest they take over the financial and other responsibility for organising Co-Liberals in two blocks of seats. I say "Blocks" because it is only the pressure that comes from say 3 or 4 contiguous Liberal Associations that will move the Unionists who are quite capable of discerning that it will be to their advantage by giving away one seat they can obtain full Liberal support say in the other three. To this end I have suggested:

(a) South of the River. The Wandsworth block of 5 seats at present all held by Tories in all of which there is plenty of Liberalism, organised in skeleton form only.

(b) North of the River. The Islington block of 4 seats, at present all held by Tories, where the same conditions rules as in the Wandsworth block.

4. I would like to point out for your private information that with the exception of Lord Ratherdean and a few others. The Committee including the Chairman of Sub-Committee, Sir Herbert Morgan, have little or no real experience of London political organisation. I am very much surprised to find that Major Goronwy Owen[117] has for two months been adopted as candidate in succession to Mr Holman Gregory. This is the first I have heard of this man. Will you kindly let me know who he is and under what circumstances he was adopted. Will you also kindly let me have a list of all candidates adopted since I became Chief Whip. I should also like some information with regard to important negotiations which I understand are proceeding both in Manchester and in Leeds with a view to a more equitable allocation of seats. Up to the present I have had no information put before me with regard to either of these matters, which have only come to my knowledge through questions put to me by members in the Lobbies which disclosed to me the fact that negotiations of the kind are proceeding.

116 Marked 'Very Private & Personal'.

117 Goronwy Owen (1881–1963), Liberal MP for Caernarvonshire 1923–45; Liberal chief whip 1931–2; soldier.

No candidate ought under any circumstances to be recommended to a local Association or to receive the official approval of the Coalition Liberal Party Organisation without my approval having been first obtained. I should also like to know who is Tee, who I am informed is a candidate for Broxtowe Division.

45. *Scovell to McCurdy, 'North Battersea', 5 December 1921*

As you know Mr. Morris our member for Battersea North is thoroughly discredited. We have however now built up a new Association there, with a first-class agent and about 2,000 supporters up to date. We cannot get much further unless we have a candidate who is urgently needed. Can I presume that Mr. Morris will not seek re-election? I don't think in any case a single person will be found to re-adopt him. There is already a Democratic Association candidate in the field whom both this and the Unionist Office wish to have nothing to do with.

46. *Scovell to McCurdy, 'Lord Leverhulme', 7 December 1921*[118]

I have ascertained that Lord Leverhulme[119] in the ordinary way sails for Africa via Liverpool on Saturday January 21st. This will mean he cannot be Chairman at the great meeting on that day which would be a pity on two grounds:

1. He has the biggest world-wide name of all our "lay" supporters.

2. The London Coalition Liberal Council are now proposing to ask him to be their President with a view to getting him to give the Devonshire House Reception on the Friday night over their name, as they are naturally anxious by this means to obtain an increase in their prestige and incidentally the money to cover the cost.

As you will be seeing Lord Leverhulme, I believe, at the Manchester dinner, would you sound him about the Chairmanship for Saturday January 21st. I am told he will in all probability be quite ready to alter his date of sailing and we shall then, I hope, be able to get over our London Council difficulties, which at the moment are, I can assure you, none too easy.

47. *Scovell to McCurdy, 'Mr Jesson MP', 23 February 1922*

I think you might care to see the following extracts from a letter I have received from Mr. Jesson, MP[120]

118 Marked 'Very Urgent'.

119 William Lever (1851–1925), 1st Viscount Leverhulme; industrialist and philanthropist.

120 Charles Jesson (1862–1926), National Democratic and Labour MP for Walthamstow West 1918–22.

48. *Extract of a Letter from Charles Jesson, MP Addressed to Colonel Scovell [undated]*

After carefully considering my present position in connection with the National Liberal Party, I have now come to the conclusion that no useful purpose can now be served by my not definitely, and wholeheartedly associating myself with the Prime Minister and his party, as his programme is practically the same as that of the National Democratic and Labour Party. The only question I am in doubt about is the compulsory settlement of industrial disputes that inflict suffering upon that section of the public who are in no way responsible for them. But as I shall be free to advocate this policy within the ranks of the Party, I realize there is no need for a separate political organisation for this purpose. My immediate difficulty, however, is my active supporters in West Walthamstow are mostly ex-labour men, Conservatives, Liberals and Socialists, and they may not be prepared to come over to the Liberal Party all at once. I am, therefore, commencing the publication of a local eight page monthly paper under the title of "The Walthamstow Democrat" for the purpose of trying to bring them round to the same way of thinking as myself. I realize, however, that this will require time and very careful handling, but I feel confident I shall be successful, providing I do not rush the matter too much.

49. *Scovell to McCurdy, 'National Liberal Council Conference', 14 March 1922*[121]

The accompanying statement has been prepared for me by the Secretary to this year's National Liberal Council Conferences. I also enclose a tabular Statement shewing the expenditure for the Organisation, London, and Provincial, 1921.

National Liberal Council Conference[122]

19th, 20th, 21st January 1922.

Summary of Cost

	£	s.	d.
Hire of Central Hall Buildings, Services and Insurance	554	16	4
Caterers-Agents Luncheon, Dinners, Furnishing and Equipment	643	18	1
Devonshire House Reception	1189	13	11
Area Expenses	956	3	4
Printing – Gooding's Account	283	17	4
Miscellaneous – Postage and all sundry expenses	529	11	7
	£4159	0	7

121 Marked 'Secret'.

122 Marked 'Secret'.

50. *Scovell to McCurdy, 'Middlesborough, Broxtowe and Peckham Seats', 24 March 1922*

1. Major Goronwy Owen, DSO, has been on our candidates list for a long time. His particulars are in the candidates' file in Downing Street. You are mistaken in thinking that this is the first you have heard of him. He was at your dinner at the Hyde Park Hotel in January last and made a short and excellent speech on that occasion in reply to your own. Mr. Holman Gregory[123] met him in my office, took him down with him to South Derbyshire and introduced him to the Constituency, where he is now making great headway, I understand.

2. As regards the negotiations in Manchester. I know nothing except what you mentioned to me last Friday and from what I gathered from Sir E. Rhodes in conversation a day or two ago. So far 25, Old Queen Street has not come into the picture. As regards Leeds nothing is known here of any negotiations and as we hold four seats out of the six – and with your cognisance Miss Grant is fighting O'Grady's seat there – it would seem as if the first move for a more equal representation would come from the Unionists. Possibly Sir W. Edge may have information which he hasn't disclosed to us here.

3. I note your wishes in respect to Candidatures. In point of fact I do not think during your tenure of office any candidatures have been settled without your knowledge except perhaps in the case of:

Middlesborough – Councillor Spence adopted locally with the approval of our Executive in Newcastle.

Broxtowe – Councillor Tee adopted locally a year ago on our recommendation (see below).

Peckham – Mr. Lesser adopted a few days ago by our local folk. He has got to see you.

4. Mr. Tee has been the candidate in the Broxtowe Division for the past 9 months. He is a well-known Liberal and non-conformist in York; an office bearer in our Organisation; an excellent preacher and a well-known Temperance advocate. He was put up for Broxtowe after others had refused with a view to rallying our folk and working up a particularly difficult Labour seat in plenty of time before the General Election, He also has the additional advantage of being able to take the pulpit in the chapels.

G.J. Scovell

Enclosed: <u>List of Adopted Co. Liberal Candidates</u>

Oldham – Alderman E. Wilson. Sir W. Edge fully informed. Chief Whip has also met Mr. Wilson on more than one occasion this year.

Burslem – Mr. Malkin. Well known to Capt. Guest also to yourself as I took him only a few weeks ago to your room in the House of Commons.

123 Henry Holman Gregory (1864–1947), Liberal MP for South Derbyshire 1918–22; lawyer and judge.

Newcastle-under-Lyme – Rev. A. Shaw. No remarks. He is well known to you.

Kingswinford – Mr. Beyfus. You have already met him more than once.

Wolverhampton [East] – Mr. Shaw. Has been a N.D.P. candidate since the last G.E. (an inheritance).

Berwick – Mr. Phillipson. Well known to you.

Newcastle East – Mr. Stone. You interviewed him specifically at the House of Commons immediately after his adoption.

Wansbeck – Major Neal, M.C. Not fully settled. The candidate is your own recommendation.

Bishop Auckland – Atherley Jones. Not fully settled. You are well acquainted with this gentleman.

Jarrow – Hay Morgan. You are fully acquainted with this candidature.

Middlesborough – Councillor Spence. You have not met this gentleman yet.

Sowerby – Mr. Roebuck. I think you have met him. His adoption approved by Sir. W. Edge a long time back

Leeds – Miss Grant. You have approved of this.

Hemsworth – Dr. Crossley Holland. Adopted before you took over.

Normanton – Mr. Bearcroft. Decided on before you took over but I don't think you have ever met. Bearcroft stood at the last G.E.

Barnsley – Col. Maurice Moore. You are already aware of this.

Broxtowe – Mr. Tee. Already commented on.

S. Derbyshire – Major Owen, DSO. ditto

Loughborough – General Spears. Well known to you

Wellingborough – ? You are arranging this candidature

Eye Division – Gerald Howard. Well known to you

Lowestoft – B. Beauchamp. " " " candidature arranged 1919

Dartford – Mr. Jarrett. Arranged 1919

Saffron Walden – Col. Harbinson. Well known to you and to your predecessor

East Ham. North – Ald. Edwards. Adopted locally; entirely on his own; I don't think either of us have ever met him.

Portsmouth – Sir T. Fisher. You are acquainted with him and the circumstances of his adoption

Elland – Sir R. Newbald Kay. Both these cases are well known to you.

Canterbury – Mrs Ogilvie Gordon

Peckham – Mr. Lesser. Already referred to.

51. *Scovell Memo to McCurdy, 'Elland Constituency', 28 March 1922*

I fear there is, as I told you in front of Sir George Younger a week or two ago, nothing we can do. The situation is out of our hands altogether.

Sir R. Newbald Kay[124] is not recognised by us. He was not, as stated, brought into the Division by our organisation but was approached, selected and adopted by the powerful Liberal Association of Elland entirely on their own.

Elland has been a traditional Liberal seat continuously since 1886.

I have done my best to get Sir R. Newbald Kay to stand down but nothing will induce him to. He and his wife have worked liked niggers and he has committed himself too far. All my information goes to show that he is going to win hands down. Even Labour recognises it.

52. *'Memorandum on the Political Position in Manchester', 29 March 1922*

The present political situation in Manchester can only be fully appreciated when its history and traditions are taken into consideration. The city has always taken pride in the fact it has led the way in political thought. This conceit has been encouraged by the fact that in all great political movements, Manchester opinions have become ultimately the prevailing view of the electorate. Manchester politicians take themselves very seriously and the intensity of partisan feeling has been shown in the frequent "swing of the pendulum".

In the General Election of 1906 Manchester's overwhelming vote for Free Trade declared on the opening day of the election, had undoubtedly considerable influence upon the remaining constituencies. The result of the General Election in 1918, when no Liberal of any description was returned, was accounted for largely by fact that the National Liberal Federation held its meetings there a month previous to the election and the electors believed that every Liberal candidate was anti-Lloyd George. Although several of the candidates who stood as Liberals pledged themselves to support the Prime Minister, the Conservative machine had successfully convinced the great mass of the electorate that these Liberal candidates were at heart pro-Asquith.

The party organisations in the City up to the outbreak of war, had for many years been maintained in a high state of efficiency. During the war the Liberal machine suffered much more than the Conservative machine. Since the General Election the split in the Liberal Party has prevented the recovery of the Liberal Federation Organisation. The leaders remember constantly the power which a united party in pre-war days enabled them to exercise both in Parliamentary and Municipal affairs, and the recollection of those days accounts a great deal for the repeated movements on their part to secure once more a united Liberal Party.

The simplest way of defining the four classes into which Manchester Liberalism is divided is by classifying them under the heads of the outstanding man in each Group.

124 Robert Newbald Kay (1869–1947), Liberal MP for Elland 1923–4; solicitor.

(a) HAWORTH LIBERALS. (Sir A.A. Haworth, Bt.)[125] formerly MP for South Manchester. One of the recognised heads of the commercial life of the city. He is bitterly opposed to the Prime Minister. A Free Trade supporter who is almost fanatical in his opposition to any concession that savours of protection. There is also a personal prejudice against the Prime Minister. He attributes his defeat at the South Manchester bye-election in March 1912 to the National Health Insurance Act. This defeat put an end for the time being to his Parliamentary ambitions. He is greatly influenced by Lord Sheffield. His followers are comparatively few.

(b) ROYLE LIBERALS. Mr William Royle[126] has for many years been an active leader of Manchester Liberalism. He is a born wire-puller and his influence in the City is extraordinary. He never seeks to be in the limelight. It may be said that his one desire is to have a united Liberal Party. He feels strongly the failure of the Prime Minister and Mr. Asquith to reconcile their differences. His followers are pretty numerous.

(c) STOTT LIBERALS. Mr. Tom Stott[127] was for many years Mr. Royle's most influential colleague. He is a great admirer of the Prime Minister, but it is inconceivable to him that the Prime Minister should lead any other than the Liberal Party. The divisions in the Party have caused him to retire into the background and it is almost impossible to persuade him to take the active part which both his influence and ability would enable him to do.

(d) RHODES LIBERALS.[128] These are the active supporters of the Prime Minister, many of them members of the Manchester Reform Club. In pre-war days they took very little active part in political affairs. Sir Edward Donner, while perhaps the most influential man In the City and a strong supporter of the Prime Minister has reached the age which makes it impossible for him to take an active part.

At the last General Election all Liberal candidates stood as Liberals, most of them supporters of Mr. Lloyd George, and though it was understood that the Unionist candidates were in favour of the Coalition agreement, Mr. Carter, the Unionist Agent, all along emphasised that they stood as Unionists pure and simple. The Manchester Liberal is a type by himself, he is not "Asquithian", he is not entirely anti-coalition, though opposed to the 'coupon' arrangement, and

125 Arthur Haworth (1865–1944), Liberal MP Manchester South 1906–12, stood for Manchester Exchange in 1918, but did not receive the coupon and was defeated by the Coalition Conservative candidate; businessman.

126 William Royle (1854–1923), merchant and chair of the executive committee of Manchester Liberal Federation 1880–1923.

127 Tom Stott stood for the Manchester Moss Side constituency in 1918 but was defeated by the Conservative candidate.

128 Sir Edward Rhodes, chairman Coalition Liberals in Manchester; see Parliamentary Archives, Lloyd George Papers LG/G/30/2/24–30, correspondence between Lloyd George and Rhodes over Liberal re-union, Nov. 1922–Apr. 1924.

he has all along been distinctly "Georgian". There are of course Liberals who are distinctly "Asquithian" and "anti-Coalition", but they are in a small minority.

When our organisers in 1919 approached the Manchester Liberals they discovered that there were four distinct sections stated above, all members or office bearers of the Manchester Liberal Federation, and the most important of them members of the Manchester Reform Club. The small sections headed by Sir A. Haworth and Mr. A.W. Royle, and closely associated with the machinery of the Manchester Liberal Federation, refused to have any dealings with us, and went so far as to endure insults in their attempt to form a compact with Labour.

The Stott Liberals who had objected to the 'coupon' arrangement, frankly opposed our attempt to organise Coalition Liberals on the plea:–

(a) That such attempt was foredoomed to failure,

(b) That it would split the Liberal party in Manchester.

The Rhodes Liberals representative of at least 70% of the membership of the Reform Club welcomed our appearance and consented to the organisation of Coalition Liberals as a consultative body within the Liberal Party, always emphasising their hope and desire that Liberals of all sections would eventually be united. With this encouragement and on all these lines an organisation was set up and despite the gloomy forebodings of some of the members, the appearance of our Organisation holding its meetings in the Reform Club did not in any way embitter the personal or political relations of the various sections of the members of the Club. Indeed, we have considerable evidence to show that this appearance of activity on our part emboldened a number of the more timorous, and gave decision to the more doubtful. The difference between the Rhodes and Stott Liberals was one more of expediency and of honest doubt than of any vital question of principle or of personality, and the Prime Minister's triumphant vindication of his active Liberalism in the Irish negotiations brought from both sections an enthusiastic declaration of their belief in him. The result was rapprochement between the Rhodes and Stott Liberals, emphasising the Haworth and Royle Liberals as a small minority of vested interests and personal animus. The way now seemed to be clear for the re-union of Liberalism in Manchester, (in spite of absorbing the Manchester Liberal Federation which at any rate could not exist much longer without those Liberals who had left or were leaving it), when suddenly the 'Younger' episode again revived the question of expediency and distrust with which the Liberals had always regarded the Conservatives. The Stott Liberals are now more than ever determined to put forward their candidates in as many seats in Manchester as possible, and the Rhodes Liberals are in the following quandary as a result. They share with the other Liberals their resentment against "Younger's action", and their suspicion of the bonafides of Manchester Conservatives as dragooned by Mr. Carter. They are still, however, true to the Coalition contract and feel that their support must be given to Coalition candidates.

The Manchester Unionists have now offered them Withington to contest at the next General Election on condition that they organise Coalition Liberals in all the other seats in Manchester. How can they, however, organise Coalition Liberals in a seat like Moss Side in support of a Coalition Unionist candidate and against a Stott Liberal who, though standing as a Liberal without qualification would, if returned to the House, undoubtedly accept the Coalition Liberal Whip? The same thing applies to Platting (Mr. Clynes' seat)[129] where there is both a Unionist candidate and a Liberal supporter of the Prime Minister, except that in the case of this seat where it was agreed jointly by the Head Officers, that we should fight, a Unionist candidate has been put forward without any reference to us.

Sir Edward Rhodes points to the danger that if the independent and purely party attitude of the Conservatives is pushed too far, there will be a wholesale transfer of our supporters to the Stott section of Liberals, and that Liberal candidates will be put up in every seat with the avowed and undisguised aim of ensuring the defeat of the Conservatives in at least some of the Manchester seats. The feeling amongst Liberals in Manchester is at present distinctly pro-Lloyd George, and anti-Conservative rather than anti-Labour. It is not expected that the Manchester Conservatives will make a concession in the matter of seats large enough to justify either the confidence of all Liberals or of our spending effort and money in the organisation of Coalition Liberals in all the Manchester seats.

To sum up, Manchester Liberals are "Lloyd George Liberals" as distinct from "Coalition Liberals", ie they will follow him as their Liberal Leader and agree with him to work with any party for the sake of the common good, but they will not be parties to any pre-arranged agreement either in the country or in the constituency. They are also continually under the influence of the hope that Liberals may be united under the leadership of the Prime Minister. The view they hold, and the line of action they are taking makes impossible any agreement with the Manchester Conservatives on the re-allocation of seats on a fairer basis. It seems that both sides will require another General Election before they are convinced that they are cutting each other's throats. Meantime our Party gains neither in seats nor in organisation, and all our Lancashire efforts are seriously affected by the Manchester lack of co-ordination.

53. *Scovell to McCurdy, 'Welsh Candidates for English Seats', 30 March 1922*

Reference the attached, Mr. C.J.M. Shaw actually took charge of London last Monday. He has been associated with the London Area Office for some three weeks prior to transfer visiting Constituencies and so on. But the receipt of your memo has coincided with a visit from Mr. Sawyer who came to press on me the claims of Mr. J.J. Davies, as candidate for South Hackney! Sawyer and Davies of course are closely allied in business to Sam Waring.

I think you know my views on the Welsh invasion – I am very sure that we shall be doing the greatest disservice to the Prime Minister and the Party if we allow the English side of the Organisation or English vacancies to be filled by too many Welshmen. Apart from the dozen or so Welsh Officials in England, we already

129 John Robert Clynes (1869–1949), Labour MP Manchester N.E. 1906–18, Manchester Platting 1918–31 and 1935–45; leader of the Labour Party 1921–2; trade unionist.

have Beddoe Rees,[130] Atherley-Jones[131] (probably), D.O. Evans, Goronwy Owen, Mrs. Coombe Tennant[132] among our English adopted candidates. Moreover, our candidates' book is as you know choc-a-bloc with Welsh aspirants.

I understand Mr. J.J. Davies is an ex-schoolmaster, and is now reading for the Bar. I hope in any case to interview him in a day or two.

54. *Scovell to McCurdy, 'Addison's Loyalty', 6 April 1922*

I notice that Dr. Addison voted against the Government in both Genoa Divisions. Hitherto I have been able to damp the ardour of certain Tories who are anxious to fight him. But am I to go to the trouble of doing this any more? Incidentally the local Liberal Association, which is not in the least Wee Free, have not yet come to a decision as to whether it is prepared to re-adopt him as it is not certain whether he is pro or anti-P.M.

Can I have your view?

55. *McCurdy to Scovell, 'Addison's Loyalty', 7 April 1922*

In reply to your memorandum of the 6th,

1. We certainly do not want to encourage Tories to fight Liberal seats.

2. I shall be delighted if the local Liberal Association will bring pressure to bear on Addison, and we will support the local Liberal Association in any action they take.

56. *Scovell to McCurdy, 'Weekly Notes', 7 April 1922*

Candidatures:

Lowestoft: The Conservative Association is meeting on Saturday evening to hear an address by a son of a well-known judge with a view to his being adopted as independent Conservative candidate. This is in opposition to Mr. B. Beauchamp.[133] The Unionists have frequently threatened to bring out a candidate and some time ago it was found possible to secure the withdrawal of a Mr. Read.

Mid Bucks: Mr. Thomas Keens[134] of Luton has been adopted as independent Liberal candidate. Mr. Keens is a chartered accountant and partner in the firm of Keens,

130 William Beddoe Rees (1877–1931), Liberal MP for Bristol South 1922–9; architect.

131 Llewellyn Atherley-Jones (1851–1929), Liberal MP for North West Durham 1885–1914.

132 Winnifred Combe Tennant (1874–1956), suffragist and spiritualist.

133 Brograve Beauchamp (1897–1976), Conservative MP for East Walthamstow 1931–45, having unsuccessfully stood as Liberal candidate for Lowestoft in 1922; parliamentary private secretary to the minister of transport 1940 and to the parliamentary under-secretary for foreign affairs 1942–3; businessman.

134 Thomas Keens (1870–1953), Liberal MP for Aylesbury 1923–4, having unsuccessfully stood for the same constituency in 1922, unsuccessfully stood for Aylesbury in 1929 and Pontypool in 1931; accountant.

Shay & Co., 25, College Hill, E.C.4. He is also secretary of the Luton Chamber of Commerce. He is one of the chief men on the Liberal Executive of the Luton Division, and is a strong Free Trader, as most of the Luton manufacturers are. Before the War he was prospective Liberal candidate for Thanet, but withdrew before the election of December, 1918. He is a good platform man.

Keighley: Mr. H.B. Lees-Smith[135] has been adopted as Labour candidate. He represented Northampton from 1910–1918 as a Liberal. He contested the Don Valley Division as an independent radical in 1918.

Barkstone Ash: Mr. H.O. Willey has been adopted as Labour candidate.

North Croydon: Mr. H. T. Muggeridge[136] has been adopted as Labour candidate.

Mossley: (Nr. Manchester). Councillor M.E. Mitchell has been adopted as Wee Free candidate against Mr. Austen Hopkinson.

Isle of Wight: Lt. Col. J.T. Woolrych[137] has been adopted as Conservative candidate.

Barnstaple: Professor Hewins[138] has been invited to meet the Executive Committee of the Barnstaple Conservative Association with a view to his adoption as a Conservative candidate for the Division. Mr. Incledon Webber has given up his candidature and Prof. Hewins takes his place. Prof. Hewins is President of the Tariff Reform League.

N.E. Derbyshire: Capt. Charles Waterhouse[139] will contest this constituency as the Unionist candidate.

Dartford: Miss Alison Garland[140] is standing as the Wee Free candidate.

Moss Side, Manchester. Mr. T.W. Mercer[141] has been adopted as Co-operative candidate.

135 Hastings Lees-Smith (1878–1941), Liberal MP for Northampton 1910–18, Labour MP for Keighley 1922–3, 1924–31 and 1935–41; postmaster general 1929–31, president of the board of education 1931, leader of the opposition 1940–1.

136 Henry Thomas Muggeridge (1864–1942), Labour MP for Romford 1929–31, having unsuccessfully contested Croydon in 1918, 1922, 1923 and 1924.

137 John Thomas Woolrych Perowne (1863–1954), unsuccessful Liberal Unionist candidate for South Molton in the elections of 1910, and unsuccessful Conservative candidate for the Isle of Wight in 1922; army officer.

138 William Albert Samuel Hewins (1865–1931), Conservative MP for Hereford 1912–18; under-secretary of state for the colonies 1917–19; economist.

139 Charles Waterhouse (1893–1975), Conservative MP for Leicester South 1924–45 and Leicester South East 1950–7, having unsuccessfully contested North East Derbyshire in 1922 and 1924; parliamentary private secretary to the board of trade 1928 and to the minister of labour 1931–4, assistant whip 1935–6, comptroller of the household 1937–9, treasurer to the household 1939, parliamentary secretary to the board of trade 1941–5.

140 Alison Garland (1862–1939), suffragist and Liberal politician who unsuccessfully contested Portsmouth South in 1918, Dartford in 1922 and Warrington in 1929.

141 Thomas William Mercer (1884–1947), Labour and Co-operative Movement worker and journalist.

Daventry: Mr. J.B.E. Campion, farmer, will stand as the Wee Free candidate.

Hanley: Mr J.H. Whitehouse[142] will be the Wee Free candidate. He represented Mid Lanark constituency in the last Parliament and was Parliamentary Private Secretary to Mr. Lloyd George 1913–1914.
At the General Election 1918 he only received 504 votes, no doubt the result of his extreme anti-War attitude.

Perth: Mr. Wm. Henderson, a prominent local agriculturalist has been chosen as independent Liberal candidate. This is a Coalition Liberal seat and Sir Archibald Sinclair's name was before the Association along with that of Mr. Henderson. The reaction of Sir Archibald Sinclair has caused a disruption in the Local Association and the office bearers have resigned.

57. *Scovell to Miss Pull, Organisation in Scotland, 10 April 1922*

Would you lay the attached draft for the new Scottish Whip (as and when he is appointed) before the Chief for his consideration.

Enclosed: The Party Organisation in Scotland, 10 April 1922

1. I wish the Scottish Party Organisation in future to be fully co-ordinated for all purposes of administration with the Central Office and to bear the same relationship to 25, Old Queen Street as is at present the case with the English constituencies, the English and Welsh Whips and the Area and Constituency Organisations.

2. All appointments to and dismissals from the Staff will continue to be made by and through the General Secretary. Questions regarding finance and administration will be decided as may be advisable in consultation with the Scottish Whip by the General Secretary.

3. The Area Heads in Scotland will receive copies of all communications affecting their work issued from 25 Old Queen Street and will be required to carry out any instructions contained therein, with such reservations of a distinctly local character as may occasionally arise.

4. The present arrangement by which Mr. Mackenzie Cameron has been withdrawn from his organising work in Scotland for special work in No.10 Downing Street will be discontinued and he will resume the work he was previously doing in Scotland. It is my intention to pay an early visit to Scotland to confer with the Scottish Organisers and consult with them upon their system or organisation and their line of policy in that respect.

Propaganda and Publicity

5. With a view to securing economy and more effective work and also to avoid overlapping, the Publicity Department at 25 Old Queen Street will undertake

142 John Howard Whitehouse (1873–1955), Liberal MP for Mid-Lanarkshire 1910–18; educator.

responsibility for this branch of the work in Scotland. Such contracts and individual arrangements as may at present exist will however be continued for the time being. Mr. Dimbleby will be responsible to me for this work and submit for my consideration such proposals as he considers desirable.

58. *Scovell to McCurdy, 'Parliamentary Candidates', 10 April 1922*

I should be grateful if your Private Secretary would make arrangements for you to have early interviews with the undermentioned.

First in urgency.

Capt. G. Garro-Jones,[143] 29, Courtfield Gardens, Earl's Court, S.W. Telephone: Western 4766.

As a reminder: Capt. G. Jones has been Private Secretary to Sir Hamar Greenwood; is leader writer for the "Daily Dispatch"; has had considerable experience of public speaking; is only 27; and is ardently anxious to fight South Hackney if we can arrange to get him adopted. I recommend his Candidature for reasons which I explained to you (vide attached letter).[144]

Less Urgent.

H. Lesser Esqre., 59, Biddulph Mansions, Elgin Avenue, W.7. Telephone: New Cross 2000.

Is a Barrister and closely connected with the numerous employees' of the Metropolitan Gas Works resident in the Peckham Division for which he has been adopted as candidate vice Sir A. Richardson. I don't think you have ever met him. A strong and energetic candidate who should win, as he will receive enthusiastic support now at the Poll from numerous electors he has legally befriended.
Perhaps Miss Pull could write and arrange the interviews.

59. *McCurdy to Scovell, 'Colne Valley', 11 April 1922*

On the facts contained in your memorandum I think we ought to support Mr. Mallalieu.[145] His record in the House is good. He is just as much entitled to call himself a Liberal as various distinguished Unionist members have to call themselves Conservatives, and I think we should take a firm stand in the matter. It would, of course, be desirable to have a word with Mallalieu on the subject and I will try and get hold of him to-day.

143 George Morgan Trefgarne (né George Garro-Jones) (1895–1960), 1st baron Trefgarne; Liberal MP for Hackney South 1924–9 and Labour MP for Aberdeen North 1935–45; private secretary to Sir Hamar Greenwood 1919–22; ennobled 1947.

144 The letter is not in the archive.

145 Frederick William Mallalieu (1860–1932), Liberal MP for Colne Valley 1916–22.

60. *Scovell to McCurdy, 'Diehard Seats', 12 April 1922*

You will remember I have more than once discussed the question of our fighting certain Die-hard seats. I appreciate your views but I want to ask you to give me a lead in the following cases which are exceptional and where a decision is urgent.

<u>Case 1 of a Die-hard in South West of England.</u>

Co-Liberals and Wee Frees are fully prepared to combine to fight the sitting member. The Labour candidate has withdrawn and it seems doubtful if there will be anything but a straight fight. Many moderate Unionists do not see eye to eye with the sitting member. In a case of this kind, surely it is better that a National Liberal should fight rather than a Wee Free?

<u>Case 2 of a Die-hard in the South West of England.</u>

Co-Liberals and Wee Frees are prepared to combine to fight the sitting member. There is a weak Labour candidate in the field. The sitting member is weak and frankly re-actionary. Here again surely it is better that we should fight rather than leave the field to a Wee Free.

In both cases it really is a question of keeping our end up and preserving our prestige in the only stronghold of Liberalism left in the South of England. While we are inactive, the Die-hard elements are putting up or contemplating doing so, candidates in our seats and the Wee Frees are creeping in on all sides.

It would seem therefore as if it is our obvious duty to defend the Coalition. It is extremely doubtful however if any moderate Unionist would dream of voting for a Wee Free and there is in both cases I have cited no possible chance of the appearance of a Coalition Unionist candidate.

61. *Scovell to McCurdy, 'Bedford Division', 12 April 1922*

The Annual Meeting of the Bedford Divisional Liberal Association has just been held. The Rt. Hon. F.G. Kellaway, MP, was present and addressed the meeting.

The following Resolutions were passed unanimously:

"That this annual meeting of the Council of the Bedford Divisional Liberal Association thanks the Rt. Hon. F.G. Kellaway, MP, for his speech, expresses its unabated confidence in him as its member, and pledges its unabated confidence in him as its member, and pledges itself to again secure his return as member for the Division at the next election."

"That the Bedford Divisional Liberal Association now assembled in annual conference congratulates the Rt. Hon. David Lloyd George on his recovery to health, expresses its unabated confidence in him as Prime Minister, and respectfully sends its best wishes for the successful issue of the Genoa Conference."

Mr Kellaway paid a warm tribute to the energies and influence of the President, Sir George Royle, and to the tact and zeal of the Agent, Mr. Ernest J. Blunt, in bringing the Association to such a high state of efficiency.

62. *Scovell to McCurdy, 'By-election Expenditure', 12 April 1922*[146]

Bye Election Finance:

1. I have not forgotten for a moment your request for an abstract of expenditure in this connection, but I have delayed bringing it across for you to see until such time as I can obtain an analysis of the expenditure in respect to Inverness and East Leicester. I find, however, that there can be no question of an analysis until these accounts have been fully settled and as soon as this has been done I will let you have an analysis table for eleven bye-elections – unless you would like a copy of the analysis table exclusive of Inverness and East Leicester. This I could let you have at once.

2. I think I had better give you in summary form a pretty accurate statement showing our expenditure and outstanding liabilities as against receipts in respect of the above:–

		£	s.	d.
A. RECEIPTS:				
4th March: Cheque		1000	–	–
29th " Cash		750	–	–
April: Temporary Loans from Gen: Sec:		300	–	–
		£2050	–	–
B. EXPENDITURE – ACTUAL:				
Inverness		1086	14	6
East Leicester		835	19	2
Bodmin		95	13	3
W. Wolverhampton		40	4	–
	Total	£2058	10	11
C. OUTSTANDING LIABILITIES:				
EAST LEICESTER:				
(a) Per F.M. for Agents, local speakers and canvassers & motors		700	–	–
(b) Election Agent (Estimated)		500	–	–
(c) Central Office Payments		50	–	–
(d) Unionist Office		170	9	2
	Total	£1420	9	2
INVERNESS				
(a) Area Head, for Agents, local speakers, motors, etc.		549	1	4
(b) Railway Account		138	–	3
(c) Central Office Payments		80	–	–
	Total	767	1	7

146 Marked 'Confidential'.

		£	s.	d.
D. TOTAL OF OUTSTANDING LIABILITIES		£	s.	d.
East Leicester		1420	9	2
Inverness		767	1	7
Owing to General Secretary		300	–	–
	Total	£2487	10	9

3. From the foregoing you will see that our East Leicester effort has cost us approximately £2,200 and Inverness £1800. I shall be grateful indeed if you will let me have a cheque for £2,500 to complete.

4. Considering the intensity of our effort both these bye-elections, in comparison with previous ones, can be considered normal, eg.:

Cardigan	£3,000
Penistone	£2,086
Bedford	£2,396
Caerphilly	£3,928
Westhougton	£2,303

63. *Memorandum on Recent Bye-Elections and the Inferences to be Drawn from the Results [undated but April 1922]*

1. East Leicester Bye-Election.

The result came as a complete surprise to all parties, and was as unexpected by Labour as by Coalitionists.

The Coalition candidate laid great emphasis on the importance of the Genoa Conference, but both his opponents refused to make this subject a matter of controversy. They adopted the attitude that a resettlement of European difficulties was equally their policy. The overwhelming defeat of the Government candidate involves more than an amalgam of causes and indicates that there has been some outstanding factor to produce this result. The engineer's lock-out, which is said to have affected 10,000 work people in the City of Leicester, many of whom are electors in the Eastern Division, is certain to have had a serious adverse effect on the candidature of a capitalist employer.

Subsidiary Reasons:

(a) Owing to the onerous duties during the past three years of Sir Gordon Hewart he was unable to give the necessary attention to purely constituency business, and failed more than once to fulfil public engagements in his constituency.

(b) The weather during the campaign has been bitterly cold and miserable with the result that it has been almost impossible to get good audiences to listen to speakers capable of putting the case for the Government. This was particularly necessary at the present time, seeing that there has been no Governmental reply to the Press "drumfire".

(c) Under pressure from local Liberal and Conservatives our choice of candidate was confined to a businessman conversant with the local staple industry.

(d) The specious promises and fantastic idealism of the Labour candidate who cannot be said to be in any way a Bolshevik.

(e) The general bewilderment of all thinking people regarding the present political situation. They are confused by the stories they read in the press which convey the impression of the Government's instability and a general lack of cohesion among its forces.

2. Recent Bye-Elections.

Won by.		Increased Percentage of Labour vote in relation to total poll.	Percentage of total electorate	Increase of poll since polled	Percentage of votes polled by General Ind. Libs.
Clayton	Labour	20	74.14 1	7.7%	–
North Camberwell	Labour	21	55.17	15.22%	–
Bodmin	Ind.Lib.	–	75.46	6.2%	42.59
West Wolverhampton	Co. U.	9.5	82.46.	19.1%	–
Cambridge	Co. U.	7	88.91	20%	17.9
Inverness	Co. Lib.	–	55.92	18.2%	27.42
Chertsey	Co. U.	–	61.01	13.00%	27.18.
East Leicester	Labour	31	70.57	4.8	–

Clayton

An industrial constituency where as a result of distinct lack of cohesion amongst the Coalition forces there was considerable transfer of Liberal voters resulting in the return of a moderate Labour candidate with an excellent local Government record.

North Camberwell

An industrial constituency, one of the few Liberal seats in London fought by a Tory candidate. We have vainly endeavoured to obtain a reversion of this seat.

Bodmin

An industrial constituency insufficiently assisted by the Government through exceptionally bad times. Strongly Liberal in character. The successful candidate was a capable politician, well known locally, and personally popular.

West Wolverhampton

An industrial constituency, which was won mainly by the personal prestige of the candidate due to the continuous employment of his workpeople, despite personal financial loss. The Coalition Liberal vote here undoubtedly saved the seat for the Coalition.

Cambridge

The Unionist candidate retained the seat thanks to the anti-Government split, but with a minority vote. The Coalition Liberals after much pressure, and in spite of the independent attitude of local Tories were eventually induced to vote for the Government candidate. This seat however can be by no means regarded as a key seat.

Inverness

A lucky win for us against the combined anti-Government forces. The narrow majority was won mainly by the attractive personality of the candidate, and by the personal prestige of the Prime Minister which was emphasised by his recent visit to the Highlands.

Chertsey

This is the most significant of recent bye-elections. The local squabbles over the candidature, the low percentage of polled votes, the general apathy, and the small majority in a typical Tory citadel (which in the last 30 years has only once returned a Liberal, then only by a majority of 99) can only be accounted for by the loss of Government prestige due to "Youngerism" and the Northcliffe press jazz band.

East Leicester.

This bye-election has been referred to above.

3. National Considerations of a More General Nature Which can be Evolved from or are Supplementary to the Foregoing Remarks

It seems to us that the present political position pivots round two or three central facts viz:–

First and foremost, unemployment, lack of trade and grievously high taxation (both direct and indirect). It must be remembered that practically every household in the country feel the effects of these in some direction or other, day by day, hour by hour. Each reacts on the other, each is complimentary and each leads to political disgruntlement. The loss of prestige by the Government, and the apparent lack of cohesion in the Coalition owing to "Youngerism", the action of the Die-hards and their more vocal as well as their more silent allies all over the Country, and last but by no means least the insistent drumfire of a powerful section of the Press. All this has resulted in the complete bewilderment, and as a consequence into a kind of "wait and see" attitude on the part of the more moderate section of the electorate. Apart from the two central facts, which for brevity we may summarise as "disgruntlement" and "bewilderment" as stated above there are one or two further considerations which we venture to think are worth stating:

(a) To the ordinary outsider The Prime Minister's hand has been off the helm while he has been in North Wales, and his enemies on the right, temporary or permanent, in and outside Parliament have taken advantage of and been busy in his absence. If we are not mistaken they will get busier still when he is at Genoa.

(b) There has been no opportunity for the Government to state its case in the provinces, particularly north of the Trent. This can only be done efficaciously by the Big Five, and all our information goes to show that this is an urgent requirement.

(c) There appears at the moment to be a left-ward trend in the political world, but we shall not be in a position to take advantage of this unless and until we roll up our sleeves and say to the Die-hard elements "Very well, we are tired of your sniping, come out into the open and we will fight". They may be the salt of the Conservative Party, but they add neither strength not savour to the Prime Minister and his policy.

64. *Scovell to McCurdy, 'Weekly Notes', 21 April 1922*

Candidatures:

High Peak: Mr. J.C.H. Robinson (Labour candidate) has withdrawn on account of extreme pressure of Trade Union work.

Peebles and South Midlothian: Mr. Archibald Crawford, M.A., Ll.B. Advocate was unanimously adopted as the prospective Coalition Unionist candidate to oppose the Rt. Hon. Sir Donald Maclean, the sitting member. Mr. Crawford, who is the youngest son of the late Mr. Robt. Crawford, D.L. Ll.D. is a graduate of Glasgow University and was called to the Scottish Bar in 1906. In 1910 he was one of a group of Progressive Unionists responsible for the formation of the Workers League.

Leith: The Scottish and National Executives of the Labour Party have refused to endorse the candidature of Mr. Robert Foulis on account of his connection with the Communist Party. Steps are now being taken to secure a new candidate.

Wolverhampton West: Mr. A.G. Walkden[147] who contested this seat at the last bye-election has again been adopted as Labour candidate.

Stalybridge and Hyde: Mr. John Lincoln Tattersall[148] of Didsbury will contest this seat as an independent Liberal.

Knutsford: Mr. Percy Butlin has been adopted as independent Liberal candidate.

Aylesbury: Sir Charles Hobhouse has accepted the independent Liberal Candidature for the above constituency.

Swindon: Sir Frederick Young[149] having announced his intention not to contest this seat at the next General Election, the local Conservative and Unionist Association has adopted Mr. Reginald Mitchell Banks, B.A., to contest this seat in their interest. Mr Banks is a son of the late Sir William Mitchell Banks, M.B., Ll.P., F.R.C.S. at Edinburgh who was well known throughout Lancashire and Cheshire.

147 Alexander George Walkden (1873–1951), 1st baron Walkden; Labour MP for Bristol South 1929–31 and 1935–45, having unsuccessfully contested Wolverhampton West in 1918 and 1922, and Heywood and Radcliffe in 1924; trade unionist.

148 John Lincoln Tattersall (1865–1942), Liberal MP for Hyde 1923–4, having unsuccessfully contested Stalybridge and Hyde in 1922; mill owner.

149 Frederick William Young (1876–1948), Conservative MP for Swindon 1918–22; barrister.

He was educated at Rugby and Christchurch, Oxford. He is a rapid and forceful speaker with a clear enunciation and fine delivery.

Saffron Walden: Dr. Dunstan has withdrawn as he has acquired a practice which occupies the whole of his time. The Labour Party are looking for another candidate.

Hertford: Mr. Edgar Carruthers, J.P., of Bishops Stortford will contest the above Division as an independent Liberal. At the recent bye-election his name was put forward but owing to the opposition of our friends he finally decided not to stand. He is a successful Scotch draper with business at Bishop Stortford, Hertford, and Colchester.

Leeds, N.: Mr David Stewart, M.A., has been adopted as Labour candidate.

Bermondsey, W.: The Rev. R.M. Kedward[150] has been adopted as independent Liberal candidate in place of Mr. H.J. Glanville, who it is understood will not seek re-election.

Carmarthen: Mr. Ross Llewellyn Williams has been adopted as the independent Liberal candidate for this constituency.

Woolwich W.: Mr. J.T. Shepherd, a well-known local Socialist had been adopted as Labour candidate. Mr. Shepherd who unsuccessfully contested West Islington at the General Election is on the Managing Committee of the Royal Arsenal Co-operative Society. For some years he had a seat on the Woolwich Borough Council.

Aston: Mr. J. Cotter, President of the Amalgamated Marine Workers, and a member of the Executive of the National Transport Workers Federation will contest this seat in the Labour interest.

Peckham: The Peckham Liberal Association has adopted Mr. Frank Roscoe as an independent Liberal candidate.

Lowestoft: Lord Sandon,[151] son of the Earl of Harrowby has been adopted as Conservative candidate in succession to Mr. G. Butler Lloyd who will not seek re-election. Lord Sandon has stated that he would support the present Coalition Government when he felt it was in the interests of the Country to do so, and has declined to declare himself a "die-hard".

Lonsdale: Mr. Hal Maden will contest this seat as an independent Liberal.

Wellingborough: Mr D. Owen Evans has been adopted as Coalition Liberal candidate for this Division.

Bishop Auckland: Mr. Egbert Atherley Jones at a meeting of a special Committee appointed by the local Unionist and Coalition Liberal Associations created a most favourable impression and will be recommended to the Associations for adoption.

150 Roderick Morris Kedward (1881–1937), Liberal MP for Bermondsey West 1923–4 and Ashford 1929–31, having unsuccessfully contested Kingston Upon Hull Central in 1918 and Bermondsey West in 1922; unsuccessful at Ashford in 1933; Wesleyan minister.

151 Dudley Ryder (1892–1987), 6th earl of Harrowby, known as Viscount Sandon from 1900 to 1956; Conservative MP for Shrewsbury 1922–3 and 1924–9; assistant private secretary to the secretary of state for the colonies 1919–20, parliamentary private secretary to the secretary of state for air 1922–3; succeeded to the earldom in 1956; soldier.

Spennymoor: Capt. Anthony Eden[152] was unanimously adopted as Coalition candidate at a joint meeting of Unionists and Coalition Liberals held at Durham on the 12th. inst.

West Birkenhead: Lt. Col. W.H. Stott,[153] C.B., has been adopted as Coalition Unionist candidate to succeed Lt. Col. Sir Henry M. Grayson who has intimated his intention not to seek re-election.

London, City: The Executive Committee of the City of London Conservative and Unionist Association met yesterday. It was decided to call a full meeting of the Association on Friday the 28th inst. when the name of Mr. Edward Charles Grenfell will be submitted as prospective Conservative candidate.

Jarrow: The National Liberal Federation has recommended to the newly formed independent Liberal Association in this constituency as a suitable candidate Mr. Young. Mr. Young was therefore invited to address the Association, and subsequently unanimously adopted.

Wirral: Mr. S.R. Dodds, M.A., Ll.B., has been invited to become independent Liberal candidate for this constituency.

Galloway: At a general meeting of the Galloway Liberal Association a motion to the effect that in view of the political opinions expressed by Major Gilbert McMicking further support to him be withdrawn was carried.

South Shields: At a specially convened meeting of South Shields Liberals, in the course of which a strong opposition to the Coalition administration was manifested, the independent Liberals endeavoured to obtain a declaration in favour of the policy of The National Liberal Federation, but this was rejected and the question of affiliation was adjourned sine die. Mr. Havelock Wilson was elected President of the Association.

65. *Scovell to McCurdy, 'Weekly Notes', 28 April 1922*

L.C.C. Bye-Election.

Kennington.

Candidates: Ald. G.W. Brittain, J.P. (Prog.),[154] A. Hudson, (M.R.), Harry Gosling, (Lab). Polling Day: Saturday 29th April

Our London Office staff is helping Alderman Brittain. The action of the local Unionists to run a candidate of their own makes the return of Ald. Brittain uncertain.

152 Robert Anthony Eden (1897–1977), 1st earl Avon; Conservative MP for Leamington 1923–57; under-secretary of state for foreign affairs 1931–4, lord privy seal 1934–5, minister without portfolio for League of Nations affairs 1935, foreign secretary 1935–8, secretary of state for dominion affairs 1939–40, secretary of state for war 1940, foreign secretary 1940–5, leader of the House of Commons 1942–5, deputy prime minister 1951–5, prime minister and leader of the Conservative Party 1955–7; ennobled 1961.

153 William Henry Stott (1863–1930), Conservative MP for Birkenhead West 1922–3 and Birkenhead East 1924–9; shipowner.

154 Progressive.

Bermondsey, West. A Joint Meeting of Coalition Liberals and Unionists held on April 19th. The Candidature of Mr. Charles R. Scriven, (C. Lib.) was heartily endorsed. The Constitutional Association meeting on the 20th passed a similar Resolution.

Hackney, South. Mr. Garro Jones has been seen by an informal Committee consisting of five Coalition Liberals and five Conservatives. The meeting was quite satisfactory and arrangements are being made for him to meet the Executive Committees of both the Coalition Liberal and Conservative Associations at an early date.

Tottenham, North. It is reported that Sir William Prescott,[155] MP, (C.U.) has decided to retire at the next election.

The Wirral. Mr. S.R. Dodds has been adopted as the independent Liberal candidate. The Hon. W. Hulme Lever, son of Lord Leverhulme, presided at the meeting and supported Mr. Dodd's candidature. He is the son of a former Mayor of Birkenhead and has a practice there as a Solicitor.

Blackburn. Sir Sydney Henn,[156] K.B.E., has been adopted as Unionist candidate to succeed Commander P.T. Dean,[157] V.C., who is retiring. He is a Unionist Free Trader.

Southport. Sir John Brunner[158] has accepted the Wee Free Candidature. In his speech he said he was not a supporter of the Coalition or of its Chief, and that "the Maurice affair was the great cause of his profound distrust of Mr. Lloyd George, His Government, his friends and his policy. It was impossible for him to have any reconciliation with Mr. Lloyd George or to have him back as leader of the Liberal Party."

Sowerby. Major R.H. Barker speaking at the Conservative Club stated that he had definitely decided not to seek re-election.

Clay Cross. Mr. C.F.G. Masterman[159] is addressing a meeting next week and it is stated that he will be invited to become the candidate in opposition to Mr. T.T. Broad on the invitation of the local Liberal Association.

Shrewsbury. Mr. Joseph Sunlight of Knutsford, a young architect in practice at Manchester and in London, has been adopted as the Wee Free candidate.

Sedgfield, Durham. Mr. E. Waddington, who for many years had been an active agent of the Unionist Party in different parts of the country and whose son is their principal Welsh agent, has been adopted as Unionist candidate in place of Colonel Burdon, MP,[160] who is retiring.

155 William Henry Prescott (1874–1945), Conservative MP for North Tottenham 1918–22; engineer and soldier.

156 Sydney Herbert Holcroft Henn (1861–1936), Conservative MP for Blackburn 1922–9.

157 Percy Thompson Dean (1877–1939), Conservative MP for Blackburn 1918–22; naval officer.

158 John Fowler Brunner (1865–1929), Liberal MP for Leigh 1906–10, Northwich 1910–18 and Southport 1923–4.

159 Charles Frederick Gurney Masterman (1873–1927), Liberal MP for West Ham 1906–10 and Bethnal Green South West 1911–14.

160 Colonel Rowland Burdon (1857–1944), Conservative MP for Sedgefield 1918–22; landowner.

Gloucester City. Capt. E. Ackroyd has been adopted as Labour candidate.

Brecon & Radnor. Mr. W.A. Jenkins of Swansea has been adopted by the Liberal Association as Coalition Liberal candidate.

Carmarthen. Mr. John Hinds, MP,[161] has been adopted by his Association as a supporter of the Prime Minister.

Perth. The Conservative Association have decided to bring forward a candidate. The Liberal Association three weeks ago adopted Mr. Wm. Henderson of Lawton, who is an independent Liberal. The seat is at present held by a Liberal supporter of the Government.

66. *Scovell to McCurdy, 'Mr Mallalieu, MP', 29 April 1922*

You will remember that you undertook to interview Mr. Mallalieu, MP, as to his position, and I have now had a letter from our Yorkshire Area Head, the following extract from which I think I should pass across to you:–

"Reference your letter of the 12th instant, I have consulted with Mr Bulmer as to the position of this Constituency, and he states that if after the Chief Whip has interviewed Mr. Mallalieu he is satisfied with the interview Mr. Bulmer is prepared to recommend to the Yorkshire Executive to give all the support in their power to Mr. Mallalieu."

67. *Memo to McCurdy, 'Visits of the Rev. J.T. Rhys', 3 May 1922*

Cornwall.

Mr. Rhys[162] found that few Ministers in Cornwall were supporters of the Government, and he is of opinion that this is due in great measure to the result of the Bodmin election and to the vigorous campaign that the independent Liberals have been carrying on ever since. He was fortunate enough however to meet the Rev. Captain Frank Edwards, Wesleyan Minister, Newquay, who is a strong supporter of the Prime Minister and has offered his assistance. Captain Edwards is in charge of 39 Churches in Cornwall, is personally known to every Methodist Minister, and on account of his popularity wields great influence throughout Cornwall. He served as a private both in the South African war and in the late war, and when disabled was sent by the Government to the United States for propaganda purposes. Mr Rhys's experiences confirm our impression that we have lost considerable ground in Cornwall and that special efforts will have to be made to regain it.

161 John Hinds (1862–1928), Liberal MP for West Carmarthenshire 1910–18; chairman of the Welsh Liberal Party 1921–2; businessman.

162 John Thomas Rhys (1867–1938), congregationalist minister, temperance reformer and journalist joined the secretarial staff at 10, Downing Street as private secretary to Margaret Lloyd George, and remained there until the fall of Lloyd George.

Yorkshire. Sheffield 26th April.

Mr Rhys attended a Luncheon at Sheffield on April 26th, at which 38 Free Church Ministers were present. A general discussion lasting about two hours took place. There was little or no hostility to the Prime Minister personally, but almost general hostility to the Government. Mr Rhys found a considerable amount of misapprehension on various matters, but, as he was able to remove these, he considers that good work was done. On the 27th April he attended a luncheon at Hull where there were present 18 Free Church Ministers. One of the leading Free Church Ministers opened the discussion in a spirit of distinct hostility to the Prime Minister, and it was evident that the large majority who were present were accustomed to follow his lead. As a result of Mr. Rhys's answers however, it was apparent that there was a considerable change in point of view, and there were many individual admissions that the questions under discussion had never been previously considered in the light in which he had put them.

On the 28th April, Mr. Rhys attended a Luncheon at Leeds at which 26 Free Church Ministers were present. Mr. Rhys found practically the same condition of things as at Sheffield and Hull, but had the satisfactory feeling that his visit had had considerable influence upon the political point of view of those present. Mr. Rowlatt, who accompanied Mr. Rhys is of opinion that these meetings have done a great deal of good. He says that the personal respect for the Prime Minister is very great and that it is admitted that he is the only man who can lead at the present juncture. There was everywhere expressed the fear that he has been inveigled into the Tory Camp, and Mr. Rhys's visit has done much to remove these suspicions.
Pencil Signature [unreadable]

68. *Scovell to McCurdy, 'Weekly notes on Constituencies', 5 May 1922*

Bye-Elections.

Clapham. Sir John Leigh's Election Address has not yet been circulated but from an advanced copy that has come into our possession he states that he has the support of many Liberal Coalitionists. He describes himself as a Progressive Conservative and an advocate of Anti-Waste and reserves complete freedom of action. Great stress is laid and detailed information given upon his munificent gifts to charitable causes.

The indications are that there will be no contest.

Candidates.

North Camberwell. Dame Helen Gwynne Vaughan[163] has been adopted as Coalition Unionist candidate.

Barnstaple. Mr W.A.S. Hewins was adopted on Friday last as Conservative candidate.

The Wrekin. General Townshend, having notified his intention not to seek re-election, the Executive Committee of the Wrekin Division Conservative and

163 Helen Charlotte Isabella Gwynne-Vaughan (née Fraser) (1879–1967), unsuccessfully contested Camberwell North in 1922, 1923 and 1924; biologist, mycologist and academic who served in both world wars.

Unionist Association has unanimously decided to recommend to the Association at a meeting to be held on May 4th the name of Mr. Howard S. Button of Cedar House, Hillingdon, Middlesex, as prospective candidate. Mr. Button is Chairman of Messrs. Alfred Button and Sons, Ltd., Uxbridge, and Deputy Chairman of Uxbridge and High Wycombe District Gas Company. He also owns and runs a farm, is a Justice of the Peace, and a member of Middlesex County Council. The local paper (*Express and Star*) stated last night that it had heard that the Independent Group do not intend to relinquish their hold on the Wrekin Division, and that Major the Hon. Christopher Lowther might possibly be the independent candidate. In a letter to Mr. Houston, the agent, and Parliamentary Secretary to General Townshend,[164] he expressed the opinion that the seat must not be allowed to go uncontested. It is stated that the Labour candidate may be Mr Frank Hodges. Any further developments will be reported immediately.

Deritend. Mr Fred Longden has been nominated as prospective Labour candidate for this Division. An adoption meeting will be held shortly. Mr. Longden is a member of the I.L.P. and was a student at Ruskin College.

Shipley. Mr. J.H. Watson of Bradford, has withdrawn from the Prospective Candidature for the Shipley Division for health reasons.

Clay Cross. Mr. Masterman met the Divisional Liberal Council on Wednesday and a unanimous invitation to become their candidate was given to him. He has promised a definite reply within three weeks.

Saffron Walden. William Cash has been adopted as Labour candidate in place of Dr. Dunstan. He is a Balliol scholar, and accountant, and a member of Executive of Industrial Christian Fellowship.

Colchester. Rev. Hughes, the Labour candidate has withdrawn, and Capt. R.L. Reiss[165] has been adopted in his stead.

Gateshead. Capt. John P. Dickie, South Shields has been asked to become the Wee Free candidate. He is in business in Newcastle representing the Ragasine Oil Company.

S.W. Norfolk. The Annual Meeting was held on Saturday last. Colonel H.J. Powell, the Conservative Central Office agent, reported as follows:

"A considerable amount of fuss was made as to whether there was to be a General Election last February or not. So far as he could see, the Coalition was unpopular where a Conservative Party was not in a position to choose a candidate of their own. He thought however, that the trouble which occurred last December and January had more or less cleared the air, because people had generally seen what the alternative would be. Coalition may not be a very popular form of Government, but he thought it was the least unpopular."

164 Charles Townshend (1861–1924), independent Conservative MP for the Wrekin 1920–2; soldier.

165 Richard Leopold Reiss (1883–1959), for the Liberals he contested Chichester in 1910 and St Pancras South East in 1918, for Labour he contested Colchester in 1923 and 1929 and Preston in 1935; town planner.

69. *Scovell to McCurdy, 'Weekly notes on Constituencies', 12 May 1922*

Bye-Elections.

Clapham. Sir John Leigh,[166] Bt., was elected unopposed for Clapham on Tuesday May 9th. Defining his position to the electors after this return, Sir John described himself as a follower of the Earl of Balfour, Mr. Austen Chamberlain and Mr. Bonar Law, but if his Leaders called upon him to support Mr. Lloyd George he would sympathetically consider the request.

London, City of. Mr. E.C. Grenfell[167] (Official Conservative) and Sir Vansittart Bowater[168] (independent Cons.) were nominated yesterday. Polling is fixed to take place on Friday next, the 19th.

Candidates.

Heywood & Radcliffe. Arrangements are being made for the adoption of Col. A. England as Coalition Liberal candidate at a meeting to be held at the end of this month.

Mossley. Miss. Jane F. Wood, the prospective Labour candidate, has withdrawn her candidature for this constituency on account of ill health.

Middlesborough. East. The Labour candidate, Mr. T. Farrah has withdrawn.

Sunderland. Major L.A. Common, D.S.O., a member of the Sunderland Town Council and a prominent Shipowner was adopted as independent Liberal candidate on Tuesday.

Hull, S.W. The Rev. David Pughe a local Wesleyan Minister has been adopted as Coalition Liberal candidate to oppose Mr. C.F. Entwistle, the sitting Ind. Liberal member.

Grimsby. It is reported that Mr. Tickler, the Coalition Unionist member for this constituency will not seek re-election.

Wrekin. Mr. H.S. Button was adopted on Thursday as the Conservative candidate for this constituency. In the course of his address Mr. Button said he would support the Coalition as long as it did not act in defiance of what he believed to be Conservative principles.

Rugby. Sir John L. Baird,[169] the sitting C.U. member has notified his intention not to seek re-election.

166 John Leigh (1884–1959), Conservative MP for Wandsworth 1922–45; mill owner and newspaper owner.

167 Edward Charles Grenfell (1870–1941), 1st baron St Just; Conservative MP for the City of London 1922–35; banker.

168 Thomas Vansittart Bowater (1862–1938), mayor of London 1913–14; Conservative MP for the City of London 1924–38.

169 Sir John Lawrence Baird (1874–1941) of Urie, 1st Viscount Stonehaven; Conservative MP for Rugby 1910–22 and Ayr Burghs 1922–5; minister of transport 1922–4, first commissioner of works 1922–4, governor general of Australia 1925–30; ennobled 1925.

Kidderminster. Mr. J. Bruce has been adopted as the Labour candidate for this division.

Rhondda, East. Mr. Arthur Davies, Barrister-at-Law, has been adopted as the Coalition Liberal candidate in opposition to Lt. Col. D. Watts-Morgan, the sitting Labour member.

Carmarthen. Mr. Daniel Johns has been adopted as Ind. Agricultural candidate to oppose Mr. John Hinds, the sitting C.L. member. Mr. H. Llewelyn Williams, nephew of the late Mr. Llewelyn Williams, K.C., will contest the seat as an independent Liberal.

Pontypridd. Mr. T.A. Lewis is to be opposed by Mr. Mardy Jones, who has now been finally adopted as the Labour candidate.

Cardigan. The Welsh papers announce that Sir John Simon, K.C., has been invited to contest Cardiganshire as an independent Liberal against Captain Ernest Evans.[170]

National Liberal Federation. The annual meeting of the Council of the National Liberal Federation is to be held at Blackpool on Wednesday and Thursday the 17th and 18th May. On Wednesday the re-election of Mr. J. M. Robertson as President and the election of Sir R. Hudson as Treasurer will be moved, together with a Motion regretting the resignation of Mr. Frank Wright as Treasurer and that of Sir. R. Hudson as Secretary, and expressing the gratitude of the Federation to those gentlemen will be moved.

70. *Scovell to McCurdy, 'Reductions in Expenditure', 15 May 1922*

Secret:

The Chief Whip:

While considering and before introducing the more drastic of the alterations in expenditure from 1st July onwards which may involve a serious weakening of our effort in the constituencies, I think it is only right to bring to your notice one aspect with which I find it very difficult to cope. This is the expenditure by the Whips on their own seats. Take first the case of Northampton. Without taking into any account the large monthly sums you are spending, this organisation is charged with:

Agent's salary	£50	per month
Miss Eastgate's salary	£21	" "
Office Exes (flat rate)	£50	" "
Total per month	£121	
Total per annum	£1452	

170 Ernest Evans (1885–1965), Liberal MP for Cardigan 1921–3; private secretary to Lloyd George and Matthew Vaughan-Davies (1840–1935), the Liberal MP for Cardigan 1895–1921.

While this sum is out of all comparison with anything we are spending on any other single constituency, yet there are serious disadvantages to such a large expenditure from my point of view, namely, that this lavish all-in expenditure is not only known and is the subject of comment far beyond the Midlands, but is having a bad effect on other constituencies. For example, the Kettering Liberal leaders say "why should we raise money to pay our way when your chest must be overflowing as evidenced by your expenditure in Northampton". Again, Wellingborough is now demanding £400 of you. Apart from your pledge our leading folk there keep one eye on Northampton expenditure and consequently make no effort to look after their finances. And then again, the example of Northampton has its baneful effect on our officials, constituencies, candidates and even members.

Take next case of Bolton. For some months past we have been spending at Sir William Edge's insistent request at the rate of £300 a month or more, Viz:–

(a) £40 a week on canvass-distribution.

(b) An Agent at £400 p.a.

(c) A Woman organiser at £260 p.a.

(d) 20,000 Searchlights a month.

This lavish expenditure is known all over the North and has an evil effect on our potential subscribers and on our officials, Agents, candidates and members.

I have already issued instructions that with a very few purely temporary exceptions all paid distribution of any kind ceases on May 15th – this week being done by voluntary workers drawn from the War or Polling-District Committees. I have so far met with no opposition or disgruntlement but when the continuance of paid distributors in Northampton and Bolton is known I may have to encounter some dissatisfaction. The expenditure on the seats of the other Whips in no case exceeds £300 p.a.

Recommendation: The question of what cut, in any, in these large figures you are going to insist on is outside my province, provided of course you relieve me of all responsibility in the matter. To this end I would strongly urge that on and after 1st June all expenditure, either personal or in connection with the seats of the Whips, should be a matter between you and them and that no charge of any kind in respect thereof should be shown on my books, either Central Office or Provincial. I trust you will appreciate that this memorandum is merely a statement of fact and not written in any critical spirit. I realise that there possibly may be good grounds why the Whips' seat should be kept in the very highest state of efficiency.

71. *Scovell to McCurdy, 'Expenditure', 16 May 1922*[171]

1. You will see by the following totals showing nett monthly expenditure from 1st January of the current year that owing to:–

171 Marked 'Secret'.

(a) The cost of the National Liberal Conference,

(b) Emergency preparations for a General Election, both in respect of Central Office and Constituencies,

The normal monthly rate of expenditure had been very considerably exceeded. Of course, in respect of (b) above, besides carrying large stocks which have been paid for and are to a great extent recoverable, we have outstanding advances in suspense against members and candidates for election envelopes etc totalling some £1,500.

Month	1922	Expenditure
January	"	£18,461
February	"	£16,701
March	"	£18,880
April	"	£17,000 estimate only

2. In April 1921 the expenditure was £14,897 less £2,500 special capital expenditure of a non-recurring nature, leaving £12,300 as the nett figure.

3. I am hopeful that on and after the 1st July that the nett annual expenditure in connection with this Organisation and distinct from items chargeable to Nos 10 or 12 Downing Street, will not exceed £110,000 p.a. Of course, this to some extent depends on Scotland where nothing can be effected till the advent of a new Whip.

4. I have already arranged that by 1st July I shall have saved £13,000 p.a. or more in "distribution" and £3,000 p.a. by dispensing with temporary woman organisers.

72. *Scovell to McCurdy, 'Searchlights', 16 May 1922*

The Chief Whip

I suggest that on grounds of economy and incidentally for the relief of the staff, August and September (the holiday months) be proclaimed as "close" months for all "Searchlights". Have you any objection?

73. *Scovell to McCurdy, 'Northampton Expenditure', 24 May 1922*

1. On and after 1st June the following will, as things stand now, be the monthly budget for Northampton:

	£	
Clarke's salary (paid by Central Office)	50	monthly.
Office allowance (via Leicester Office)	25	"
Rent & Rates (via Leicester Office)	15	"
Woman Organiser salary & expenses	25	"
Per month	£115	
Per annum	£1380	

2. I now suggest that from 1st July the budget should be amended to read as follows:–

	Monthly £
Clarke's salary	50
Office allowances	15
Rent & Rates	15
Woman Organiser, maximum of three days only.	15
per month	£95
per annum	£1140

3. If you concur I will notify our Leicester office accordingly.

74. *Scovell to McCurdy, 'Northampton Expenditure', 25 May 1922*[172]

I am sorry to bother you once more over Northampton, but I have learned to-day, quite casually, that there is a little difficulty there in connection with Clarke which you can easily rectify. It appears that you are apt to leave Clarke to pay all bills out of his own pocket and keep him waiting too long before repaying him. As he now gets only £25 a month from us, the fact of having this money out for three weeks or so makes things somewhat difficult for him. So if you can possibly arrange to give him an advance cheque for the month or arrange for him to be paid a little more promptly for items which he has been forced to disburse on your behalf, I think it would help matters along. I rather fancy he has been put to a great deal of expense lately over his wife, and is, therefore, out of pocket all round. Please do not say a word about this to Clarke as he has made no complaint and there may be nothing in it. You will, however, know at once if any difficulty like this really existed.

75. *Scovell to McCurdy, 'Expenditure', 25 May 1922*[173]

Just to say that Sir W. Sutherland has put across to me a bill for £562 odd for calendars for his Constituency which he wishes me to pay. I presume I had better do so. The account is due for early payment. It is only fair to say that his Constituency has not cost this organisation much during the past two years or more.

172 Marked 'Personal & Private'.

173 Marked 'Secret'.

76. *Scovell to McCurdy, 'Weekly notes on Constituencies', 26 May 1922*

Candidatures.

S.E. Southwark. Colonel Alexander[174] has been adopted at a meeting of the local Liberal Association as Coalition Liberal candidate. He made a most favourable impression.

E. Aberdeenshire. The Unionist Association have passed a resolution approving of the continuance of the Coalition and undertaking to support Sir Henry Cowan.[175] A local cinema proprietor, Mr. J. Falconer is spoken of as the Labour candidate, and Mr. Frederick Martin as an independent Liberal candidate.

Croydon. Mr. T.W. Dobson,[176] ex-MP, for Plymouth has been adopted as Wee Free Liberal candidate.

The Eccles Division. Mr. F.H. Robey, son of a former Liberal Member for the division has been adopted as Wee Free candidate. Mr. John Buckle[177] of Leeds will be the Labour candidate.

Wallsend. Major. A.J. Dudley Ward has withdrawn his candidature. He threatened to stand as an independent Unionist against Mr. Matt Simm.[178]

Stockton. It is stated that an independent Liberal has agreed to fight Captain Watson, but no name has yet been disclosed.

South Leicester. Ald. A. Hill will be the Labour candidate. He is the Secretary of a local branch of the National Union of Boot and Shoe Operatives.

Deritend. Mr. Fred Longden has been adopted as Labour candidate.

Coventry. Mr John Edward Darnton,[179] of Mackerye End, Herpenden, Berkshire, has accepted the invitation of the Coventry Liberal Association to become the independent Liberal candidate.

Mr. Darnton is interested in the woollen industry at Bradford, and was President of the Liberal Four Hundred in the Taunton Division of Somerset. He contested the Taunton Division on two occasions unsuccessfully. He is related to Mr. Percy Illingworth and changed his name during the War from Schunck.

174 Maurice Alexander (1889–1945), Liberal MP for Southwark South East 1922–3; unsuccessfully stood for election again in 1923, 1924 and 1931.

175 William Henry Cowan (1862–1932), Liberal MP for Guildford 1906–10 and East Aberdeenshire 1910–22, and Conservative MP for Islington North 1923–9.

176 Thomas William Dobson (1853–1935), Liberal MP for Plymouth 1906–10; unsuccessfully contested East Nottingham in 1912, Plymouth Drake in 1918 and Croydon South in 1922.

177 John Buckle (1867–1925), Labour MP for Eccles 1922–4; trade unionist.

178 Matthew Turnbull Simm (1869–1928), National Democratic and Labour Party MP for Wallsend 1918–22; unsuccessfully contested the seat for the Lloyd George Liberals in 1922.

179 John Edward (1869–1940), baron von Schunck; unsuccessfully contested Coventry for the Liberals in 1922, coming third.

77. Scovell to McCurdy, 'Merseyside', 1 June 1922[180]

Owing to the coming readjustments of our finances I have been brought face to face with the question of policy in respect of our Merseyside operations.

1. The movement in Merseyside commenced in 1920, but has been under the nominal direction of Mr. Max Muspratt[181] of Liverpool rather than this office. Mr. Muspratt loaned us the services of his private Secretary (Mr. Quilliam) to carry out the work of organisation and by doing so on this basis made things extremely difficult for us, as everything had to be left to the last named to do or to muddle as the case may be.

2. Your predecessor subsequently made an abortive attempt with Mr. Muspratt to have him placed on a more definite and paid basis. We here have had endless trouble in respect of his accounts and his financial arrangements have been far from satisfactory but for obvious reasons we have had to be patient.

3. Over a period of seventeen months I find we have made grants to Mr. Quilliam totalling some £2,600: in addition some £1,300 has been found by local people, £400 of which was subscribed by Mr. Max Muspratt himself, and there are now outstanding commitments approximating £600. In the main however we have been subventing an organisation for the promotion of Municipal Candidatures and payment of expenses in connection therewith. In this connection you will, of course, recollect that Mr Muspratt himself is leader of the Liberal Party on the Liverpool Council; incidentally, we have no seat in Liverpool and I doubt whether we shall ever have one.

4. As previously indicated I now find the total liabilities of the office are approximately £600 and I propose to liquidate this as quickly as possible after I have cleared up several outstanding points of considerable moment. In the meantime I have given definite instructions that the whole staff with the exception of two whose salaries only total £30 per month are to be paid off immediately.

5. Now in respect to the policy for the future. I think it would be mistake to close down absolutely in toto from the 1st July, but I would make the following proposals:

- (a) that we should take over direct and absolute control of the Liverpool office,
- (b) reduce it to a skeleton, so that it does not cost at the outside limit more than £500 a year,
- (c) the whole administration of this office to come directly under us and that Mr. Quilliam be pushed out at all costs, with, of course, a suitable letter of thanks.

6. After the next three months have elapsed we could then consider whether further steps would not be desirable but I think in the meantime it would be a great

180 Marked 'Secret'.

181 Max Muspratt (1872–1934), Liberal MP for Liverpool Exchange 1910, lord mayor of Liverpool 1916–17; chemist.

mistake if by winding up the whole organisation we lost all of the records and other interesting information which it now contains. Moreover, a complete cessation would possibly have an unfortunate effect in the mind of Sir A. Salvidge.[182]

78. *Scovell to McCurdy, 'Weekly notes on Constituencies', 2 June 1922*

Garden Parties, etc. Great interest is being shown in the visit which Dame Margaret Lloyd George[183] has promised to make to Bristol, Devon and Cornwall in July.

North Eastern Area. Arrangements are being made for a large picnic to include our supporters from all the constituencies in Durham and Tyneside to be held in Lambton Park by permission of the Earl of Durham on Wednesday June 21st.

Bradford. A Garden Fete is being arranged on Saturday June 24th in the grounds of one of our principal supporters at which it is anticipated there will be from 1,500 to 2,000 people present. The Minister of Pensions has been invited to be present and speak.

Bosworth. A summer outing to Llandudno is being arranged.

Constituency Report.

Crewe. The Annual Meeting of the Association was addressed by Sir Joseph Davies, who spoke strongly in support of the Coalition. It was one of the most successful meetings ever held. Most of the Officers elected are strong supporters.

Candidates.

Heywood & Radcliffe. Colonel England, after addressing a large meeting of Liberals was unanimously adopted as Coalition Liberal candidate.

The Wrekin. Major Christopher Lowther[184] is announced to speak at a series of meetings at which he will be supported by the following: Sir Cecil Beck, MP,[185] Admiral Sueter, R.N., C.B., MP,[186] Col. Claude Lowther, MP,[187] Sir Thomas Polson.[188] His campaign is being organised by Mr. Houston who, in the past has been closely associated with Bottomley.

182 Archibald Tutton James Salvidge (1863–1928), prominent Conservative politician in Liverpool.

183 Dame Margaret Lloyd George (1864–1941), wife of David Lloyd George from 1888.

184 Christopher William Lowther (1887–1935), Conservative MP for Cumberland 1918–22; unsuccessfully contested Wallsend in 1922.

185 Arthur Cecil Tyrell Beck (1876–1932), Liberal MP for Wisbech 1906–10 and 1910–22; vice chamberlain of the household 1915–17.

186 Murray Fraser Sueter (1872–1960), Conservative MP for Hertford 1921–45; naval officer.

187 Claude William Henry Lowther (1870–1929), Conservative MP for Eskdale 1900–6 and 1910–18, and for Lonsdale 1918–22.

188 Thomas Andrew Polson (1865–1946), MP for Dover 1921–2; writer.

Romford. Alderman A. Emile Davies,[189] L.C.C., has been adopted as Labour candidate.

Maidstone. Mr. Hugh Dalton[190], M.A., D.Sc., has now been adopted as Labour candidate.

79. *Scovell to McCurdy, 'Finances', 5 June 1922*[191]

The Chief Whip

Bolton Constituency Finances

1. I have not had an opportunity of going into things with Sir W. Edge and our Lancashire organisers and the following proposal is submitted for your consent in respect of this constituency:–

(a) that the salary (£34 p.m.) of the Bolton Agent, Mr. Cobden Vickers, should be continued to be paid, as heretofore, by our Manchester Office.

(b) that a monthly cheque for £50 should be sent to Sir W. Edge on the first week of each month, commencing 1st July, by the Central Office or your good self as you may prefer, which cheque Sir William Edge[192] will pass across to the Treasurer of his Association to help to meet all other expenses, such as Office expenses, rent, etc., Searchlights. Distribution. Pay and expenses of a woman organiser, (presumably Miss Fawcett). Any debtor balance to be found by local subscription.

(c) That no charges beyond the Agent's bare salary are to fall on our Manchester Office, otherwise my 1st July estimate will go awry.

2. It will therefore be seen that under this scheme, the annual charge levied against this Organisation in respect of Bolton will amount to:–

Agent	408	p.a.
Monthly allowance	600	
	£1008	p.a.

I have sent a copy of this memorandum to Sir William Edge, with whom you will doubtless discuss the matter.

189 Albert Emile Davies (1875–1950), Labour politician who unsuccessfully contested Romford in 1922, 1923 and 1924, and Manchester Moss Side in 1931; leader of the Labour Party on London county council 1924–5 and chairman of the council 1940–1.

190 Edward Hugh John Neale Dalton (1887–1962), baron Dalton; Labour MP for Peckham 1924–9, Bishop Auckland 1929–31 and 1935–59; under-secretary of state for foreign affairs 1929–31, minister of economic warfare 1940–2, president of the board of trade 1942–5, chancellor of the exchequer 1945–7, chancellor of the duchy of Lancaster 1948–50; chair of the Labour Party 1936–7.

191 Marked 'Secret'.

192 William Edge (1880–1946), Liberal MP for Bolton 1918–23 and Bosworth 1927–45; industrialist and close associate of Lloyd George.

80. *Scovell to McCurdy, 'Weekly notes on Constituencies', 9 June 1922*

Bye-Elections:

Banbury. The Labour Party held a meeting last night at Banbury. They agreed that it was undesirable to contest the seat at the present bye-election unless in the event of there being a three-cornered contest.

There are no indications of any activity on the part of the Wee Frees. The local Conservative leaders are also prepared to give Sir Rhys Williams[193] their support.

Nottingham E. The Labour Party have appointed a small Committee to obtain a suitable candidate when it is understood the name of various candidates will be considered. The Conservative agent declined to give any information as to who they were. The local opinion is that the Wee Free candidate's chances will be improved in a three-cornered contest. The Conservative agent is quite confident of holding the seat.

Moray & Nairn. No change in the situation. Contest unlikely.

Newbury. No contest.

Constituency Reports.

West Ham-Silvertown. Mr. E.E. Leech of Bury St. Edmunds has been adopted as Working Man Unionist candidate for the Silvertown constituency. He is a working whitesmith and very active in Friendly Society work as a member of the St. Edmunds' Lodge of the Manchester Unity of Oddfellows and President of the Bury St. Edmunds' Co-operative Society. He served during the war from 1914 to 1919 and became a sergeant in a Suffolk regiment. It is understood that his election expenses will be the first charge on a fund being raised by the Association of Conservative Clubs.

Rochester-Gillingham. Col. Maurice Spencer,[194] C.M.G., has been adopted Labour candidate. He has been associated with the Sidney Webbs[195] for many years and has quite a good army record.

St. Rollox-Glasgow. Mr. J. Arnold Fleming,[196] a local manufacturer has been adopted as Wee Free candidate.

Galloway. Major McMicking[197] has announced his intention of retiring at the General Election.

193 Rhys Rhys-Williams (1865–1955), Liberal MP for Banbury 1918–22; contested Pontypridd unsuccessfully in 1922; soldier.

194 Maurice Spencer (1863–1940), Labour politician who stood unsuccessfully for Gillingham in 1922, 1923 and 1924 and for Bournemouth in 1929; soldier, intelligence officer.

195 Sidney Webb (1859–1947), 1st baron Passfield; Labour MP for Seaham 1922–9; president of the board of trade 1924, secretary of state for the colonies 1929–31, secretary for dominion affairs 1929–30; ennobled in 1929.

196 John Arnold Fleming (1871–1966), Liberal politician who unsuccessfully contested Glasgow St Rollox in 1922; chemist, journalist, writer and philanthropist.

197 Gilbert McMicking (1862–1942), Liberal MP for Kircudbrightshire 1910–18 and Galloway 1918–22; soldier.

Newport. The Conservatives have selected Mr. Reginald Clarry[198] who will stand as an opponent of the Coalition.

Stourbridge. Mr Sylvan Mayer, K.C., has resigned the Labour candidature owing to the attitude of the extreme section in the constituency.

81. *Scovell to McCurdy, 'Weekly Notes on Constituencies', 16 June 1922*

Bye-Elections:

Nottingham E. Nomination Date, Wednesday June 21st.

Candidates:

Mr. J.P. Houfton, J.P.[199] of Mansfield Woodhouse, Director of the Bolsover Colliery Company. (Coalition Unionist).

Mr. Cecil Roberts,[200] of Nottingham, Editor of the "Nottingham Journal". (Ind. Liberal).

Mr. A.H. Jones, J.P. of Shrewsbury, member of Central Board of the Co-operative Union. (Co-op. Labour).

Electorate:	Men…	16,593.
	Women…	13,769.
	Total…	30,362.

The Unionist Agent is confident of a good majority and says that Mr. Roberts will be a bad third. Mr. Roberts has the advantage of being a local man. Mr. Jones, little or nothing is so far known. He has only just been adopted and is quite unknown locally. Mr. Roberts has already given offence to the local teetotallers by an unfortunate remark of his which he explained he had intended to be facetious.

Moray & Nairn. A small group of independent Liberals have made an effort to secure a candidate, and the name of Sir John Simon has been mentioned. Mr. Wm. Webster, of Edinburgh, the Wee Free Organiser has made it known that unless there are indications of much greater support than have so far appeared a candidate will not be provided.

Banbury. The Liberal Association have adopted Sir Rhys Williams. There will be no opposition to his return.

198 Reginald Clarry (1882–1945), Conservative MP for Newport 1922–9 and 1931–45.

199 Sir John Plowright Houfton (1857–1929), Conservative MP for East Nottingham 1922–3 after winning the by-election; colliery owner.

200 Edric Cecil Mornington Roberts (1892–1976), journalist and writer, editor of the *Nottingham Post* 1920–5, did not proceed to contest the seat.

Candidatures:

Middlesborough, E. Mr Martin Connolly,[201] a working riveter on the Tyne and a member of the Boilermakers Executive has been adopted Labour candidate.

Deritend. Mr. J.W. Dennis,[202] Unionist, has decided to retire.

Derbyshire, N.E. Major G.H Bowden,[203] Ind. Unionist, has withdrawn his candidature. Mr. Frank Lee, Assistant Secretary of the Derbyshire Miners' Association has been adopted as Labour candidate.

Rugby. Captain Euan Wallace, M.C., will be the Unionist candidate.

Cardiganshire. Mr. Hopkin Morris,[204] barrister, has been adopted as Wee Free candidate.

Dundee. The Liberal Association resolved by a majority of 81 to 41 to support the Candidature of Mr. Churchill and Mr. MacDonald, Coalition Liberals.

Tottenham, N. Mr. C.D. Roberts, prominently connected with the Tottenham Hotspur Football Club has been adopted by the Constitutional Party as candidate in succession to Sir W. Prescott, MP, who will not stand at the General Election.

Huntingdon. Great efforts by the Die-hards have been made to capture the Conservative organisation in Huntingdon, but without success. Lord Sandwich was approached but he refused to countenance this movement. A public meeting was called, and about 100 were present, including men of all parties. The Conservative agent states that the movement will fizzle out in a short time.

Cardiff, S. Mr. E.A.C. St Aubyn Arney, K.C., has been adopted as the Conservative candidate.[205]

82. *Scovell to McCurdy, 'Cinema Trade and Entertainment Tax', 17 June 1922*

Further to my Minute of June 12th I now have had some further additional information from one of our most consistent supporters:

(a) That there is serious misgiving in the Trade that the Chancellor of the Exchequer has bluffed the deputation that waited on him on Wednesday last.

201 Martin Henry Connolly (1874–1945), Labour MP for Newcastle-Upon-Tyne East 1924–9, having unsuccessfully contested Middlesborough East in 1922 and 1923; trade unionist.

202 John William Dennis (1865–1949), Conservative MP for Birmingham Deritend 1918–22.

203 George Robert Howland Bowden (1873–1927), Conservative MP for North East Derbyshire 1914–18; he was not awarded the coupon in 1918; engineer.

204 Rhys Hopkin Morris (1888–1956), Liberal MP for Cardiganshire 1923–32 and Carmarthen 1945–56; lawyer and magistrate.

205 In fact, the sitting Conservative MP James Hubert Cory (1857–1933), who represented Cardiff in 1915–18 and Cardiff South in 1918–23, contested the seat successfully in 1922 and unsuccessfully in 1923.

(b) That 12.5% flat rate would be found to be acceptable to both the Kinema Trade and other interests as well, eg. Theatre Proprietors, in place of the present obviously unfair incidence on the cheapest seats. At the moment the demand is for a 10% flat rate.

(c) That, although the Chancellor would lose in the direction of the Entertainments Tax, he would recoup some part of his losses by increased receipts in respect of Corporation and Income Tax.

(d) 12.5% on gross box office receipts appears to equal 14.3% on net receipts of proprietors, on which the present tax is based.

(e) It would seem highly desirable, if an alteration is to be made, that it should be done before the House debates the subject, so that the wind is taken out of the sail of the Die-Hard group and the Labour Party, all of whom, I am told, are ready to champion the cause.

(f) On dit that there are powerful financial interests at work who, for obvious reasons, ardently desire to see the shares of these big concerns at a lower figure than they are to-day.

(g) I have seen, and forward, some samples of the propaganda that the Trade has ready prepared.

G.J. Scovell

P.S. Please understand I am perfectly disinterested in this matter except from the point of view of:–

(a) political friendship with the trade.

(b) the danger of a pernicious anti-Govt. campaign.

83. *Scovell to McCurdy, 'Cinema Tax and Entertainment Tax' [Undated but circa June 1922]*

It has come to my knowledge that the cinema theatre owners are preparing an extensive propaganda campaign against the Government. They have already opened fire and there are traces of their work in the Press. At the present time they are holding their hands until after their interview with the Chancellor of the Exchequer on the 14th. inst., but unless they are satisfied or at any rate placated as the result of that interview, they will go ahead. I understand that Captain J.W. Barber is running the campaign from 80, Wardour Street, W. From the political point of view, they can make an effective case, and they can give that case a publicity which no other body in the country can equal, and which it will be extremely difficult to counter. By posters, which perhaps do not matter very much, and by announcements on the screen, which would matter a very great deal, they would draw attention to the fact that the 2d. tax on a 5d. seat is 40% of the seat price whereas the wealthy man's box in a West End theatre of the "legitimate" variety, works out at only 11 per cent of the seat value.

Doubtless they will also press the point which is being made by the Labour Party all over the country that remissions of taxation this year go for the most part to Income Tax payers, and these are always identified for propaganda purposes with the wealthy. It isn't true, but it is effective politically. The Chancellor of the Exchequer appears to have deliberately minimised the probable income of this year and maximised the probable expenditure. An income of only one per cent more, and an expenditure of one per cent less than he anticipates would give him a large surplus. If this view be correct, if instead of a surplus of less than one million there is a reasonable chance of a surplus of three or four millions, could not the Chancellor take the risk of modifying the Entertainments Tax so as to choke off the campaign? Mr. Hilton Young in the House of Commons said that Sir Robert was prepared to modify the tax to suit the cinema people provided that the modification did not diminish the total yield. Isn't some further concession possible? I think it would be advisable to keep direct political propaganda off the films. Once that starts, the Labour Party will have a pull, since cinema proprietors if they are to "propaganda", will have to take the line of least resistance and most profits – that is to say they will have to please their clients, most of whom are workers. So far as indirect propaganda is concerned, if their views could be met now it would be of great political advantage to us in the next twelve months. The trade says that ninety per cent of cinema proprietors are financially on the rocks and affirm that the main cause of it is the Entertainments Tax. From what I hear the first is, I think, not greatly exaggerated while the second is true in part.

On the political aspect of the situation, reflection is certainly necessary from the point of view of the Government. May I emphasise ever so strongly that a little practical sympathy now will possibly lead to a good quid pro quo later if asked for or needed.

The attached article from Mr. Jesson's papers is a specimen of what they are doing and saying.

Outline of Tax To-Day

On 3d.	seats	additional	tax	is	1d.
" 4d.	"	"	"	"	1d.
" 4.5d.	"	"	"	"	1.5d.
" 5d.	"	"	"	"	2d.
" 6d..	"	"	"	"	2d.
" 7d.	"	"	"	"	2d.
" 9d.	"	"	"	"	3d.
" 1/-	"	"	"	"	3d.
" 1/2–1/8		"	"	"	4d.
" 7/6	seats	"	"	"	1/–
" 10/6	"	"	"	"	1/6

Sample of Large Poster

THE WORKING MAN'S CINEMA

for 3½ years since the War has Contributed the bulk of the

ENTERTAINMENTS TAX

On an unfair scale.

A 5d. seat is taxed 2d. = 40%

A 9d. " " " 3d. = 33.33%

WHEREAS IN THE WEALTHY MAN'S THEATRE

A 10/6d. seat is taxed 1/6 = 14.5%

A £2 box " " 4/6d = 11.25%

THIS UNDEMOCRATIC DISTRIBUTION MUST CEASE

PUNISHING THE WORKER.

The entertainment tax is unjust because

IT PENALISES THE WORKER

The tax on the 5d. Cinema seat is 40% or 8/– in the pound.

The tax on the £2 Theatre box is 11.25% or 2/3 in the pound.

WHY SHOULD THE WORKER PAY THE HIGHER PROPORTION OF TAX ON HIS PLEASURES THAN THE WEALTHY MAN?

LET ALL PAY EQUALLY

84. *Scovell to McCurdy, 'Weekly Notes on Constituencies', 23 June 1922*

Bye-Elections:

Nottingham E. The Labour Party are very active, their open-air meetings are well attended. The points they are making are:–

1. The Budget concessions favour the rich man, but do nothing for the poor.

2. Mine owners made huge profits during the war and continue to charge excessive prices for household coal. They contrast the price paid for export with coal for home consumption.

The Wee Frees are not at all happy. They consider that the change of candidate will result in Graham getting a very small poll, and make their cause look ridiculous.

S. Hackney. The Selection Committee had eleven names submitted to them of possible candidates. They have selected four who are to be invited to meet the

Committee, viz., Sir Charles Ruthven, Lt. Col. Bennett Dampier, Garro Jones, Esq., and if he consents, Sir Charles Russell.[206] The Committee insist that the candidate must be prepared to pledge support to the Government.

Candidatures:

Rugby. The Conservative candidate, Captain Euan Wallace has stated that he will stand as a Conservative supporter of the Coalition. At his adoption meeting Sir John Baird, MP, was present.

Leicester E. Captain H.A. Evans[207] has met the Coalition Executive of both the Unionist and Liberal Associations with a view to his adoption as candidate.

North Dorset. The Conservative Association at its Annual Meeting declared itself anti-Coalition. The new President made a bitter attack upon the Prime Minister. The candidate, Mr. Cecil Hanbury[208] stated that he held no brief whatever for the Coalition Government, in fact he was a keen critic and that the Coalition had made a muddle of things all round.

Stockton. Major Strother Stewart[209] has been adopted as Wee Free candidate. He was defeated at Workington in 1918.

North Islington. Miss E. Picton Turberville has been adopted as Labour candidate.

North Bristol. Colonel Henry Guest[210] has been adopted by both wings of the Coalition as the candidate in place of Mr. Stanley Gange[211] who is retiring.

Hulme Division, Manchester. Colonel J. Nall, MP,[212] has publicly stated that by an unanimous vote of the Conservative Association his anti-Coalition attitude has been endorsed. He says "I am now against the Government policy and administration in practically every direction at home and abroad".

206 Charles Russell (1863–1928), solicitor. His father Charles Arthur Russell (1832–1900), baron Russell of Killowen, had been the Conservative MP for Hackney South 1885–94, attorney general 1886 and 1892–4, lord of appeal in ordinary 1894, and lord chief justice of England 1894–1900.

207 Henry Arthur Evans (1898–1958), Liberal MP for Leicester East 1922–3 and Conservative MP for Cardiff South 1924–9 and 1931–45.

208 Cecil Hanbury (1871–1937), Conservative MP for North Dorset 1924–37, having successfully contested the seat in 1922 and 1923.

209 Robert Strother Stewart (1878–1954), Liberal MP for Stockton-on-Tees 1923–4, having unsuccessfully contested the election for Workington in 1918 and Stockton-on-Tees in 1922.

210 Christian Henry Charles Guest (1874–1957), older brother to Freddie Guest and Oscar Guest MPs, Liberal MP for East Dorset 1910, Pembroke and Haverfordwest 1910–18, Bristol North 1922–3, Plymouth Drake 1937–45; soldier.

211 Edwin Stanley Gange (1871–1944), Liberal MP for North Bristol 1918–22.

212 Joseph Nall (1887–1958), Conservative MP for Manchester Hulme 1918–29 and 1931–45; industrialist.

85. *Scovell to McCurdy, 'Central Portsmouth', 23 June 1922*

Central Portsmouth

The position here has not materially altered since the date of the last memo – February 16th. There are still the three candidates in the field:–

Co. Lib.	Sir Thomas Fisher
Cons.	Alderman Privett[213]
Wee Free.	Sir Thomas Bramsdon[214]

It is suggested that Ald. Privett is persisting in his candidature in Central Portsmouth, so that he may have first claim on South Portsmouth in the event of the sitting member's (Major Cayzer)[215] resignation at the General Election which is likely. The fight is really between Sir Thomas Fisher and Sir Thomas Bramsdon. The latter is a strong candidate on account of his local influence and popularity, but Sir Thomas Fisher has been making great headway, and has recently considerably strengthened his position by providing employment and repairing some of his ships in Portsmouth dockyard.

86. *Scovell to McCurdy, 'Expenditure', 26 June 1922*

I think I ought to let you know that, with the exception of Bolton's finances (in respect of which I have been unable, so far, to arrive at any definite or satisfactory arrangement with Sir William Edge) I can now see my way, as from 1st July, to reduce our expenditure to the figures I gave you in my memorandum of the 24th May. I should, however, mention that, in order to obtain such a huge cut in expenditure, besides having to lay out over £2,000 of retrenchment money, I have had to settle up all kinds of liabilities which were outstanding, so if the bank approaches you with respect to any overdraft you will, I trust, appreciate that economies on the scale which I have carried out cannot possibly be effected without considerable outlay.

Mr. Dimbleby has been very helpful in speeding up the submission to the various area offices of accounts for literature, Searchlights, and other material of that kind, supplied from this office during the previous four or five months which had not hitherto been paid for. As at present seen, I do not think the reduction of expenditure which becomes operative at the end of this month will lead to any marked loss of efficiency now that most of our adopted candidates are well in the saddle.

213 Frank John Privett (1874–1937), Conservative MP for Portsmouth Central 1922–3, after victory over the Lloyd George Liberal candidate Sir Thomas Fisher by just seven votes.

214 Thomas Arthur Bramsdon (1857–1935), Liberal MP for the borough of Portsmouth 1900, 1906–10 and Portsmouth Central 1918–22 and 1923–4; solicitor.

215 Herbert Robin Cayzer (1881–1958), 1st baron Rotherwick; Conservative MP for Portsmouth South 1918–22 and 1923–39 after standing down briefly to allow Leslie Wilson, the chief whip, to get into parliament via a by-election in 1922; ennobled in 1939; shipping interests.

87. *Extract from Unionist Central Office Report on Newcastle, 3 July 1922*[216]

Mr. Shortt[217] was returned on the "Lloyd George" wave at the last General Election with the united support of the Unionist vote. Since that date, practically all the leading Liberals who supported his candidature, including his election agent, Councillor Harry Benson, have gone back to the Asquithian fold, and he is left now with a very thin skeleton of Liberal supporters and practically no organisation. We ourselves have a strong Women's Unionist organisation in all the wards of that division numbering nearly five hundred subscribers, who are well organised and exceedingly active. Our Men's Unionist War Associations in the five wards in this division are fairly strong, in addition to which we have several strong Unionist Labour branches in that constituency. We have also an old established Unionist Club in that division with a large membership and we are opening another Unionist Club on the borders of that division and the Central division at the end of this month, which we all hope will have three hundred paid members by the opening day. The Coalition Liberals are depending upon our organisation in the event of a Bye-election. The Labour candidate, Councillor David Adams, who is a good fighter, has money, and is well known in the division.

The Hon. R.D. Denman,[218] formerly MP for Carlisle, is a "Wee Free" candidate and has recently been nursing the division. The Coalition Liberals are unable to secure a suitable local candidate. I have discussed the position on several occasions with them pointing out that unless they can get a strong local candidate or an outside man whose name is a household word, they will lose the seat at a bye-election, and this would have its effect upon the adjoining (i.e. Central Division) which is represented by Sir George Renwick, Bart. Both Sir George and myself have urged them to bring strong Coalition-Liberal influence on Sir William Noble, Bart.,[219] a well-known and popular Ship-owner, who lives practically in that division and who has a large Chapel following, and would, we feel sure, be a most acceptable candidate. He would also, we believe, be the means of influencing many Asquithian voters, as he is an outstanding feature in the commercial life of the North and Newcastle Quayside.

A few weeks ago, I had one of the Coalition Lieutenants from London, along with the local organising Agent, Mr. T.J. Fletcher, interviewing me on this question and they informed me that one of their chief men from the Central Office was coming down to see Sir. W.J. Noble, as the local office has failed to make any impression on him. Whether they have seen him or not, I do not know. He got his baronetcy through Downing Street, and that is where the pressure should come from.

216 Forwarded to Scovell on 8 July. Signature of person forwarding document is unreadable but probably that of the area agent for Newcastle and Northumberland.

217 Edward Shortt (1862–1935), Liberal MP for Newcastle-upon-Tyne 1910–18, Newcastle-upon-Tyne West 1918–22; home secretary 1919–22; lawyer.

218 Richard Douglas Denman (1876–1957), Liberal MP for Carlisle 1910–18 and Labour MP (National Labour 1931–45) for Leeds Central 1929–45.

219 William Joseph Noble (1863–1935), 1st baron Kirkley; shipowner; ennobled 1930.

The local Coalition Liberal Office suggested a Miss Baxter Ellis as a woman candidate for the division. I then called a joint meeting of the Western Division Women's Unionist Executive, when the question was carefully discussed and a resolution was unanimously passed that a woman candidate, whether Unionist or Coalition Liberal, would have no prospect of success in that division at the present time. If they cannot find a strong Coalition Liberal candidate, a strong Unionist candidate might be found, if acceptable to the Coalition Liberals, which I very much doubt.

88. *Scovell to McCurdy, 'Weekly Notes on Constituencies', 30 June 1922*

Bye-Election.

Nottingham E The result was declared last night as follows:

Mr. J.P. Houfton. (C.U.)	10,404
Mr. A.H. Jones. (Lab)	5,431. – 4,973
Mr. T.G. Graham. (I.L.)	4,065

The *Daily Chronicle* in its announcement misdescribes the party of two of the candidates. Jones is described as independent Liberal and Graham as Labour. This conveys the wrong impression that the independent Liberals polled more than Labour.

Candidatures.

S.W. St. Pancras. Mr. Fred Easton has been adopted as Labour candidate. He is editor of the "National Newsagent" and a member of the Printing and Paperworkers' Union.

Westhoughton. Mr Jas. Tonge[220] has been unanimously adopted as the Coalition candidate by both Liberals and Unionists.

Blackpool. The Labour candidate Mr. J.C. Martin has withdrawn.

Withington, Manchester. The Sitting Conservative member, Mr. Carter[221] will not contest the seat again.

Sir Edward Rhodes is doing all he can to obtain the consent of the Conservative Organisation to their giving support to a Coalition Liberal. They however are not inclined to do so. The present Lord Mayor, Mr. E.D. Simon[222] of Manchester will stand as an independent Liberal, if the election does not take place until after November.

220 James Tonge (1837–1923), unsuccessfully contested the Westhoughton constituency as an independent Liberal in 1918, at a by-election in 1921, and as a Lloyd George Liberal in 1922.

221 Rei Albert Deakin Carter (1856–1938), Conservative MP for Manchester Withington 1918–22.

222 Ernest Emil Darwin Simon (1879–1960), 1st baron Simon of Wythenshawe; lord mayor of Manchester 1921–2; Liberal MP for Withington 1923–4 and 1929–31, unsuccessfully contested Penryn and Falmouth in 1931 for the Liberals and Combined English Universities in 1946 as an independent candidate, joined the Labour Party in 1946; ennobled 1947; writer and industrialist.

Garden Party, Bradford. The success of this gathering was interfered with to some extent by the stormy weather. Mr. J.W. Pratt, MP, was the principal speaker. There was quite a good attendance and the press gave good reports of the speeches.

89. *Memo to the Chief Whip, 'Newcastle West', 6 July 1922*

The position in this constituency is substantially the same as on the date of my last report to you, 13th April 1922. There has been considerable activity in the division and the organisation is in a healthy condition. Our difficulty still remains what it has always been – there is, as yet, no candidate in the field. As I reported to you, I submitted several names for consideration, but both our people and the local Conservatives still urge the desirability of having a local man. I have discussed the position frequently with Sir Alfred Palmer on his visits to London, and I propose paying a long overdue visit to Newcastle early next week for the purpose of discussing the position on the spot with representatives of both wings of the Coalition and if possible prevailing on them to decide on a candidate. I am now in a position to suggest the name of a local gentleman who, I think, will be acceptable to both wings and will be, from every point of view, a very suitable candidate.

I understand that the Hon. R.D. Denman, the independent Liberal candidate is making no impression whatsoever. Mr David Adams, the Labour candidate, who is one of the war's mushroom shipowners, has been very active but is by no means popular. I have just seen our Newcastle organiser, who happens to be in London, and he always says that, provided a vigorous candidate with local connections, there is a reasonable chance of holding the seat.

90. *Scovell to McCurdy, 'East Nottingham', 14 June 1922*

We are informed that after weighing the rival claims of two men, the East Nottingham Conservative Association decided on J.P. Houfton of the Bolsover Colliery, The Hall, Mansfield Woodhouse. He fought North East Derby as a Liberal at a bye-election in May 1914, and failed by about 300 votes to win a three cornered fight. He is a strong Coalitionist. His adoption took place on Monday 12th inst. The independent Liberal candidate is Mr. Cecil Roberts, proprietor and Editor of the *Nottingham Guardian and Express*.

At a meeting last night the 13th inst. it was decided to run Mr. A.H. Jones, J.P. of Shrewsbury, as Labour Party Trade Council, and Co-operative Board candidate.

91. *McCurdy to Scovell, 'MacCallum Scott', 15 June 1922*

In arranging for clerical assistance for Mr. MacCallum Scott the possibility of Mr. Towyn Jones[223] resigning from the Welsh Whip-ship should be borne in mind, – his successor would certainly need assistance also.

223 Josiah Towyn Jones (1858–1925), Liberal MP for Carmarthenshire East 1912–18 and Llanelli 1918–22; congregationalist minister.

I should be glad if you would have a word with Miss Pull about this, as it is very desirable that before an addition to the staff is made, the most practical form of assistance should be understood.

92. *Scovell to McCurdy, 'MacCallum Scott and Organisation in Scotland', 16 June, 1922*

Reference the attached, I have had a long discussion with Mr. MacCallum Scott on this very subject. He tells me he will need a whole time man –

(a) to do his personal work; and

(b) to be capable of joining him in Scotland during the vacation, when he can give plenty of time to the question of Organisation in Scotland.

For this purpose, we have arranged as follows:

(a) pending the time when we can find a desirable single young man i.e. typist, shorthand writer and a Scotsman, probably to be drawn from one or our offices up North, he is going to employ a purely temporary woman typist whom he knows of, to be paid by the week.

(b) he proposes to send Mr Cameron, who has been assisting Sir William Sutherland, back to Scotland, to do organising work there.

(c) he has not quite made up his mind yet as to whether his clerical assistant shall be lodged in 25 Old Queen Street or 12 Downing Street.

Of course, the possibilities to which you refer somewhat complicates affairs, but Mr. MacCallum Scott made it quite clear to me that he would require the services of a whole timer.

93. *Scovell to McCurdy, 'Essay Competition', 5 July 1922*

Attached is draft of memo on the Essay Competition which I discussed with you. Do you approve?

G.S. Scovell

Essay Competition

Subject, Conditions, Classes and Prizes

Limited to Certified Agents, Trainee Agents, Organisers, Full time staff of the Party Organisation.

I. Subject

The intensive and complete organisation of a constituency (which to the Agent is virgin ground) in the available time at his disposal, in this case not less than six months before an Election, (bye or general), and the carrying out of all election duties up to and including the submission of Election Accounts to the Returning Officer.

II. Conditions

(a) For the purpose of this essay it will be presumed that the Agent takes up his duties on 1st January 1922, that a candidate is not finally adopted until the end of March 1922, and that the writ for the election is moved on 1st July 1922.

(b) The words "intensive and complete organisation" are intended to cover a wide field apart altogether from the more mechanical or routine duties of an Election Agent, and embrace such points as the working up of the Women's side; how the local Press is to be tackled; how the candidate is to endeavour to capture the goodwill of all classes and interests; how voluntary workers can be collected, enthused, etc, and how distributors can be arranged for etc; due regard being had throughout to the greatest economy.

(c) Each essay must be submitted by one person, but there is no objection to collaboration with one or more men or women Agents or Organisers within the area: collaboration with people outside the Area will disqualify. A list giving the names of collaborators, if any must be submitted in a sealed envelope on which is inscribed a "nom de plume". The leader or person submitting the essay will head the list with his name and address.

(d) Essays must not exceed 3,000 words and must be typed on foolscap paper – one side only.

(e) Essays must reach this office addressed to the General Secretary not later than 15th October, 1922.

III. Classes

The competition will be divided into two classes viz:

Class A. The complete development of an Organisation in a purely Urban and industrial constituency of 6 Wards.

Or

Class B. The complete development of an Organisation in a Constituency which is partly Urban say with 3 Urban districts of 7,000 voters each, the remainder being purely rural, with say altogether 30 polling districts.

Each competitor may choose one or other of A. and B. but not both.

IV. Prizes

Prizes will be allotted as follows:–

Class A 1st prize. £20 2nd prize. £10

Class B 1st prize. £20 2nd prize. £10

2nd Prizes will only be awarded provided three or more compete in each class.

V. General

The judges in awarding prizes will take into account:–

(a) Not so much the literary style of the essay as its methodical arrangement;

(b) The number of new and practical ideas or suggestions or the adaptation of old ideas to the present situation each essay question contains.

(c) Any failure to give in detail a method or methods of overcoming difficulties in respect to small but necessary points of organisation;

(d) Clear signs that every economy has been considered.

94. *Scovell to McCurdy, 'Weekly Notes on Constituencies', 7 July 1922*

Bye-Elections.

Gower. Nomination date, Wednesday July 12th, Polling Thursday July 20th.

Candidates: Mr. D.H. Williams, (C.L.), Mr. D.R. Grenfell, (Lab.)[224] (Miner's Agent)

The Campaign opens to-day.

Pontypridd. The writ for this Bye-election was moved yesterday. Mr. T.A. Lewis will be opposed by T.I. Mardy Jones,[225] the political agent for the South Wales Miners' Federation.

Northern Liberal Federation. The Annual Meetings of the Northern Liberal Federation will be held at Middlesborough on the 15th July. The speakers will include the following: Mr. Walter Runciman,

Mr. Aneurin Williams, MP,[226] Mr. Trevelyan Thomson, MP,[227] Col. P. Williams, MP,[228] Hon. R.D. Denman. (Ind. Lib. candidate for Newcastle, West).

Eastern Counties Liberal Federation. The Annual Meetings of the Eastern Counties Liberal Federation will be held at Grantham on Friday 14th July.

Candidatures:

Edinburgh, W. Mrs Hamilton More Nisbet is to be invited to contest this constituency as an independent.

St. Helens. (Lancs). Mr. Edward Wooll[229] has been invited to address the St. Helens Unionist Party on the 20th instant with a view to his adoption as Unionist candidate.

Worcester. Viscount Deerhurst, the adopted Unionist candidate for this constituency has been forced to withdraw because he was asked to declare himself independent, not only of the Prime Minister but also of Mr. Chamberlain. The Conservative Executive have now chosen the Hon. Henry Lygon, half-brother of the present Earl Beauchamp, as independent Conservative candidate.

224 David Rhys Grenfell (1881–1968), Labour MP for Gower 1922–59; miner.

225 Thomas Isaac Mardy Jones (1879–1970), Labour MP for Pontypridd 1922–31; miner.

226 Aneurin Williams (1859–1924), Liberal MP for Plymouth 1910, North West Durham 1914–18, Consett 1918–22.

227 Trevelyan Thomson (1875–1928), Liberal MP for Middlesborough West 1918–28; iron and steel merchant.

228 Penry Williams (1866–1945), Liberal MP for Middlesborough 1910–18, Middlesborough East 1918–22 and 1923–4.

229 Edward Wooll (1878–1970), unsuccessfully contested St Helens in 1922 and Hull Central in 1923 for the Conservative Party; barrister, soldier and writer.

95. *Scovell to McCurdy Via Miss Pull, 11 July 1922*

If Bolst[230] is finally selected as a Coalitionist candidate for South Hackney despite our endeavours otherwise I presume you will have no objection if we run his contest, providing it doesn't cost us a penny – rather than let the Tories grab him and the future of the seat. Reply as given to me. Despite my dislike, I can see no other course.

96. *Scovell to McCurdy, 'Weekly Notes on Constituencies', 14 July 1922*

Bye-Elections.

Gower. The local people have not been severe in their demands for speakers (MP's) and we have been able to satisfy their requirements in this direction. Sir Alfred Mond Bt. MP, will be the principal speaker on the 18th. Polling takes place on the 20th.

Pontypridd. We have secured a large number of speakers (MPs) to speak in support of Mr. T.A. Lewis[231] as the attached list will show, and Mr. Lewis in very pleased with our efforts in this matter. Polling Day is Tuesday the 25th.

Candidatures.

Leyton West. The Unionist candidate Major J.C. Walker is retiring, in consequence of which we have asked the Unionist Central Office to endeavour to get Mr. E. Alexander who at present is standing as an independent Conservative in the neighbouring constituency East Leyton adopted as his successor.

Hartlepools. Mr. W.A. Jowitt,[232] K.C., has been adopted as independent Liberal candidate for this constituency. He is the only son of the late Rev. W. Jowitt, Rector of Stevenage, Herts; and is the youngest K.C. at the Bar.

Newcastle Central. Major Walter Hedley, the independent Liberal candidate has withdrawn. His reasons are of a purely private character. No other candidate has been adopted in his place as yet.

230 Captain Clifford Charles Alan Lawrence Erskine-Bolst (1878–1945), served in the Black Watch regiment and Royal Highlanders 1914–18. Elected Unionist MP for Hackney South in a by-election in Aug. 1922 after the sitting MP, Horatio Bottomley, was expelled from the House following his conviction for fraud. Re-elected in 1922, he lost the seat in the following year. He was returned in 1931 at Blackpool, and stood down in 1935.

231 Thomas Arthur Lewis (1881–1923), Liberal MP for Pontypridd 1918–22, University of Wales 1922–3; barrister.

232 William Allen Jowett (1885–1957), 1st earl Jowett; Liberal MP for the Hartlepools 1922–4 and Preston 1929, and Labour MP for Preston 1929–31 and Ashton-under-Lyne 1939–45; solicitor general 1940–2, paymaster general 1942, minister without portfolio 1942–4, minister of national insurance 1944–5; ennobled 1945; lord chancellor 1945–51.

East Aberdeenshire. Mr. Fred Martin[233] is to be invited to attend a General Meeting of the Liberal Association with a view to his adoption as independent Liberal candidate for this constituency.

Barrow. Mr. D.G. Somerville[234] has been invited to address the Barrow Unionist Executive Committee with a view to his adoption as Unionist candidate for the Barrow Division, in succession to Sir R. Burton Chadwick[235] the sitting member, who will contest Wallasey at the next election.

97. *Scovell to McCurdy, 'Weekly Notes on Constituencies', 21 July 1922*

Bye-Elections:

Pontypridd. Report attached.[236]

Eastern Counties Liberal Federation. There was a fairly large attendance at the 25th Annual Meetings of the Eastern Counties Liberal Federation held at Grantham on the 14th instant. The meetings were not enthusiastic and Lord Lincolnshire who usually puts vim into the proceedings was absent. Last year's Office Bearers were re-elected. Mr. Lyle-Samuel[237] was the principal speaker at lunch. Both he and Mr. Geoffrey Howard were pessimistic. By far the best speaker at the evening meeting was Major Harry Barnes, MP. The discussion on agriculture was poor and divergent views were expressed from the body of the Hall.

Candidatures:

South Hackney. Captain C. Erskine-Bolst was adopted as Prospective Coalition candidate at a combined meeting of the Unionist Coalition Liberal and independent Parties in this constituency on Wednesday the 19th.

Sth Derbyshire. Mr. H.D. Lorimer was adopted on Saturday last as Prospective independent Conservative candidate for this constituency. He is the son of the late Sir William Lorimer. We have already adopted a candidate for this division in the person of Major Goronwy Owen to succeed Mr. Holman Gregory, K.C., the sitting member, who will not seek re-election.

233 Frederick Martin (1882–1950), Liberal MP for East Aberdeenshire 1922–4, unsuccessfully contested the seat for the Labour Party in the 1931 and 1935 general elections.

234 Daniel Gerard Somerville (1879–1938), Conservative MP for Barrow-in-Furness 1922–4 and Willesden East 1929–38.

235 Robert Burton-Chadwick (1869–1951), Conservative MP for Barrow-in-Furness 1918–22 and Wallasey 1922–31; parliamentary secretary to the board of trade 1924–8, counsellor to the British embassy at Buenos Aires 1940–7; shipping magnate.

236 No report is attached.

237 Alexander Lyle-Samuel (1883–1942), Liberal MP for Eye East Suffolk 1918–23. In 1919–20 he was involved in an eventually successful legal action as he pursued damages against *The National News* and others who had spread salacious rumours relating to his private life.

Plaistow. (West Ham). Mr. F.G. Penny[238] will contest this seat in the Conservative interest. Mr. Penny unsuccessfully contested the recent L.C.C. bye-election at East Woolwich. He has held a number of public offices, including the membership of the Woolwich Borough Council from 1910–1919.

Hertford. Ald. E. Carruthers, the independent Liberal candidate has withdrawn.

South Leicester. Mr. R. Wilberforce Allen who unsuccessfully contested E. Leicester as an independent Liberal at the recent bye-election, has accepted an invitation to become prospective independent Liberal candidate for the South Division of Leicester.

East Leicester. The local Coalition Liberal Association has adopted Capt. H.A. Evans as Coalition Liberal candidate for this constituency.

Evesham. (Worcestershire). Mr. R. Aldington[239] has been adopted as Labour candidate for this division.

Colne Valley. At a private meeting of the Executive Committee of the Colne Valley division Conservative Association, held on Saturday last, Mr. Tom Brook was adopted as prospective Conservative candidate for this constituency.

98. *Scovell to McCurdy, 'Camborne', 25 July 1922*

I had a long talk with Beddoe Rees at No.10 last night. He tells me he does not desire on business and geographical reasons to continue very much longer in his candidature at Camborne. We have, therefore, now to look out for a successor. I have discussed the question very fully with Mr. Millman and we have both come to the conclusion that the best fellow to fight the seat is a Mr. A.J. Penny, an ex-civil servant; member of the National Liberal Club and 1920 Club and Alderman of the Surrey County Council and member of the Borough for Wimbledon. He is an excellent speaker and a man whom I expect you know.

Our reasons for hitting on him are as follows:

(a) He is building a house for himself in Devonshire near Exeter;

(b) His brother writes for the Western Morning News and other local papers in the South West of England;

(c) Penny knows his Politics from A to Z

(d) As he has retired from the Civil Service he has ample time to give to the nursing of this seat.

238 Frederick George Penny (1876–1955), MP for Kingston-on-Thames 1922–37; parliamentary private secretary to the financial secretary to the war office 1923, Conservative whip 1926–37, lord commissioner of the treasury 1928–9, vice-chamberlain of the household 1931–2, comptroller of the household 1932–5, treasurer of the household 1935–7, honorary treasurer of the Conservative Party 1938–46.

239 Robert Aldington (1872–1956), unsuccessfully contested Evesham for the Labour Party in the 1922, 1923, 1924 and 1929 general elections.

(e) He also possesses a two seater car.

(f) He is a West country man and a thorough Liberal.

The main thing is that he ought to be able to devote time, and according to Beddoe Rees this is everything.

Given a candidate who can devote time to nursing this Constituency between now and the General Election there is no reason why the seat should not be ours. Have you any objection to my approaching him? I should like to get this matter settled if I can before I go off on the 8th prox.

99. *Memorandum to McCurdy, 'Unemployment in Camborne and Redruth', 26 July 1922*

Mr. McCurdy.

I understand that at the large meeting held at Redruth at which Dame Margaret spoke, she used the following words in connection with the terrible unemployment distress in the tin industry in Camborne and Redruth:– "I can assure you that when I go back to London after all I have heard here, I shall put your case before the Government. I do not say I can do much, but I will present it with the best of hearts."

It has been represented to me to-day by one of our leading supporters in the County of Cornwall that the result of her talk with the Prime Minister on the subject should be sent down to Cornwall. Perhaps you would like to consider the matter and take such steps in connection therewith as you think desirable.

100. *Scovell to McCurdy, 'Weekly notes on Constituencies', 28 July 1922*

Constituencies.

St. Helens. Mr. Edward Wooll, barrister of Liverpool on July 24th was adopted as prospective Conservative candidate for this division, at present represented by Mr. James Sexton.

Reigate. Influential members of the Unionist Party in this constituency being dissatisfied with the policy of the Government and with the attitude of Brig. Gen. G.K. Cockerill,[240] have formed themselves into a provisional Committee with the object of taking steps for running an independent Conservative candidate at the General Election.

Harrow. Mr. Mosley, MP,[241] has decided to stand as independent candidate at the next General Election.

240 George Kynaston Cockerill (1867–1957), Conservative MP for Reigate 1918–31; career soldier.

241 Oswald Edward Mosley (1896–1980), Conservative and later independent MP for Harrow 1918–24, Labour and later New Party MP for Smethwick 1926–31; founder of the British Union of Fascists (1932) and later its leader.

Shoreditch. Dr. Addison, MP, was adopted as independent Liberal candidate for Shoreditch by the Shoreditch Liberal Association on July 27th.

East Aberdeenshire. Mr. Fred Martin was adopted on the 19th instant as prospective Liberal candidate by the East Aberdeenshire independent Liberal Association.

W. Leyton. On July 18th Mr. J.D. Cassels[242] was adopted as prospective Coalition Unionist candidate for West Leyton in opposition to the sitting member, Mr. A.E. Newbould, (Ind. Lib). The adoption meeting was attended by members of the West Leyton Conservative Association.

Sutton, Plymouth. It is reported that Lady Astor is likely to have an opponent at the next General Election. A meeting of the newly-formed Imperial Conservative Association in Plymouth has been called and will be addressed by Dr. H.W. Bayly of Harley Street, London with a view to his adoption as candidate.

Gloucester. Capt. Ackroyd, the prospective Labour candidate for this constituency has resigned.

Coventry. Mr. John Edward Darnton of Harpenden, Hertfordshire, has been adopted as prospective Liberal candidate for Coventry. He has unsuccessfully contested Taunton twice.

101. *Scovell to McCurdy, 'Payments to Towyn Jones', 29 July 1922*

This office has hitherto had to pay Mr. Towyn Jones £300 each half year. The last payment was made on 1st July 1922. Would you let me know what you now wish done about it.[243]

102. *Scovell to McCurdy, 'Newcastle West', 29 July 1922*

Sir William Edge has now ascertained from Sir George Renwick[244] that Mr. Arthur Lambert, Deputy Mayor of Newcastle City, would be an ideal candidate for Newcastle West. We have therefore asked Mr. Lambert to come down on Tuesday and see Sir William Edge and possibly yourself. In the meantime, I have heard from Newcastle to the effect that there is no possible chance of Mr. Lambert standing, mainly on financial and for business reasons. I have now come to the conclusion that there is no use proceeding any further along those lines. In accordance with your suggestion, I am now in favour of approaching Colonel Brown and endeavouring to persuade him to go up to Newcastle and have a look round. I do not think there will be any difficulty at all in getting him adopted if he will only consent to stand. There is a large number of ex-soldiers in the constituency, but, at the same time, there is a distressing amount of unemployment. I would most strongly recommend that everything possible be done to dissuade the 'Powers that

242 James Dale Cassels (1877–1972), Conservative MP for West Leyton 1922–9 and Camberwell North West 1931–5; judge and journalist.

243 A scribbled note from McCurdy states 'cease payment'.

244 George Renwick (1850–1931), Conservative MP for Newcastle-upon-Tyne 1900–6 and 1908–10, and Newcastle-upon-Tyne Central 1918–22; shipping industry.

Be' from bringing on a contest there. I am afraid, however, that it will be inevitable, but it is just as well for 25 Old Queen Street to make it clear that the result, no matter how good the candidate, will be most uncertain.

Fifty per cent of the Constituency is situated in the region of the famous Elswick and other engineering works. I think this is quite enough to show you what a dangerous seat it is.

Copy of this sent to Sir William Edge.

103. *Dimbleby to Scovell, 'Publications', 28 July 1922*

You will recall that in June we announced that the publication of the "Searchlight" would be suspended during July and August. It will be necessary, therefore, to prepare plans during August for re-issue in September, if such a course is decided upon. In view of the fact that the Chief Whip is leaving for his holiday on the rising of the House, we have very little time in which to decide upon the new procedure. After giving the matter careful thought, I have come to the conclusion that the only way we can give the local people the freedom of action they are demanding, and at the same time meet the objection offered by the Chief Whip to paying for matter of the "Parish Magazine" type, which the local editors insist upon our using on pages 1 and 4, will be to limit publication in future to the two middle pages only. By doing this we should be able to retain uniformity of policy in all the "Searchlights" throughout the country, and at the same time we should be able to supply local producers with a partly printed sheet at such a rate that they would be able to print their own local pages and publish the complete article for a price certainly not higher than that which has hitherto been paid to us.

If we can secure circulation of 100,000 we can supply partly printed pages to the local people for something under 15/– a thousand, and they would be able to get the sheet completed, so far as pages 1 and 4 are concerned, and folded ready for distribution at something in the neighbourhood of 21/– per thousand where three and four thousand copies are required. In that way they would effect a considerable economy.

In view, however, of the fact that an arrangement of this kind might mean consultation with the area heads concerned, and the holidays seem to be extending well into September, I suggest that it might be well to notify all areas that there will be no "Searchlight" during September. That will give us a complete holiday interval, and afford ample time for consideration of the new form.

104. *Scovell to McCurdy, 'Publications', 29 July 1922*

I forward you herewith copy of a memorandum I have had from Mr. Dimbleby,[245] subject as above. Personally, on the ground of expense, I am very anxious not to produce any further issues of the Searchlight, anyway, until October at earliest. By that time:

245 See document above.

(a) The holiday season will be well over.

(b) We shall be in a position to see how the various Areas are working on their rationed expenditure.

(c) After conference with the Area Heads, we shall be in a position to have their views as to whether it would be better to print off say 5,000 for one Constituency than 1,000 copies for five Constituencies.

Incidentally, I would mention that they have only budgeted for one thousand copies per month per Constituency. They may, therefore, prefer an occasional issue of larger dimensions rather than a monthly one of 1,000 copies. I am strongly in favour of Mr. Dimbleby's suggestion in the second paragraph, marked "X". I constantly hear grumbles that the local printers are being ignored. I shall be very glad if you would give these points your consideration, and perhaps I could speak to you on the policy you wish pursued in the matter.

105. *Memorandum on Coalition Liberal Party Organisation [undated but circa July 1922]*

Points to Remember:

1. That the only organisation existing in April, 1919 was:

In London:

A skeleton Publicity Department, London only.

Mr G.W. Thompson, and one room:

A women[']s organisation dispersed all over the country, not necessarily working in any of the constituencies.

In Provinces:

Five Area Agents, all U.K.A. men and with one exception all useless:

No loyal Constituency Agents:

No Area or Constituency Councils:

No organised supporters:

2. We now have:

A Central Office co-ordinated within itself and linked up with a network of National Liberal Councils covering the whole of Great Britain, a co-ordinated Woman's and Publicity side and an Agent and an organisation in every one of our constituencies for which we are responsible and some additional ones besides:

A substantial candidate List:

A Speaker's Panel of some 150 Men and Women:

Organised means of distributing literature by hand or by post:

Whereas formerly our bye-elections were largely run by Unionists, we now are self-contained in every direction:

(a) Whereas early in 1919 we could assemble 10–20 representative men or women from the provinces for a conference in 1922 we have 2,000 duly elected delegates representative of the three kingdoms:

(b) In attaining these results we have had to increase our staff nearly three times and are now only nearing finality:

(c) During 1922 no less than 160,000 copies of a localised Searchlight have been distributed on an average each month in our English constituencies:

(d) We now have means of submitting a report on every constituency in Great Britain, whereas in 1919 we had practically none.

(e) National Liberal Councils for Scotland England and Wales, each with their own constitution are now formed or are in course of formation. A co-ordinated executive has also been set up:

(f) With two exceptions candidates are in the field in every one of our 170 seats:

(g) The detailed development of the Publicity side requires separate citation:

(h) Junior formations and Debating Circles are now being formed:

(i) The Universities have not been lost sight of:

(j) In 1920 approximately 800 meetings were held under our auspices, addressed by women only. Figures for men are not available. In the same year 2,000,000 pamphlets were distributed:

(k) In 1921 the figure of meetings of all kinds advanced to well over 2,000 in the year: In the current year figures to hand show the number of meetings will exceed 3,000 – a marked advance year by year.

Special Note

Throughout 1919 and 1920 this Organisation was required to devote the whole of its attention to area as distinct from constituency work, & to some extent helping the few loyal Liberal Associations that existed. Up till the end of 1920 we were hardly permitted to enter any of our own constituencies for fear of a local split. Even today we are, for this very reason, practically barred from active work in such vital centres as Leeds and Sheffield.

106. *Scovell to McCurdy, 'Committee of Inquiry', 31 July 1922*

Consequent on our talk at Downing Street this morning I think it is only fair to you to say that if the Committee which has been set up to look into certain matters connected with this Organisation considers, after due reflection, that someone else can steer the ship better than I can, I once more reiterate that I am prepared to make way without demur. Moreover, from what I gathered from you this morning it appears that a complete and far-reaching change in "organising" policy is contemplated. In my humble opinion any scheme entailing the wholesale scrapping of Area offices at this juncture will lead us to a disaster for which I should not care to be in any way responsible. Before I conclude I should like to make it clear that in writing thus I do not admit for a moment that either the policy or the work of this Organisation, for which I have been responsible since its inception in 1919, is or has been other than of which my colleagues and myself have reason to be justly proud. I frankly confess that the real motive that has actuated me in so readily offering to make way on more than one occasion in the past year is the perpetual undermining of confidence in the Organisation on the part of outsiders which acts as a blight on the enthusiasm of a loyal and excellent staff.

107. *Clipping from Leicester Mercury, 31 July 1922, enclosed in Leicester Coalition Liberal Office to Scovell, 'Committee of Enquiry', 31 July 1922*

"National Liberal" Organisation

Sir Alfred Mond, Dr Macnamara, and Mr. Kellaway are now acting in the position of a sort of Advisory Committee to consider the position of the "National Liberal" organisation. It is no secret that the results of the work so far as the constituencies are concerned has not been satisfactory to the Prime Minister. The failure to hold Pontypridd is only one indication of weakness. Since the Central Hall gathering in January the organisation has not made by any means as much progress as was hoped, and there has been a certain amount of friction with the Unionist bodies in divisions which are represented by Coalition-Liberals in the House of Commons. The business of the three Ministers will be to consider how matters can be improved. Mr McCurdy's position is, of course, involved.

108. *Scovell to McCurdy, Committee of Enquiry, 1 August 1922*

Since sending across to you my letter of yesterday I have been turning things over in my mind and I have come to the conclusion that in view of the wide publicity given by the Press to the setting up of a Committee it would be inimical to my own interests to resign at the present moment unless some way out was found by which any reputation I possess was fully safeguarded from garbled statements and inuendoes in the Press and elsewhere. In this direction the situation today has been rendered radically different from what it was some weeks back when I told you not to hesitate to retrench me if in the interests of the machine you thought fit to do so. In short, while ready to leave the ship I am not prepared for one instant to sacrifice myself or my reputation in the mind of the Press or the public on the altar of Welsh bye-election reverses for the results of which I am no more responsible than the office cat. I feel perfectly sure you will appreciate my point of view in the matter and doubtless your ingenuity and experience can suggest a satisfactory way out.

109. *Scovell to McCurdy, 'Weekly notes on Constituencies', 4 August 1922*

Bye-Election:

South Hackney. Mr. Holford Knight[246] has been adopted as the Labour candidate. Captain Erskine-Bolst has appealed to this office for help which we are giving him as far as is possible or advisable.

Meetings:

Bolton. Particulars are attached of a Children's Demonstration to be held to-morrow. On September 9th, a great Lancashire Coalition Liberal Demonstration will be held at Rivington Park, and Lord Leverhulme's grounds will be open.

Romford. Arrangements are being made in connection with Dame Margaret Lloyd George's visit to East Leyton and Romford in October. The Rt. Hon. Robert Munro has been asked to be the principal speaker.

Torquay. The local Unionist Association have definitely gone over to the Die-hards. At their Annual meeting they adopted the report that "in the interests of the Country they should return to their own political fold and serve under their own shepherds". The Central Office Area agent warned them to go warily and pointed out that what they had to secure was the National rather than Party interest.

Constituencies.

Upton. Mr David Margesson[247] has been adopted as Coalition candidate.

Gorton, Manchester. Mr. William Heap has been adopted as Conservative and Unionist candidate.

Cheltenham. Mr. Cuthbert Plaistowe has been adopted as independent Liberal candidate.

Batley & Morley. Mr J.A. Compston, K.C., Recorder of Leeds has been adopted as Liberal candidate in succession to Mr. Gerald France, MP,

The Wrekin. Mr. R.E. Jones, an official of the A.E.U. will be the Labour candidate.

Tiverton. Mr. Brown has been adopted as Labour candidate.

Stourbridge. Mr. S. Mayer the Labour candidate has retired.

Woodbrige. Mr. Henry Harben, the Labour candidate has withdrawn.

Fulham E. Mr. M. Gordon Liverman has been adopted as independent Liberal candidate.

246 George Wilfrid Holford Knight (1877–1936), Labour MP (National Labour 1931–5) for Nottingham South 1929–35.

247 (Henry) David Reginald Margesson (1890–1965), Conservative MP for West Ham, Upton 1922–3 and Rugby 1924–42; parliamentary private secretary to the minister of labour 1922–3, assistant whip 1924–6, whip and junior lord of the treasury 1926–9, chief whip and parliamentary secretary to the treasury 1931–40, secretary of state for war 1940–2; ennobled 1942 as Viscount Margesson of Rugby.

South Oxfordshire. Sir Henry Rew[248] has been adopted as independent Liberal candidate.

Whitby. Captain Herbert has announced that he will stand as an independent Conservative candidate.

North Leeds. Mr. Hugh M. Butler,[249] has decided to contest the seat at present held by Major Farquharson[250] as an independent Conservative.

Pudsey & Otley. At an Annual meeting of the Conservative Association a resolution demanding a Conservative candidate met with strong support. An amendment however referring the matter to the Executive was carried.

110. *Scovell to McCurdy, 'Weekly notes on Constituencies', 11 August 1922*

Bye-Election.

South Hackney. Captain Bolst's campaign is now in full swing. His Election Address however will not be out for a day or two. Large numbers of outdoor meetings have been held, but indoor meetings will not commence until to-night. The hoardings are covered with large posters. Mr. Jesson, MP, and Mr. Green, MP, have promised to speak in support of Captain Bolst. The Conservative Head Office have sent a number of staff speakers, and we have done the same. Up to now the Labour candidate does not appear to have gained much of a foothold.

Constituencies.

Heywood and Radcliffe. Colonel England is undertaking a programme of outdoor meetings beginning on August 15th and ending on September 1st.

Yarmouth. The Labour Party have adopted Councillor A. Whiting[251] of Barking. He was the Labour candidate for Romford at the last election.

Plymouth. Sir George Younger stated in his letter that the Central Office recognises Lady Astor as the official Coalition candidate. The Plymouth Liberal Party have decided not to oppose Lady Astor.

Brentford and Chiswick. Mrs. Oliver Strachey has been adopted as independent candidate.

The Labour Party. Sidney Webb writes in the Labour Magazine reviewing the position of their Party. He states "they intend contesting 450 seats as compared with 361 at the last election". He says "how many members of Parliament that will mean, it is impossible to predict".

248 Robert Henry Rew (1858–1929), unsuccessfully contested Henley for the Liberals in 1922 and 1923; statistician.

249 Hugh Myddleton Butler (1857–1943), Conservative MP for Leeds North 1922–3; ironmaster.

250 Alexander Charles Farquharson (1864–1951), Liberal MP for Leeds North 1918–22; barrister, doctor and soldier.

251 Arthur Whiting (1878–1938), unsuccessfully contested Yarmouth in 1922 and Chorley in 1935 for Labour; socialist.

The *Yorkshire Observer* has given great prominence during the week to the party-political situation. There are long letters from Sir William Bulmer[252] and Sir James Hill[253] who is recognised as the Wee Free local leader.

111. *Scovell to McCurdy, 'Weekly notes on Constituencies', 18 August 1922*

Bye-Elections.

South Hackney.

The Communists organise opposition to all the Coalition public meetings, but it is thought that the effect of this will have been detrimental to the Labour candidate's chances. In the South Ward which was allotted to our workers the canvass returns are four to one in favour of Captain Bolst. It has not been possible to obtain a result of the canvass as a whole, but it is confidently stated that the seat will be retained. The forecasts of the majority vary so much that reliance cannot be placed upon any figure given. The Coalition candidate has done very well and suited himself to the exceptional circumstances of the constituency.

Constituencies.

Leigh. Sir John Holden, the prospective Conservative candidate has withdrawn. The explanation given is that he is unwell. It is understood that the Conservative Party will secure another candidate.

Chester-Le-Street. Lt. Col. D.F. Todd,[254] a doctor in practice in Sunderland and who has been prominently identified with the Unionist cause in Durham County for many years, has been adopted as Coalition candidate.

Leyton West. Mr. James D. Cassels has been adopted as Coalition Unionist candidate. He is a barrister, and was engaged on the editorial staff of the Morning Post. For two years he was in the Press Gallery. He joined the Army as a private in the early days of the war, but secured a commission.

Bolton. Sir William Edge and Mr. Ainsworth have been adopted by the Conservative Association as joint Coalition candidates.

High Peak. Frank Anderson,[255] Railway Clerks' Association has been adopted as Labour candidate.

East Dorset. The Coalition Association have arranged a series of Garden Parties covering the whole of the constituency. They began on Tuesday August 8th, and will conclude on Saturday August 19th.

252 William Bulmer (1881–1936), mill owner, public servant and football player.

253 James Hill (1849–1936), Liberal MP for Bradford Central 1916–18, lord mayor of Bradford 1908–9; wool merchant.

254 David Fee Todd (1864–1945), soldier and doctor.

255 Frank Anderson (1889–1959), Labour MP for Whitehaven 1935–59, had unsuccessfully contested High Peak in 1922 and 1923 and Stetford in 1929 and 1931; railwayman.

112. *Scovell to McCurdy, 'Weekly notes on Constituencies', 25 August 1922*

Candidatures.

East Fulham. Mr. Percy Gates (C.U.) has withdrawn his candidature.

Peckham. Mr. Frank Roscoe (Ind. Liberal) has withdrawn his candidature.

Mile End. Col. C. Whaley Cohen (Ind. Liberal) has withdrawn his candidature.

Barrow in Furness. Mr D.G. Somerville has now been adopted as Coalition Unionist candidate.

Tynemouth. Mr. G.H. Humphrey[256] is spoken of as the Labour candidate.

Saffron Walden. Mr. R.L. Gilmour, (Ind. Liberal), has withdrawn.

East Leyton. Mr. E. Brotherton-Ratcliffe has been adopted as independent Liberal candidate. It is reported that he is a nephew of Colonel Sir Edward Brotherton Bt.,[257] Unionist MP for Wakefield.

Reigate. Lt. Comm. R. Hope, Labour candidate has withdrawn.

Manchester, Exchange Division of. It is now reported that Sir J.S. Randles, MP[258] will not seek re-election and that Sir Edwin F. Stockton, ex-President of the Manchester Chamber of Commerce will be invited to become a candidate.

113. *Scovell to McCurdy, 'Weekly notes on Constituencies', 1 September 1922*

Candidatures:

Wells, Soms. Sir Harry Greer[259] the sitting member will not contest the seat at the next election.

East Fulham. Sir Henry Norris is retiring and Sir Harry Greer, the present member for Wells, will be the Conservative candidate.

Reading. Major The Hon. E. Cadogan[260] who is taking the place of Colonel Leslie Wilson[261] as Conservative candidate has stated that:– "I am a Conservative and

256 George Harold Humphrey had unsuccessfully contested the seat as an independent in 1918.

257 Edward Allen Brotherton (1856–1930), 1st baron Brotherton; Conservative MP for Wakefield 1902–10 and 1918–22; ennobled 1929; industrialist.

258 John Scurrah Randles (1857–1945), Conservative MP for Cockermouth 1900–10, Manchester North West 1912–18 and Manchester Exchange 1918–22; businessman.

259 Harry Greer (1876–1947), Conservative MP for Clapham 1918 and Wells 1918–22; businessman.

260 Edward Cecil George Cadogan (1880–1962), Conservative MP for Reading 1922–3, Finchley 1924–5 and Bolton 1940–5; army officer.

261 Leslie Orme Wilson (1876–1955), Conservative MP for Reading 1913–22 and Portsmouth South 1922–3; parliamentary secretary to the ministry of shipping 1919–21, to the treasury 1921–3, governor of Bombay 1923–8, of Queensland 1932–46; Royal Marines officer.

an Imperialist. I am not an adherent of the Coalition. The contingency I look forward to is the return of the Conservative Party, with a working majority, led by a Conservative Prime Minister. I need hardly point out that only one who professes Conservative and Imperialist principles would have any claim upon my allegiance".

Lambeth, Norwood. Councillor Kirby has been adopted as Wee Free candidate.

Paddington. Mr H. Roberts, the Labour candidate has withdrawn.

Warrington. Sir Harold Smith[262] will not seek re-election.

Bosworth. Mr. A.E. Hawley, the prospective independent Conservative candidate died recently.

Wansbeck. Mr. Matthew Davey, a working man has been adopted as Wee Free candidate.

Bedford. Mr. E. Backhouse,[263] the prospective Labour candidate has been killed while mountaineering in Switzerland.

Plymouth. The Plymouth branch of the National Organised Unemployed Workers[264] have adopted Mr. George Ebury,[265] their Organiser, as candidate against Lady Astor.

Bedwellty. Captain Bagram has been adopted as Coalition Unionist candidate.

Merioneth. Mr. J. Jones Roberts has been adopted as Labour candidate.

Caerphilly. Major Allan McLean[266] has been adopted by the Unionists. He has addressed the Liberal Association with a view to securing their support.

262 Harold Smith (1876–1924), Conservative MP for Warrington 1910–22 and Liverpool Wavertree 1922–3; brother of Lord Birkenhead.

263 Edward Backhouse (1875–1922).

264 National Unemployed Workers Movement formed in 1921 by figures within the Communist movement in Britain. Its principal activities included the organisation of hunger marches in the 1920s and 1930s. It suspended its activities to draw attention to the plight of the unemployed in 1939 and was formally wound up in 1946.

265 George Ebury (1867–1939) turned to socialism in Glasgow in 1884, later working as a carpet designer in Heckmondwike until he was sacked in 1908 after getting elected as a socialist councillor. He became increasingly involved in radical activities, moved to London in 1911, and became national organiser for the British Socialist Party. With the formation of the Communist Party of Great Britain he became its Yorkshire organiser, before moving to Plymouth where he became the treasurer of the N.U.W.M. After the First World War he was widely regarded as the leading Communist in Plymouth, and was adopted by the local branch of the N.U.W.M. as an unofficial Labour candidate before the adoption of the official candidate Frederick George Woulfe-Brenan. Ebury seems to have been persuaded to withdraw rather than risk a split in the Labour vote. He remained active in Plymouth politics until his death in 1939 despite splitting with the Communist Party.

266 Allan McLean (1875–1959), Conservative MP for South West Norfolk 1923–9 and 1931–5; barrister.

Forthcoming Speaking Engagements:

Sowerby Division. Mr. J.W. Pratt, MP, has consented to speak at a Garden Party on Saturday 23rd Sept.

Merthyr Tydvil. Mr. J.W. Pratt, MP, has consented to speak at a Meeting with Sir Edgar Jones on Thursday September 28th.

Torquay. The Marquis of Salisbury[267] has promised to speak for the Devonshire Unionists on November 24th.

114. *Scovell to McCurdy, 'Weekly notes on Constituencies', 8 September 1922*

Candidatures.

East Fulham. The Labour Party have adopted Alderman J. Palmer[268] as their candidate.

Scarborough & Whitby. Captain Sitwell[269] has resigned the Wee Free Candidature on personal grounds. He has promised to do everything in his power to help a new Wee Free candidate.

Leeds, Central. Counc. D.B. Foster, former President of the Trades Council and an active member of the Union of Democratic Control during the War, has been adopted as Labour candidate. Mr. Armitage, Coalition Liberal, is the sitting member, and Mr. Arthur Willey has been adopted as Conservative candidate.

The Wrekin. Mr. R.E. Jones, Secretary of the Sheffield Branch of the A.E.U. will be the Labour candidate.

North Lanark. J.C. Carrol of London has been adopted as the Wee Free candidate. He opposed Dr. Macnamara at the Bye-election.

Meetings: The Duke of Northumberland[270] has promised to speak in support of the Die-hard candidate, who is opposing Lady Astor at Plymouth.

267 James Edward Hubert Gascoyne-Cecil (1861–1947), 4th marquess of Salisbury; Conservative MP for Darwen 1885–92 and Rochester 1893–1902; under-secretary of state for foreign affairs 1900–3, lord privy seal 1903–5, president of the board of trade 1905, chancellor of the duchy of Lancaster 1922–3, lord president of the council 1922–4, lord privy seal 1924–9, leader of the House of Lords 1925–9; succeeded to title 1903.

268 John Palmer unsuccessfully contested East Fulham for Labour in 1922, 1923, 1924 and 1929.

269 Francis Osbert Sacheverell Sitwell (1892–1969), unsuccessfully contested Scarborough and Whitby for the Liberals in 1918; writer and army officer.

270 Alan Percy (1880–1930), 8th duke of Northumberland; soldier, newspaper owner and Diehard Conservative.

115. *Scovell Memorandum to McCurdy, 'Election Prospects by Seat', 11 September 1922*[271]

The question which this memorandum endeavours to answer may be stated as follows:– Suppose that a complete dissolution of the existing Coalition has taken place, and that the Conservative Party fights a General Election as an absolutely independent force, under its own leaders, with its own programme, and with its organisation both at Headquarters and in every Constituency throwing its whole weight in its own favour; under these conditions how many of the seats now held by Coalition Liberals would be retained in such a General Election? In other words, it is assumed that in all the seats held at present by Coalition Liberals – 126 in number – and in which Coalition Liberals have been adopted as candidates – 40 in number – there will be:

(i) An official Conservative candidate,

(ii) A Coalition Liberal candidate,

(iii) A Labour or Wee Free candidate, if not both.

Under these conditions it is practically certain that the following seats now held by Coalition Liberals would be retained at a General Election for one or more of the following reasons:

(a) The personal influence of the Sitting member or candidate.

(b) The close personal interest which the member or candidate has taken in the constituency.

(c) The attention which has been given to the local organisation.

(d) The strong Liberal traditions of the Constituency.

Wales

Carnarvons Burghs	The Prime Minister
Swansea, West	Sir Alfred Mond
Cardiganshire	Captain Ernest Evans
Carmarthen	Mr John Hinds.
Flint	Col. T.H. Parry[272]
Pembroke	Major Gwilyn Lloyd George[273]
Welsh University	(Provided a candidate of equal standing with Mr. J.H. Lewis is found).

271 Presented prior to his meeting with the prime minister that day.

272 Thomas Henry Parry (1881–1939), Liberal MP for Flint Boroughs 1913–18 and Flintshire 1918–24; soldier and lawyer.

273 Gwilyn Lloyd George (1894–1967), 1st Viscount Tenby; Liberal MP for Pembrokeshire 1922–4 and 1929–50, Newcastle-upon-Tyne North 1951–7; parliamentary secretary to the ministry of food 1941–2, minister of fuel and power 1942–5, minister of food 1951–4, home secretary 1954–7; ennobled 1957.

Scotland

Argyll	Sir Wm. Sutherland
Kilmarnock	Hon. Alex Shaw[274]
Banff	Sir Charles Barrie[275]
Dundee	Mr Winston Churchill
Dunfermline	Mr John Wallace[276]
Inverness	Sir Murdoch Macdonald[277]
Ross	Mr. J.I. Macpherson[278]
Moray & Nairn	Mr. T.M. Guthrie[279]
Orkney & Shetland	Sir Malcolm Smith[280]

England

Middleton & Prestwich	Sir W. Ryland Adkins[281]
Leeds, Central	Mr Armitage[282]
Leeds, South	Sir Wm. Middlebrook[283]
Northampton	Mr C.A.McCurdy
Bristol, North	Col. Henry Guest
Carlisle	Mr W.T. Carr[284]
Dorset, East	Capt. F.E. Guest
Isle of Ely	Captain Colin Coote
Cornwall	Sir Clifford Cory
Bolton	Sir Wm. Edge

274 Alexander Shaw (1883–1944), 2nd baron Craigmyle; Liberal MP for Kilmarnock Burghs 1915–18 and Kilmarnock 1918–23; succeeded to the barony in 1937.

275 Charles Coupar Barrie (1874–1940), 1st baron Abertay; Liberal MP for Elgin Burghs 1918, Banffshire 1918–24 and Southampton (1931–40); ennobled 1940.

276 John Wallace (1868–1949), Liberal MP for Dunfermline Burghs 1918–22 and 1931–5.

277 Murdoch Macdonald (1866–1957), Liberal MP for Inverness 1922–50; civil engineer.

278 James Ian Stuart Macpherson (1880–1937), 1st baron Strathcarron; Liberal MP for Ross and Cromarty 1911–35; under-secretary of state for war 1916–19, chief secretary for Ireland 1919–20, minister of pensions 1920–2; ennobled 1936.

279 Thomas Maule Guthrie (1870–1943), Liberal MP for Moray and Nairn 1922–3.

280 Malcolm Smith (1856–1935), Liberal MP for Orkney and Shetland 1921–2; business-man.

281 William Ryland Dent Adkins (1862–1925), Liberal MP for Middleton 1906–18 and Middleton and Prestwich 1918–23; barrister and judge.

282 Robert Armitage (1866–1944), Liberal MP for Leeds Central 1906–22; lord mayor of Leeds 1904–5.

283 William Middlebrook (1851–1936), Liberal MP for Leeds South 1908–22; solicitor.

284 William Theodore Carr (1866–1931), Liberal MP for Carlisle 1918–22; bakery business.

Stockport	Mr Harry Fildes[285]
London	Mr J.D. Gilbert
"	Sir William Pearce
"	Mr E.A. Strauss[286]
Luton	Mr C.B. Harmsworth[287]
Sudbury	Major S.G. Howard[288]
Barking	Captain A.E. Martin
Southampton	Sir I. Philipps[289]
Stretford	Sir Thomas Robinson[290]
Sheffield	Sir Tudor Walters[291]

Totals:	
Wales...	7.
Scotland...	9.
England...	20.
Total:	36.

The only seats at all likely to be won at an election held under the anticipated conditions would be the Forest of Dean, where it is understood that Mrs. Coombe-Tennant has by her personal influence secured the goodwill of the people quite apart from party lines of demarcation and the possibility of Mr. Winston Churchill carrying with him the Coalition Liberal candidate in the double-barrelled seat at Dundee.

This represents the minimum fighting force of the direct followers to Mr. Lloyd George after a General Election fought under conditions which are deliberately assumed to be the worst possible. No account is taken of the effect that would be produced if Mr. Lloyd George took the field with a popular programme containing new and surprising elements; and, again, no account is taken of the political effects of any improvement in the industrial situation, both of which are incalculable.

285 Henry Fildes (1870–1948), Liberal MP for Stockport 1920–3 and Dumfriesshire 1935–45.

286 Edward Anthony Strauss (1862–1939), Liberal MP for Abingdon 1906–10, Southwark West 1910–18, Southwark North 1918–23, 1927–9 and 1931–9; agricultural merchant.

287 Cecil Bisshopp Harmsworth (1969–1948), 1st baron Harmsworth; Liberal MP for Droitwich 1906–10 and Luton 1911–22; under-secretary of state for the home department 1915, under-secretary of state for foreign affairs 1919–22; ennobled 1939; businessman.

288 Stephen Goodwin Howard (1867–1934), Liberal MP for Sudbury 1918–22; farmer.

289 Ivor Philipps (1861–1940), Liberal MP for Southampton 1906–22; army officer.

290 Thomas Robinson (1864–1953), Liberal and late independent MP for Stretford 1918–31.

291 John Tudor Walters (1866–1933), Liberal MP for Sheffield Brightside 1906–22, Penryn and Falmouth 1929–31; paymaster general 1919–22.

116. *Scovell to McCurdy, 'Weekly notes on Constituencies', 15 September 1922*

Newport Bye-Election: see Separate report.[292]

Candidatures:

Bewdley. Mr. Sardius Hancock,[293] of Glenfield, Newtown, Malvern has been adopted as prospective Wee Free candidate for this division. He is a man who has acted as Liberal agent for some years and his candidature cannot be looked upon seriously.

Sedgefield, Durham. Mr. C.H. Brown, a prominent Liberal in Newcastle has been adopted as Wee Free candidate for this division.

Tiverton. Mr. Fred Brown of the National Union of Agricultural Workers and one of their district organisers will be the Labour candidate. It has been officially endorsed by the National Executive of the Labour Party.

Honiton. Major A.C. Morrison-Bell, MP,[294] has announced that he will contest the constituency as an independent Unionist and Conservative candidate.

Meetings:

Newcastle, W. The Home Secretary is addressing a meeting in Newcastle this weekend. A telegram has been received that he has been recalled to London for the Cabinet Meeting to-day, Friday, and asking that a substitute should be sent. Endeavours are being made to get Mr. J.W. Pratt, MP, to do.
Aberdeenshire. Sir Donald MacLean is speaking in Aberdeenshire.

The Scottish Liberal Federation have announced their Annual Conference will be held at Dumfries on October 6th and 7th. Mr Asquith, Lady Bonham Carter and Sir Donald MacLean are expected to be present.

117. *Scovell to McCurdy, 'Weekly notes on Constituencies', 22 September 1922*

Candidatures:

Mossley. Mr. D.B. Lawley of Blackburn, has been adopted as Labour candidate for this Division. Mr. Lawley is a blind man, having lost his sight whilst working as a miner in British Columbia.

Wycombe. The independent Liberal candidate, Mr. T. Arnold Herbert, K.C., is retiring.

Uxbridge. Dr. A. Herbert Hart is standing as an independent candidate.

292 Not amongst the Scovell papers.

293 Sardius Hancock (1865–1955), unsuccessfully contested Bewdley as the Liberal candidate in 1922 and 1923 and again in 1929 as the Labour Party candidate; methodist and chicken farmer near Worcester.

294 Arthur Clive Morrison Bell (1871–1956), Conservative MP for Honiton 1910–31; soldier.

Aberdeenshire. Mr. Fred Martin will be the independent Liberal candidate for East Aberdeenshire. Mr. Martin is blind.

North Aberdeen. Mr. W. MacKenzie Cameron, one of our Organisers, has been invited to become the National Liberal candidate. The Sitting member is Frank A.H. Rose and the Wee Free candidate Mr. James Johnstone.

Dundee. Mr R.R. Pilkington, K.C.,[295] has been adopted as Wee Free candidate.

Meetings:

Mr. Asquith has promised to speak at Peterborough in October. Comm. Hilton Young has promised to speak on behalf of Sir Thomas Fisher at Portsmouth on Friday, November 24th.

General:

National Union of Landworkers.

In the Eastern Area certain members of the Agricultural Labourers' Union, being dissatisfied with that Union, have broken away and formed the National Union of Landworkers. The General Secretary is H.R. Lovell, J.P., of Huntingdon, and Mr. Sam Peel, a former prominent Labour worker in North Norfolk, is the President of this new Union, which has been attacked by prominent Labour men such as Mr. George Edwards, MP,[296] and Mr. W.R. Smith, MP.[297]

118. *Scovell to Miss Pull, 'Leeds', 26 September 1922*

I spoke to Mr. McCurdy this morning re. the attached. Mr. Burke is Chairman of the South East Leeds Liberal Association, but I have ascertained that he carries very little weight in the other Divisions of Leeds.

Sir Rowland Barran,[298] who is one of the most influential of our Liberal Leaders in Leeds, tells me that he does not think Arnold a very suitable candidate.

Enclosed Draft Reply in Scovell to Pull, 'Leeds', 26 September 1922

Dear Mr. Burke,

I must apologise for not having replied before this to your letter of the 17th instant. I have delayed doing so until I have made some enquiries into the position in Leeds Central. After careful consideration, I think it would be most inadvisable on my part to give any appearance of interference in the affairs of that Division, unless or until I am approached officially by the local Leaders. I gather, however, that the Executive of the Central Leeds Liberal Association have the whole question

295 Robert Rivington Pilkington (1870–1942), Liberal MP for Keighley 1923–4; King's Counsel.

296 George Edwards (1850–1933), Labour MP for South Norfolk 1920–2 and 1923–4; trade unionist.

297 Walter Robert Smith (1872–1942), Labour MP for Wellingborough 1918–22 and Norwich 1923–4 and 1929–31; parliamentary secretary to the ministry of agriculture and fisheries 1924, chair of the Labour Party 1933–4; trade unionist.

298 Rowland Hirst Barran (1858–1949), Liberal MP for North Leeds 1902–18; manufacturer.

of the choice of a candidate well in hand and I do not anticipate the Association meeting with any difficulty in finding a suitable candidate to represent them.

May I take this opportunity of saying personally how grateful we are for the interest you have taken in Miss Grant's Candidature in the South Eastern District of Leeds.

119. *Scovell to McCurdy, 'Weekly notes on Constituencies', 29 September 1922*

Candidatures:

Newark, Notts. C.A. Hacking, D.S.O., the Unionist candidate has resigned. It is stated that the Marquis of Titchfield[299] will be the new candidate.

Warwick & Leamington. Mr. Percy Cole, the Labour candidate has withdrawn. The reason given is the inability of the Iron, Steel and Kindred Trades Association to give him adequate financial support.

Deritend, Birmingham. Mr. John S. Crooke, manufacturing jeweller will be the Unionist candidate.

Lancaster. Mr John E. Singleton, K.C.,[300] has been adopted as the prospective Unionist candidate. Captain Brian Bibby having resigned.

Glasgow, Central. Sir George Paish,[301] will be the Wee Free candidate in opposition to Mr. Bonar Law.

Clay Cross. It is confidently asserted that Mr. C.F.G. Masterman will be the Wee Free candidate in opposition to Mr. T.T. Broad.[302] A new agent has been appointed and a series of meetings in the division are announced at which Mr Masterman will be present.

South Islington. Sir Charles Higham, MP[303] has announced that he will retire at the end of this Parliament.

Clapham. Mr. Ernest Villiers[304] will be the Wee Free candidate. He was formerly member for Brighton.

Meetings:

Portsmouth. Owing to the impossibility of obtaining a suitable hall on Friday November 24th, Commander Hilton Young has been asked if he will give another date.

299 William Arthur Henry Cavendish-Bentinck (1893–1977), marquess of Titchfield, 7th duke of Portland; Conservative MP for Newark 1922–43; junior lord of the treasury 1927–9, lord lieutenant of Nottinghamshire 1939–62; succeeded to the dukedom in 1943.

300 John Edward Singleton (1885–1957), Conservative MP for Lancaster 1922–3; judge.

301 George Paish (1867–1957), economist.

302 Thomas Tucker Broad (1863–1935), Liberal MP for Clay Cross 1918–22; unsuccessfully contested Leyton East in 1923; congregational minister.

303 Charles Frederick Higham (1876–1938), Conservative MP for Islington South 1918–22; publicist.

304 Ernest Amherst Villiers (1863–1923), Liberal MP for Brighton 1905–10.

The Eastern Counties National Liberal Council are arranging their Annual Meeting and they have invited Captain Guest to be the principal speaker.

General:

Thirsk & Malton. The Conservative Association at a meeting last week passed a resolution expressing satisfaction with the announcement that Mr. E.R. Turton[305] is prepared to contest the division at the next election as a Conservative and Unionist, as they are of the opinion that this is the wisest policy to be pursued.

120. *Scovell to McCurdy, 'Weekly notes on Constituencies', 6 October 1922*

Bye-Election:

Newport. Mr. Lyndon Moore[306] has issued his address. Copy attached. The meeting held at the workers Liberal Institute was well attended. There was considerable enthusiasm. The proceedings are fully reported in the "South Wales Argus". Three Ward Meetings were held on Wednesday night and three last night. There was also a meeting of Liberal Women yesterday afternoon at which the speaker was Mrs. Lloyd Atkinson, a well-known South Wales active Liberal woman worker. The attendance was small however, only fifty being present. The Ward organisation is now complete and the canvass cards have been issued in seven out of the ten wards.

Candidatures:

Shipley. Yorks. Mr. William McKinder,[307] district organiser of the National Union of Distributive and Allied workers will be the Labour candidate. Mr. J.H Watson, District Secretary of the Textile Workers, Bradford, having resigned on account of ill-health.

Canterbury. Mr. F.L. Baker, the Labour candidate, has withdrawn. He states that he is not in agreement with the Agricultural policy of the Labour Party.

Houghton-le-Spring. Captain William Shaw[308] of Bournemouth, formerly Sheriff of Poole, will be the Coalition Unionist candidate. During the War he got into trouble through food hoarding. The defence he made was that this had been done by his wife during his absence in America. She was heavily fined.

Smethwick. Major R.M. Thompson, Coalition Unionist has withdrawn his candidature and Mr. A.H. Addenbrooke Simcox,[309] I.C.S., B.A., has been adopted. He has many local interests.

305 Edmond Russborough Turton (1857–1929), Conservative MP for Thirsk and Malton 1915–29.

306 William Lyndon Moore, deputy chair of the Newport Liberals.

307 William Mackinder (1880–1930), Labour MP for Shipley 1923–30 after unsuccessfully contesting Shipley, suffering with a lack of funds; trade unionist.

308 Walter William (1898–1927), Conservative MP for Westbury 1924–7 after unsuccessfully contesting Houghton le Spring in 1922.

309 Arthur Henry Addenbrooke Simcox (1870–41) stood unsuccessfully for Smethwick in 1922 for the Conservative Party; civil servant.

Tynemouth. Mr. West Russell, Barrister,[310] has been adopted as the Coalition Unionist candidate. Mr Charles Percy is retiring. He has had a varied career – first in business then a Minister of the Church of Scotland; Chaplain in the Army and a Barrister.

Hampstead. Mr. L.S. Fletcher, Barrister,[311] has been adopted as the independent Liberal candidate.

West Islington. Major Despencer-Robertson[312] has been adopted by the West Islington National Unionist Association. The present member, Sir George Elliot, states that he will stand as an independent Conservative.

Meetings:

Portsmouth. Lt. Comm. Hilton Young has promised to address a meeting in the Town Hall at Portsmouth on Tuesday November 21st.

Edinburgh. Junior National Liberal Association.
The opening meeting was held on Tuesday October 3rd. Mr H.G. Purchase, MP[313] acted as substitute for Mr. J.W. Pratt, MP who was compelled to cancel his engagement at the last moment.

Yorkshire National Liberal Council.
Sir Alfred Mond has promised to attend and speak at this meeting on Friday November 3rd.

121. *Scovell to McCurdy, 'General Election Rumours', 11 October 1922*[314]

I see and hear on all sides rumours of a General Election. I am therefore moved to submit to you as a purely personal expression of opinion, reinforced by what I have heard from members of Parliament and others that to hold an election at the present juncture would, from a tactical point of view, be a serious error.

First of all, and most important in my opinion, is the fact that were we to have a General Election in the next few weeks it would give colour to an impression that we were petrified by fear of the forthcoming Unionist Convention.[315] People would begin to ask where is our "audacity"? Secondly, it will give rise to the idea that the P.M. is unduly sensitive to and can be scared by a neurotic press. Thirdly, at the present moment the country is in a thoroughly nervy condition in consequence of

310 Alexander West Russell (1879–1961), Conservative MP for Tynemouth 1922–45.

311 Lancelot Sackville Fletcher (1881–1968), unsuccessfully contested Hampstead for the Liberal Party in 1922; barrister.

312 James Fitzwarenne-Despencer-Robertson (1886–1942), Conservative MP for West Islington 1922–3 and Salisbury 1931–42, having unsuccessfully contested West Islington in 1924 and 1929; soldier.

313 Henry George Purchase (1873–1945), Liberal MP for Kennington 1918–22, unsuccessfully contested Kidderminster 1923 and 1924, Leicester South 1929, Gainsborough 1931 and Blackpool 1935; barrister.

314 Marked 'Personal and Private'.

315 Party Conference.

the frantic noise of the Press jazz-band on the Turkish crisis.[316] Heads want time to cool, and in a few weeks the full re-action will be on us. It appears as if it had already begun in France. Fourthly, for the last six or seven years the plain man has been forced to live on excitement. He therefore does not want to be rushed. At the present time he requires a soporific. Let him have his soporific in the form of ministerial explanations and then give him a General Election.

Turning to the Home situation, there are several other factors of a less philosophical kind. Firstly, in some quarters there is a feeling that we are within reach of a slight upward trend in trade. In a few months, if we get over our present difficulties, this trend may be more marked; if so, we cannot be the losers.

Secondly, if we go to the country now we must have something tangible in our hands, but have we the goods at the moment? I am advised on all sides, that the electorate will show little gratitude for the Government's part in foreign affairs, but they will be really grateful if it is only possible to reduce the Beer duty and lighten the Sugar load. If too a further reduction in the Income Tax, however small, is possible in addition to beer and sugar, the prospects of the situation will be still more improved.

In conclusion, I would like to emphasize ever so strongly that in my humble opinion, and only after consultation with others, that if at all possible the appeal to the country should be deferred until after the production of the Budget with some concessions on the lines indicated. If this is hopelessly improbable, I would still suggest that we await in calmness the full force of the re-action, that is to say – till the time when the jazz-band players both of the Press and the Conservative caucus have exhausted themselves. I am convinced that the present pace, anyway so far as the Press is concerned, cannot last long.

316 Also referred to as the Chanak (Çanakkale) Crisis (Sept.–Oct. 1922). Lloyd George's post-war championing of Greek ambitions for territory in Asia Minor at the expense of the Turkish government unravelled in Aug.–Sept. 1922 as the Greek army was defeated in western Anatolia. With the capture of Smyrna (Izmir) on 9 Sept. the Greek army was forced to evacuate its forces, with help from the Royal Navy. Turkish nationalist forces then moved towards Constantinople (Istanbul) and towards the perimeter of British occupation forces at Chanak on the Dardanelles. By mid-September it was apparent that part of the cabinet was ready to see Britain go to war with nationalist Turkish forces if it came to a clash at Chanak. This contributed to the growing instability of the coalition. Some Conservatives, including the foreign secretary Lord Curzon of Kedleston (1859–1925), were concerned that Lloyd George might be about to plunge the country into war and call an election, in order to extend the life of the coalition. The sense of alarm at Lloyd George's willingness to take that risk caused concern throughout the Empire, and contributed to the outcome of the Carlton Club meeting on 19 Oct. The fall of the coalition coincided with the nationalist Turks signalling that they were willing to seek a negotiated settlement to avoid war. This led to the Lausanne Conference of 1922–3, and the Lausanne Treaty, providing a post-war peace settlement for Turkey.

122. *Scovell to McCurdy, 'Weekly notes on Constituencies', 12 October 1922*

Candidatures:

Chichester. Commander Hope[317] has been adopted as Labour candidate. For some time he was the adopted candidate for the Reigate Division who recently retired.

London University. Mr. H.G. Wells[318] will be the Labour candidate.

Cambridge County. A Tory Die-Hard effort has been made to capture the Conservative Association – so far without success. A joint meeting of Unionists and Coalition Liberals was held on Saturday last. After a very frank discussion it was agreed to invite Mr. Montagu, MP,[319] to attend a joint meeting of the Executive Committees of the Conservative and Liberal Associations first of all and then decide whether a larger meeting was considered desirable.

West Islington. W.J. Lewington[320] will be the Labour candidate.

Withington. Dr. Thomas Watts[321] of Birkdale, Southport and King Street, Manchester, has been adopted as the Conservative and Unionist candidate.

North Lonsdale. Mr. T.M. Scott,[322] Middlesborough, will be the Labour candidate.

North Leeds. Mr. E.O. Dodgson,[323] a nephew of Sir Mark Oldroyd,[324] who was for many years MP for Dewsbury, will be the Labour candidate.

Batley & Morley. The Liberal Association have adopted Mr. J.A. Compston,[325] K.C., the Recorder to Leeds, as candidate. Mr. Gerald France[326] having decided to retire. In the speech which he delivered at a public meeting held on the day of his adoption, he spoke of the necessity there was to return to Party Government.

317 Richard Henry Kennard Hope (1886–1962), unsuccessfully contested Chichester in 1922 and Isle of Ely in 1923 for the Labour Party; naval officer.

318 Herbert George Wells (1886–1946), stood unsuccessfully for London University in 1922 and 1923 for the Labour Party; writer and visionary.

319 Edwin Samuel Montagu (1879–1924), Liberal MP for Chesterton 1906–18 and Cambridgeshire 1918–22; under-secretary of state for India 1910–14, financial secretary to the treasury 1914–15, chancellor of the duchy of Lancaster 1915, financial secretary to the treasury 1915–16, minister of munitions 1916, secretary of state for India 1917–22

320 W.J. Lewington unsuccessfully contested Islington West for the Labour Party in 1922.

321 Thomas Watts (1868–1951), Conservative MP for Manchester Withington 1922–4 and 1924–9.

322 Thomas Marshall Scott unsuccessfully contested the Lonsdale constituency in 1922 for the Labour Party. This replaced the North Lonsdale constituency which had been abolished in 1918.

323 Edwin Oldroyd Dodgson (1864–1941), unsuccessfully contested Leeds North in 1922 and 1923 for the Labour Party; manufacturer.

324 Mark Oldroyd (1843–1927), Liberal MP for Dewsbury 1888–1902; manufacturer.

325 John Albert Compston (1862–1930), unsuccessfully contested Batley and Morley for the Liberals in 1922; King's Counsel.

326 Gerald Ashburner France (1870–1935), Liberal MP for Morley 1910–18 and Batley and Morley 1918–22; businessman and importer.

Clay Cross. Mr. C.F.G. Masterman has now definitely announced that he will be the independent Liberal candidate.

123. *Scovell to McCurdy, 'Montagu's Seat', 13 October 1922*

If you have time I think you would be interested to read through this document which contains a somewhat rough account of a Joint Meeting of Delegates from both wings of the Coalition in Montagu's seat.

Minutes of Joint Meeting of Delegates from Cambs. County Liberal and Cambs. County Unionist Association, at the Lion Hotel, Cambridge, Saturday, October 7th 1922.

Major C.W. Stanley in the Chair.

Present for Unionists: Major C.W. Stanley, Messrs. Mapey, Binney, E.G. Frost, A.E. Saunders, R. Stevenson, W. de L. Devereux (Sec).

Present for Liberals: Messrs. H.G. Few, W. Randall, J. Chivers, S. Gibson, D. Ingle, Mrs Marcus Dimsdale, F.H. Flanders (Sec).

The Minutes of the last Meeting were read and confirmed.

The Chairman (Cons) in opening paid tribute to Mr. Henry Green for the services rendered to this Committee and other public causes and expressed himself and on behalf of those present very sincere regret that so grave an illness prevented him being with them, – Mr. Few and the meeting generally sympathetically approved and the Secretary was asked to write to Mr. Green.

The Chairman (Cons) referring to the business of the Meeting said that he could only repeat what had been said on the last occasion of our meeting together, that the members of the Unionist Association held such various opinions regarding the continued support of Mr. Montagu that they felt they could not pledge themselves either way – they had arrived at no definite decision. That he understood the Liberals since their last meeting had been in conference with the member and without further words he would leave the meeting open in general discussion.

Mr. Few (Co-Lib) explained that the result of meeting Mr. Montagu had been to convince those who heard him that Mr. Montagu's attitude and opinion remained the same and that he would not allow it to be altered by happenings of a personal nature. Mr. Fordham (Co-Lib) explained that the member was still receiving the Government whip. Mr. Gibson (Co-Lib) felt we had better be perfectly frank with each other and said that the result of the Liberals meeting with Mr. Montagu was that they had been perfectly satisfied and that they pledged themselves to continue their support, and that now they come, having cleared the element of doubt as to the member's attitude, and ask for the same recognition from the Unionist's wing that was given at the last Election, and that unless some serious divergences of view arose they (the Liberals) felt justly entitled to expect such recognition. Conditions had not changed and he could not see that the time for any breach had arrived. He asked, are we going to work together? Mr. Binney (Cons) thought it was quite possible that the P.M. would resign, he thought all parties would like a change. He was sure Mr. Montagu did not love him after the way he had been treated. He felt it would be much easier to work together with the P.M. out of the way. Mr. Mapey (Cons) felt it a matter of honour that the Unionists continued the relationship – they had pledged themselves to the support of a Coalition candidate, and if Mr. Montagu is a Coalitionist they had no option but to support him. He would rather see their Association split in twain than go back on their word, – It may be said they cannot pledge their association, if that turned out to be so then he would pledge every individual Coalitionist member and would pledge himself wholeheartedly to support Mr. Montagu even though he might not like him personally. He had no room for a Conservative candidate as opposed to a Coalition candidate, he felt if a Conservative candidate was introduced Labour would be let in. He would continue his support until such time as his leaders saw reasons for acting otherwise. Mr. Saunders (Cons) wondered what would be the position if the Coalition split up. He felt we were being badly treated by what the policy is to be, and thought the people at the top should clearly define the position, otherwise drifting on as we are we should find ourselves losing more and more to Labour, who were the only party putting a definite policy before the Electorate. Mr. Chivers (Co-Lib) thought that everything was in the melting-pot, but intermingled with the four parties in the state, was a party of reasonable people which if we could only give it a name and policy we should find to be the dominating one. Mr. Saunders (Cons) thought the Unionists would be in a very awkward position if the Die Hards decided to run a Conservative candidate. He would be prepared to support a Conservative Coalitionist though he was fed up with the word 'Coalition'. He is called by some a Die Hard, but he is not, whilst those present may say they will support Mr. Montagu, others belonging to the Unionist Association say they will not. He feels that as a body they must agree. He is not prepared to break away, but he would again urge the necessity of having a definite common policy which can be placed before the Electorate. Mr. Binney (Cons) – If you go back to party you go back to the practice of outbidding one another in promises to the Electorate. Mr. E.G. Frost (Cons) owned that there are some members of the Unionist Association (he thought they might be counted on the fingers) who disagree with continued support of Mr. Montagu. He believes, however, that Coalition Liberals and Coalition Unionists are out to fight Labour. He thought they should be able to pledge the Unionist Committee to support Mr. Montagu, and do all they can to bring the members of the Association to see that they must sink their personal feelings in order to keep out the Labour candidate. Mr. Fordham (Co-Lib). In the Die Hard movement in the County. Is the objection to Coalition or Mr. Montagu? Mr. Binney (Cons) Many have a great objection to the Prime Minister. Mr. Frost (Cons) Personal dislikes must not be allowed to rule the Committee. Mr. Gibson (Co-Lib). We have heard that Mr. Montagu still receives the Government whip, and is still an acknowledged supporter of the Government and it is quite fair to assume his candidature would be endorsed by Headquarters. He, Mr. Gibson, would like to know what is the attitude of the Unionist Association to the Die Hard Movement? We are satisfied it was not the result of Local Unionist Association action, and can understand that it placed the Association in an awkward position. – The question will, however, have to be faced sooner or later. He would suggest that before any definite action is taken Mr. Montagu be invited to meet this Committee or a larger body representative of both wings of the Coalition.

Mr. Mapey (Cons) – the Unionist Association have adopted no official attitude to the Die Hard Movement though he would point out that from correspondence that has passed the inference to be drawn is that the Die Hards consider the Unionist Association pledged to Coalition and Mr. Montagu. Mr. Stevenson (Cons). This is the first I have heard of this Die Hard Meeting – did they decide to run a candidate? Mr. Binney (Cons). I was at the meeting. It was thought that Mr. Montagu should be opposed, but no candidate was chosen – they had not gone so far as that yet.

There was some discussion as to what form the Joint Meeting should take. Mr Mapey (Cons) feared giving an opportunity for a noisy minority to advertise themselves. It was eventually decided on the proposition of Mr. Gibson (Co-Lib) seconded by Mr. Mapey that Mr. Montagu be invited to meet the two Executive Committees in joint conference with a view to arranging a larger meeting if it was thought desirable.

124. *Memorandum to McCurdy Enclosing Memorandum on 'Bedfordshire, Luton Constituency', 18 October 1922*

Mr McCurdy.

I think you had better see the attached memorandum dealing with Mr. Harmsworth's seat. May I say that this Office, including the Home Counties Area Office, was totally unaware of Mr. Harmsworth's intentions until they saw them in the Press this morning.

General Secretary Very Urgent Bedfordshire – Luton

Mr. Cecil Harmsworth has suddenly announced to his local Association that he will not seek re-election, and a meeting of the Association is called for to-morrow might I have had no intimation of this apart from the press paragraphs. The organisation has always steadfastly refused to carry on any propaganda, and we probably should be defeated if a vote were taken amongst the Liberals on the subject of the Coalition. There are two outstanding Liberals in the town who might be selected as candidates. One is Milner Gray, who received the coupon at the General Election in Wellingborough, Northamptonshire, and afterwards fought as an independent Liberal at the St. Albans bye-election, and was third on the poll. The other man is Thomas Keens, a member of the Beds. County Council and Secretary of the Luton Chamber of Commerce – a rather strong body of traders. Mr. Keens was recently adopted as independent Liberal candidate in the Aylesbury Division against Rothschild,[327] where he has no chance. Both are very capable, and good platform men. Before the last General Election, Keens had been adopted as Liberal candidate at Thanet, but he withdrew his candidature on the understanding that the sitting member – Norman Craig – would support the Government.

It is possible that the Association, in view of the present turmoil, may defer the selection of a candidate until the atmosphere is more clear, when a plain Liberal

327 Lionel Nathan de Rothschild (1882–1942), Conservative MP for Aylesbury 1910–23; banker.

could be selected who would suit both sections. The Conservatives are reported to have a candidate in the background, and may now rush him into the field. Have we a strong candidate whom we could put forward if necessary? The town of Luton is the biggest factor in the constituency. The much smaller town of Dunstable, with similar interests, ranks second, and the rest is made up of small villages. The predominant interest in the place is Free Trade, owing to the fact that the straw plait industry, straw hat making, dyeing, and other dependent industries, are all dependent upon free imports. Engineering is also strongly represented in the town which contains a number of capable businessmen. Percy Alden[328] is the Labour candidate and, having been an old Radical MP, may now capture some of the votes which otherwise would have been retained by Mr. Harmsworth. Mr. Harmsworth's Agent is Mr. Cotchin who is really past work and hardly gets out of doors now-a-days, though he keeps in touch with people over the telephone. His assistant, Parsons, is quite an able man, quite capable of running an election, and with full knowledge of all the constituency.

125. *G.M.P (on behalf of McCurdy) to Scovell, 'Hall Caine', 19 October 1922*[329]

Sir William Sutherland has more than once mentioned the name of Hall Caine, Jnr., to Mr. McCurdy as a very desirable candidate for some such constituency as Battersea. Have you any information about Mr. Hall Caine. If so, will you let the Chief have it, together with your views.

126. *Scovell to McCurdy, 'Hall Caine', 20 October 1922*

I have seen Mr. Hall Caine[330] on three or four occasions. His health is now much better and I should think he would be a good candidate for a London seat, as and when the opportunity offers, but, at present moment, there is simply nothing for him. During the past two years his health has been very bad and he spoke with an American accent which would hardly commend itself to the Electorate, but now he is physically much better and has certainly lost a great deal of his American twang. As I have already indicated, I think he would make an excellent "stunt" candidate for London and nowhere else.

328 Percy Alden (1865–1944), Liberal MP for Tottenham 1906–18, Labour MP for Tottenham South 1923–4; joined Labour in 1922 then unsuccessfully contesting Luton, rejoined the Liberals in 1927; social worker and land reformer.

329 The identity of G.M.P. is not known, but the use of the phrase 'the Chief' in the letter implies that he was someone within the Coalition Liberal Party office at 25, Old Queen Street.

330 Derwent Hall Caine (1891–1971), Labour MP for Liverpool, Everton 1929–31; actor, son of Thomas Henry Hall Caine (1853–1931), writer and propagandist, and brother of Gordon Hall Caine (1884–1962), Conservative MP for East Dorset 1922–9 and 1931–45.

127. *Memorandum to McCurdy, 'Election Rally in Leeds', 22 October 1922*

As there appears to be some question as to the political complexion of the audience in the Majestic Cinema at Leeds yesterday, I think I had better let you know at once that with few exceptions the audience was solely confined to Liberal supporters of Mr. Lloyd George. Tickets were allotted as follows:

(a) To all of our Ministers, members and candidates.

(b) To all the Area Delegates on the National Liberal Council for England.

(c) Tickets in bulk from 20 to 30 in number were issued to each Area Office in England, Scotland and Wales for distribution to enthusiastic supporters of the Party who were prepared to travel as far as Leeds.

(d) The great mass of remaining tickets, to the number of some 2,000 were divided up among the Party's Organisations in Yorkshire.

(e) The only complimentary tickets allotted to Unionists so far as known here were –

Newspaper Editors, like Mr. Mann[331] of the *Yorkshire Post.*

Lord Halifax.[332] A very old gentleman's special request.

Mr Rupert Beckett[333] Chairman of the Conservative Party in Leeds

and to a few other leading Unionists in Yorkshire Constituencies where we are holding the representation or have candidates in the field and on whose help and cooperation we must rely against Labour in the coming fight.

In my judgement, the grand total of all Unionists present could not possibly have exceeded 3% of the whole. In conclusion, may I remark that some misapprehension may possibly have arisen first through the regrettable fact that unauthorised publicity was given to the fact that Lord Halifax was to be present and to the inevitable feelings of envy, etc., aroused in the many thousands who endeavoured to obtain tickets in vain, and also to the terrible haste in which the meeting had to be organised, entailing some important Liberals getting seats in the gallery instead of in the stalls.

128. *Memorandum to McCurdy, Election Rally in Leeds, 22 October 1922*

In submitting the attached forecast of possible losses in Conservative seats, I should like to point out the serious difficulty this office is labouring under. First, for many months now our area heads have been instructed to confine their attentions as far as possible to our own seats and not bother with Conservative seats. Second, the situation in respect of political conditions and candidatures is changing almost

331 Arthur Henry Mann (1876–1972), editor of the *Yorkshire Post* 1919–39, chairman of the press association 1937–8, governor of the BBC 1941–6.

332 Charles Lindley Wood, 2nd Viscount Halifax (1839–1934), Anglo-Catholic ecumenist.

333 Rupert Eveyln Beckett (1870–1955), banker.

daily so that it is impossible amidst the general pressure to arrange for this office to be kept absolutely up to date.
Thirdly, the general bewilderment due to the enlarged electorate.

1. Total number of seats at present held by Conservatives – 350.

2. Number of Conservative candidates – 412.

Forecast of Possible Changes

	Seat	Sitting member		Forecast
Scotland:	Edinburgh., N.,	Jameson		Wee Free
	Fife	Sprot		Wee Free
	Forfarshire	Shaw		Wee Free
	Linlithgowshire	Kidd		Wee Free
	Midlothian	Hope		Labour
	Dumbarton	Raeburn		Labour
	Dumfries	Murray		Wee Free
	Shettleston	Adair		Labour
	Springburn	Macquisten		Labour
	Coatbridge	Buchanan		Labour
	N. Lanark	Maclaren		Labour
	Stirling	Hope, H.		Labour
	Totals:	Wee Frees	5	
		Labour	7	
			12	
Wales:	Llandaff & Barry	Cope		Labour
England: Northern & Western Counties				
	Accrington	Gray		Labour
	Ashton-u-Lyne	de Frece		Labour
	Barrow	Chadwick		Labour
	Macclesfield	Remer		Wee Free
	Northwich	Dewshurst		Wee Free
	Stalybridge	Wood		Wee Free
	High Peak	Hill-Wood		Wee Free
	Farnworth	Bagley		Labour
	Lancaster	Hunter		Wee Free
	Manchester			
	Ardwick	Hailwood		Labour
	Hulme	Nall		Wee Free
	Mosside	Hurst		Wee Free

Rochdale	Law Wee	Free
Rossendale	Waddington	Labour
Birkenhead	Grayson	Labour
Liverpool	Hall	Labour
Cleveland	Goff	Labour
Bradford		Labour 2
Hull one seat		Labour
Dewsbury	Pickering	Labour
Wakefield	Brotherton	Labour
Holderness	Wilson	Wee Free
Keighley	Clough	Wee Free
Skipton	Roundell	Wee Free
Cumberland	C. Lowther	Wee Free
Whitehaven	Grant	Labour
Durham	Hills	Labour
Sedgefield	Burdon	Labour
Gateshead	Surtees	Wee Free
Tynemouth	Percy	Wee Free

Totals:	Wee Frees	14
	Labour	17
		31

England: Midlands & Eastern Counties

Lincolnshire –

Grantham	Royds	Wee Free
Kesteven	Willoughby	Labour
Brigg	Maclean	Labour
Horncastle	Hotchkin	Wee Free

Leicestershire –

Harborough	Keith Fraser	Labour

Nottingham –

Bassetlaw	Hume-Williams	Labour
Nuneaton	Maddocks	Wee Free
Coventry	Manville	Labour
Rugby	Baird	Labour
Stafford	Ormsby-Gore	Labour
Oswestry	Bridgeman	Labour
Tiverton	Carew	Wee Free
N. Dorset	Colfox	Wee Free

	Westbury	Palmer	Wee Free
	Frome	Hurd	Labour
	Swindon	Young	Labour
	Gloucester	Bruton	Wee Free

Totals:	Wee Frees	7
	Labour	10
		17

<u>England: Home Counties</u>

Basingstoke	Holbrook	Labour
St. Albans	Freemantle	Labour
Enfield	Bowles	Labour
Huntingdon	Locker-Lampson	Wee Free
Kings Lynn	Jodrell	Labour
Yarmouth	Fell	Wee Free
Oxford City	Marriott	Wee Free

<u>London:</u>

Tottenham, N.,	Prescott	Labour
Tottenham	Malone	Labour
Finsbury	Archer-Shee	Wee Free
Islington, S.,	Higham	Wee Free
Bow & Bromley	Blair	Labour
Woolwich, E.,	Gee	Labour
Edmonton	Warren	Labour
Gravesend	Richardson	Labour
West Ham – Upton	Wild	Labour

Totals:	Wee Frees	5
	Labour	11
		16

<u>Summary</u>

	Wee Frees	Labour
Scotland	5	7
Wales	–	1
England:		
Northern Western	14	17
& Midlands & Eastern Counties	5	11
	31	36 = 67

129. *Scovell to McCurdy, 'Visit to West of England of Lloyd George', 24 October 1922*

In case Mr. Lloyd George visits the West of England, the Mayor of Bath has suggested to me that the Freedom of Bath should be conferred at 12 noon. He also points out that a meeting could be held in the Bath Theatre in the afternoon and then Mr. Lloyd George could proceed to Bristol for an evening meeting. He is very anxious that the visit should be fixed for not later than the first week in November. Mr. Ernest White happens to be Mayor this year. He is one of our most enthusiastic supporters.

[Pencil note]: Would you let Mr J.T. Davies know?

130. *McCurdy to Scovell, 'Dissolution Honours', 26 October 1922*

You brought to my notice a few days ago the case of Dr. Henry Jackson.[334] I should be very grateful if you would let him know that I should like nothing better than to be in a position to put his name through for recognition in the going-out list. Unfortunately, owing to the strict limitation in the numbers, and the length of the list before me, I have found it quite impossible to do so. But, as I have already indicated, I shall be grateful if you would let him know how sorry I am that I have been unable to assist him on this occasion.

131. *Guest to Scovell, 'Committee of Inquiry', 27 October 1922*[335]

We have been such friends in the last three years that I am proposing to write quite openly to you, more particularly as you will have to make a rapid decision and there will be no opportunity for discussion on the subject. I am merely stating bald facts and not attempting to argue the merits or demerits of the situation which has arisen and of which I have suddenly become apprised. They mean to get rid of you – of course in strict observance of the terms of your contract and I am sure that if you do not resign you will be asked to do so. This being the case, I want you to take advantage of the moment to get into Parliament, which I know you have often wanted to do and, at the same time, make this the excuse for your resignation. You may feel that it is impossible to do this while the contest is in progress and that things in the office would suffer in consequence. I think, as a matter of fact, that now that the placing of candidates is practically finished the rest of the necessary work for the Campaign will automatically proceed without failure, even if you were not there. I think the mere fact that this is possible reflects great credit on the way in which you have got the machine into running order, but, for the moment, I am thinking of you and with your knowledge of what vacancies and opportunities exist you ought to be able to take advantage of some opening which has prospects of success.

334 Jackson (mayor of Wandsworth) to Scovell, 22 Oct. 1922. Jackson said that he had supported the Coalition Liberal organisations in the five constituencies covered by the borough.

335 Marked 'Secret'.

I am in a position to inform you that if you were, say tomorrow morning, to inform the Chief that it was your desire to jump at an opportunity of such a character and to name the place and at the same time assure him that the machine would function in spite of your absence, the request would receive immediate approval. Of course, if you really feel that your absence would be letting down the whole show and that disaster in many directions would most certainly ensue, then the proposal must be abandoned. I cannot believe that this is the case. Remember also, that there remain 6 or 7 days before Nomination and that if your plans were carefully laid almost every outstanding electoral problem which concerns the office might be solved or placed in reliable hands. Anyway, I urge you to consider this most seriously and not lose a moment by indecisions.

132. *Scovell to McCurdy, 'Resignation', 30 October 1922*

I am sending you a copy of a letter which I have addressed to J.T. Davies for submission to Mr. Lloyd George. I have purposely taken this course in the hope that it will ease matters for you. Please understand that I have no personal grievance and that my decision is final. I feel certain that I can depend upon you to safeguard the interests of the excellent staff here and in the provinces.

133. *Scovell to J.T. Davies, 'Resignation', 30 October 1922*

Early in 1919 when I was in the Demobilisation Section of the War Cabinet Secretariat under Sir Eric Geddes and on the eve of taking up a lucrative and permanent post in the commercial world, I was invited by the then Chief Coalition Liberal Whip to take on the task of building up of the scattered Liberal adherents of Mr. Lloyd George throughout the country. I confess that partly as the scion of a very old Liberal family which for over 100 years has served the State and Party with distinction in various directions but mainly out of admiration of Mr. Lloyd George's wonderful services to progress and his country during the Great War, I found it difficult to refuse in spite of the dark picture my intimates drew for me to the permanence of a political career of this kind. Within the limitations imposed upon me, I think I can claim that my task has now been completed, this in the face of difficulties which, from my reading of history and in the light of a varied organising experience over a period of twenty years, I feel can safely be said to have been unparalleled.

As the circumstances ruling at the time of my appointment have now completely changed, and in view of the possibility that Mr. Lloyd George may be glad of this opportunity of retaining near him someone who has had the good fortune to serve him much longer than I have, I have decided, after very careful consideration and with a sure feeling that it will be without detriment to the cause which I have had at heart since 1918, to ask for my release at the earliest possible moment after the General Election. I need hardly say that this decision of mine is quite irrespective of the result of the coming contest. I should be glad therefore if you will lay this letter before Mr. Lloyd George at the earliest opportunity.

Before closing there is one very reasonable request I should like to make and that is on behalf of the London and Provincial staff of 25, Old Queen Street, whose untiring efforts and patient loyalty to the Cause and to myself during the past three or four years can never be sufficiently recognised. May I have Mr. Lloyd George's assurance that their individual claims to just and appreciative consideration will not be overlooked in the event of changes consequent upon the General Election.

I am sending a copy of this letter to Mr McCurdy and to Captain Guest as the person originally responsible for my appointment.

Believe me, Yours very truly,
[unsigned]

P.S. May I add that whatever I may be doing in the future, the experience and information I have gathered and any influence I am able to use with the many political friends I have formed in all parts of the country during the past four years will always be at the service of Mr. Lloyd George.

134. *McCurdy to Scovell, Resignation, 31 October 1922*

I have just got your note & copy of the letter you have sent to Mr Lloyd George. I appreciate what the difficulties have been (I have shared some of them) & I do very fully appreciate the really fine work you have done, & if ever I can be of service to you I hope you will use me as a friend. I will do my best to look after the interests of the staff.

135. *Scovell to Frances Stevenson,*[336] *15 November 1922*

Our confidential conversation yesterday, when you were very kindly speaking about my pending departure, was suddenly interrupted. If it doesn't bore you, for your personal information I should like to summarise my main reasons for departure. The details I expect you can fill in.

First: The perpetual intrigues against this organisation or its personnel which have redoubled in intensity during the past eight months and which have had the most baneful effect of the spirit of our paid or voluntary workers.

Second: The setting up of a Secret Committee of Investigation in July/August of the present year and the press jazz music which it brought forth – obviously inspired from some interested quarter. I may say that no one on the staff has yet been able to understand the meaning of this Committee or seen its report.

Third: In my opinion our poor display of "grit" as evidenced partly by our dealings with the Conservative Party during the past two years and partly by the narrowness of our battle front in the present contest which, by the way, has incensed many of our most prominent supporters.

336 Frances Stevenson (1888–1972), nanny, secretary and long-term mistress to David Lloyd George, who she married in 1943 following the death of his wife, Margaret; became countess Lloyd George of Dwyfor.

Fourth: The complete lack of courtesy and tact displayed by the sudden foisting on the organisation of a totally unqualified stranger in the middle of the Election without warning, consultation or discussion or (as far as I know) rhyme or reason. Please understand I have nothing personal against Sir Alfred Cope – in point of fact I am sorry for him in these most difficult circumstances.

I have no personal grievance against anyone and don't believe in complaining or explaining so I won't bother you with more. I feel convinced there is plenty of other work of a useful kind ready at hand for me to do.

136. *Unnamed [Possibly G. Gunn of Edinburgh] Draft Letter (dictated to McCurdy), 'Liberal Reunion', [Not dated but early November 1922]*

Now that the elections are over the results tabulated and known, it is time for us to take stock and decide as to the future. May I as one who has devoted the past two weeks to electioneering in the constituencies submit my views? The most significant of all the various aspects that was manifested to me, was the overwhelming desire of Liberals that the ranks of the party should be strengthened by the wings united. The country generally is tired with the personal issues that has divided the Liberal Party. Now that the Coalition has been ended Liberals consider the past quarrels should be forgotten, in face of the dangers from the reactionary and revolutionary parties Otherwise Liberals as a party will become an effete party. No future Coalition will ever be tolerated as such, save in exceptional circumstances. The discomfiture of having to bear with the taunts, jeers and sneers through the alliance with the Conservatives has been hard to bear, and will not again be borne readily. The unhappy spectacle of Liberal fighting Liberal with other candidates in the field, and the losses thereby occasioned have caused pain and vexation to those who believe in the principles of the Party. They regard it as a crime that their interests should be sacrificed because of internal quarrels. They are not concerned with the merits of either Mr. Asquith or Mr. Lloyd George, but throughout the Kingdom they are concerned lest their party is sacrificed to what they regard as a personal feud, for which both leaders are to blame.

The weakness – as regards ourselves – most apparent is the academic sectional heads rather than the practical Election chiefs.

[PAGE 2 – Missing]

... must have the flair. There is too much suspicion of the Whitehall training at Headquarters also. Had experienced men been in charge many of the candidates could never have been selected. They belonged to the days when Liberal candidates had to be local preachers, and the nonconformists were wholly Liberal. The days of religious domination are over. Men are wanted: mere amiabilities are not enough. Grit, ability and personality alone can serve. Labour has at least served to interest and help educate the worker. Trade Unions have also served in this direction, but more than all has the Great War. Men had little to do in the long hours on duty save to think. The thinking has been revolutionary in effect. Great names serve little. Ex-service men are apt to be iconoclastic more and more.

I have nothing in any way but praise for Col. Scovell as far as my own experience goes, but the machinery generally must be overhauled, and a policy be at once adopted for future work upon.

It is generally believed that Sir Geo. Younger has outmanoeuvred the Leader in all ways, and it is felt that the non-intervention of a lot of extra candidates must have been due to some such reason as

1. A belief that the Conservatives would only be returned by so few that to function an alliance would be necessary: that such alliance (if they were not unduly irritated) could be effected with the Nationals, and thus enable a minority to rule as the Irish did for so long.

2. That funds were being conserved to permit of the party being a permanent one, and that the leader would not welcome the re-union of Liberals.

3. The questions sent out for submission to candidates have been interpreted as evidencing a desire for power, and to yet bring into being a centre-party.

At the beginning of the year a centre-party could well have been formed. Now it can never be. The Tories have seen their danger. They are firmly against it. Their machine is in the hands of men who will never again let go the control. The rank and file of the Tory Party are glad to be rid of an alliance with our Leader, they have tolerated yet hated him all the time. They are forgetting the virtues and remembering the Hated foe of over twenty years ago. No such split is possible in their ranks as exists in our own.

Now that the recriminations are over the feeling is that both sections can agree a truce. The desire of the great mass of Liberals is that there should not only be a truce but also a serious attempt made to get the Liberals of both sections united with a leader chosen by the majority of elected members after a full and free discussion, all pledging to abide by the result. The belief has been again and again expressed that both sectional chiefs are great enough to sink differences: that Mr. Asquith's age would not permit him to lead at any length of years: and that the real obstacle to re-union is the permanent officials.

The advantages of unity are obvious.

137. *Scovell to McCurdy, 'Resignation', 16 November 1922*

Now that the General Election is over and having regard to the extremely difficult position I have been placed in by the unexpected arrival on the scene of Cope and the wide newspaper publicity that has been accorded to this event, I don't think I am asking too much if I request you to let me get away at the earliest possible moment. As you can well understand, the whole position here is absolutely impossible for me (and for Cope) under the present circumstances.

As regards my personal contract (the original of which is with the Solicitors) the details are as follows:–

(a) Four months' notice on either side.

(b) Twelve months retrenchment clause.

While, as I have already indicated, there is no personal grievance I can honestly claim I have more than fulfilled my contract. However, I leave the "filthy lucre" aside and am going to leave all that to you.

138. *Scovell to Area Heads, 'Resignation', 16 November 1922*

Some short time back I wrote to the Powers that be requesting that I should be relieved of my post as head of this Organisation as soon as the Election was over. As I understand my desire has been granted, I feel I must at once write to you both to take farewell and to express my wholehearted gratitude to you and to your staff for your splendid co-operation and devoted labours during the past few years. I really cannot thank you all enough. I have received nothing but kindness at the hands of each and all and the teamwork has been too splendid for words, and an example to any other Organisation.

139. *Scovell to Councillor William Wykes (Honorary Secretary of the Leicester Coalition Liberal Association), 'Leicester East Constituency', 21 November 1922*

Thank you very much indeed for you letter of the 17th instant. I cannot tell you how delighted I am over young Evans winning East Leicester. I think both you and I deserve a chaplet of laurel leaves, considering that we were the conspirators who produced young Evans. I think it is perfectly splendid. You will be amused to hear, this quite privately between us, that I gave him a devil of a lecture a few days ago, warning him that on no account must he suffer from a swollen head, begging him to lie doggo in the House, and urging him with all my persuasive powers to consolidate his position in East Leicester. I told him to get down among the people and not bother about the 'nobs', because goodness knows when we may not have another General [election]. You will have to act as his candid friend, keeping him informed all the time of what he is to do and what he is not to do. You must be most awfully pleased at the turn of events, and I don't wonder. You have behaved like a brick all the way through.

It is perfectly true that I am shortly going. I have had eleven years now of very strenuous and responsible work and I really must take a rest, but I hope that occasions may arise in the future when we shall meet. After all, a discussion on the future of politics is a very interesting topic at the present moment, because I am absolutely up the proverbial tree and I expect you are the same.

140. *Colonel G. Gunn to Scovell, 'Reflections on the Election in Scotland', 21 November 1922*

During the election stir I have been frequently thinking of you, and wishing that I could spend an hour or so with you, in order to compare notes. Well, it is now all over, and in the East of Scotland the National Liberals have been able to hold their own. But, I am sorry to see this evening that Sir Malcolm Smith has been defeated in Orkney and Shetland. I did not expect this result. I took part in the bye-election in Orkney, and I thought Sir Malcolm Smith would have been able to hold his own. The weather was stormy on election day in the Islands and the poll was a small one, and so possibly there may be some explanation. So far as local qualifications were concerned Sir Malcolm Smith seemed to have had the advantages in his favour.

I helped Sir Murdoch MacDonald in style. There was a keen struggle in Inverness-shire, but MacDonald came out of it with a largely increased majority. The contest in Caithness & Sutherland interested me very much. I spent August and September in my native county. Several individuals asked me to move, but I took no steps so far as I was personally concerned. The local leaders would do nothing in Sutherland. It now transpires that Harmsworth had been playing with them for a long time. He would not say what he intended to do, though written to repeatedly. He would always reply but would never say definitely whether he would come forward himself. At the last moment he tried to foist his son on the constituency, and when the Committee would not approve he offered to retire in favour of Mackinnon Wood,[337] Holmes and others – apparently all Wee Frees!! As these suggestions did not meet with local acceptance he, at the last moment, decided to come north again and contest the seat. In Caithness a movement had been set on foot to invite Sir A. Sinclair to come forward. Of course, from my local information one may allow that the Caithness Unionists, and Sinclair's own estate people, were mainly responsible for the call to Sinclair – But, at the same time it is perfectly clear that Sinclair played a perfectly fair and straight game. All along, Sir W. Sutherland, and afterward MacCallum Scott, would not authorize the office here to move a hand or foot for fear as Harmsworth was concerned – Therefore the opposition to Harmsworth was of local origin. Why the Whips took up that attitude you, perhaps can explain? It was all very mysterious to me. Were they afraid of the Harmsworth press and influence? I was present at Harmsworth's meetings at Golspie on Nov.6, and at Rogart, on the following day. Indeed, I had a long talk with the distinguished man while he was still in his bed on Nov 7! I corrected him with regard to a serious blunder he made at the meeting the night before when he spoke on a rather acute local land question, "resumption". I attended also Sinclair's meeting at Rogart on Nov. 7. When he made a very good appearance. Both he and Lady Sinclair[338] told me that the Scottish Whip has asked him (Sinclair) to withdraw in favour of Harmsworth – in order to allow Harmsworth to have a walk over. This was an astonishing incident in view of the fact that Harmsworth was a most inefficient member. Golspie is the second most populous centre in Sutherland – yet he never at any time spoke, or held a meeting there, till the 6th of this month! No wonder one heckler asked "How is it you have been so late in coming"? In the whole of Scotland, possibly in the British Isles, was there such a curious case as that of Harmsworth in Caithness and Sutherland? Sinclair deserved his

337 Thomas Mackinnon Wood (1855–1927), Liberal MP for Glasgow St Rollox 1906–18; financial secretary to the treasury 1911–12 and 1916, secretary of state for Scotland 1912–16, chancellor of the duchy of Lancaster 1916.

338 Lady Marigold Sinclair (née Forbes) (1897–1975).

victory. Lady Sinclair told me that the Harmsworth people threatened Winston with opposition in Dundee owing to a letter he had written backing Sinclair!

I fear I may be boring you with particulars of one seat, but I think it is a unique case. The West of Scotland has done badly – all the National Liberal members, barring 3, come from the East. I have been in close touch with things all this time. MacNicol and Miss Pressley Smith have done their part well I think, but their task was an uphill one. I am non-plussed as to what is now to happen. Hope you are well and fit? I may say I thoroughly enjoyed my stint in Inverness-shire and that there are no new fields left for me!

141. *Scovell to Colonel G. Gunn, 'Reflections on the Election', 23 November 1922*

Thank you very much for your letter of the 21st instant which, needless to say, I was more than delighted to get. Well, we have got through this Donnybrook Fair of an Election and considering all things I think we have done very well. As you know, I am not a complacent person, but I have heard nobody, except the ignorant and uninformed, animadvert in any way on the result. After all, we were without a policy, without a real and definite lead, we were limited in the scope of our organisation, and the real truth is that the country wanted a change and personally I think they were perfectly right to do so. It seems to me that the people of this country are very often shrewder or even wiser than their leaders. I am convinced, from everything I have seen during the last month, that it won't hurt Lloyd George and Winston Churchill to be out of office, or even out of Parliament, for a year. I am inclined to think that the Tories won't last the full course. They are not a homogenous lot, but I see no reason why there should be any alteration in the status quo for at least a year, provided L.G. & Co. lay doggo. I think this last is essential, otherwise the country might get justifiably annoyed.

I was very interested to hear your account of the Sinclair-Harmsworth fight. I don't think it will do Harmsworth any harm to be out of the House for a bit. Oddly enough, his son is tacitly with us, and is not an Asquithian. I think, perhaps, you are rather hard on MacCallum Scott in your remarks on his attitude to Leicester Harmsworth. It is not very easy for any whip to take a strong line in the case of a sitting member. It is true, as you say, that he may have been inefficient, but God knows, there are many others in the same boat. The case of Walter Waring[339] and J.D. Hope[340] is something different. Moreover, too, you must remember that Harmsworth has great newspaper interests behind him, and an open attack on him in the North of Scotland might have led to considerable trouble in the South West of England, where we also have interests.

Well, as you probably know, I am about to retire from this very onerous post. I really don't see why I should be persuaded to go on. I have now been in harness

339 Walter Waring (1876–1930), Liberal MP for Banffshire 1907–18, Blaydon 1918–22 and Berwick and Haddington 1922–3.

340 John Deans Hope (1860–1949), Liberal MP for West Fife 1900–10 and Haddingtonshire 1911–22.

for eleven years and I have had a very strenuous time, and with all the intrigues and the unnecessary worries and the incompetent people one has to deal with, plus the lack of policy and decision, not to mention the ridiculous state of affairs during the General Election, I am absolutely fed up, and I intend to become master of my own soul for some months to come. I hope to clear out very shortly indeed and probably go abroad. I am very glad to see that Dudgeon's brother got in. Some quite good young men have come to the House on this occasion. Why on earth didn't you arrange to defeat Sir W.S.? If you had, you would have deserved well of the Party, Great Britain, the Empire and the world.

142. *Statement of Bank & Cash Accounts on Transfer from Lieut. Col. G.J. Scovell to Sir A. Cope, 25 November 1922*

Bank Balance as per Pass Book made up as at 25th Nov 1922					£14,174 0 6
Deduct cheques drawn but not yet paid:–					
June	Sir R. Williams	25	–	–	
Nov.	T.J. Fletcher	160	–	–	
Nov.	"	290	–	–	
"	Partridge & Cooper.	2	12	2	
"	E.L. Spears.	65	11	3	
"	Cash.	200	–	–	
"	T.H. Gill & Son.	104	12	–	
"	Gt. Western Rlway	76	6	11	
	Fleet Delivery	21	–	–	
"	M.T. Simm	50	–	–	
"	A. Shaw	175	–	–	
"	D. McNicol.	300	–	–	
"	Yeats & Co	60	12	–	
"	Carter Paterson & Co	3	18	8	
"	D. Macdonald	66	–	4	
"	Cash	100	–	–	
"	A.C. White	130	–	–	
"	G.J. Scovell	125	–	–	
"	Ditto	59	–	–	
Plus cheques signed by Sir A Cope on 25th Nov:					
Nov.	Topical Film Co.	170	–	–	
"	H.N. Rowlatt.	406	14	4	
"	G.W. Thompson	8	10	–	

"	Miss Pickering	15	–	–
"	Cash	200	–	–
		2,814	17	8

Balance as shown by Cash Book on 25/11/22.

	£11,364	2	10

Statement of Cash as per Cash Book at 25/11/22:

Receipts	£3,652	14	4
Expenditure	£2,940	4	8½
Balance	£712	9	7½

Bonus List: G.E. 1922

General Secretariat			
1. P. Smullian	£5	–	–
2. Miss Kinder	£1	10	–
3. Miss Bailey	£1	5	–
4. Mrs Lee	£1	–	–
5. B. Mitchell	£1	–	–
6. F. Brundle	£1	–	–
7. H. Robinson	£3	–	–
Chief Agent's Branch:			
8. Mrs Rose	£3	–	–
9. Miss Bartlett	£3	–	–
10. G. Marrett	£3	–	–
11. T.P. O'Hara	£2	–	–
12. Mr McIlroy	£2	–	–
13. A.E. Parnell	£2	–	–
Press and Publicity Branch:			
14. Miss Thorne	£5	–	–
15. F. Burns	£2	–	–
16. Miss Johnson	£1	–	–
17. Mrs Dance	£1	–	–
Publications Branch:			
18. E.J. Thornbury	£12	–	–
19. Mr. King	£1	–	–
20. Mr. Inglis	£1	–	–
21. Mr Buck	£2	–	–
22. Miss Vallis	£3	–	–

23. Sgt-Major Bursey	£2	–	–
24. J. Forrest	£2	–	–
25. R.K. Mabberley	£2	–	–
Records Branch:			
26. Miss Anderson	£5	–	–
27. Miss Elkington	£3	–	–
28. Miss Holt	£2	–	–
29. Miss Fowle	£2	–	–
30. Miss Horwill	£2	–	–
31. Miss Gough	£2	–	–
32. Miss Bacon	£2	–	–
33. Miss Weir	£1	–	–
L.G.L.M. Branch:			
34. Miss Parker	£1	–	–
Distribution Dept:			
35. W. Croxford	£12	–	–
36. Mr. Steele	£5	–	–
37. Mr. Jackson	£5	–	–
Z. Dept:			
38. S. Watts	£2	–	–
39. L. Gallichan	£2	–	–
40. Miss Hutchings	£2	–	–
41. Miss Fowle	£1	–	–
42. H. Stanley	£2	–	–
43. J. Mabberley	£1	–	–
44. J.C. King	£1	–	–
45. Mr Hoskens	£1	–	–
46. Mrs Rickinson	£1	–	–
47. Miss Anderson	£1	–	–
48. Miss Hopkins	£1	–	–
49. Miss Neves	£1	–	–
Special Bonuses	£75	–	–
Extra G.E. Bonus List			
Miss Dalley............................	£1	–	–
Mrs Perryman.........................	£1	–	–
Miss Hems............................	£1	–	–
Mrs Frost...............................	£1	–	–

J.J. Irvine................................	£2	–	–
B. Goodacre..............................	£2	–	–
W. Hems.................................	£2	–	–
W. Rickinson...........................	£5	–	–
H. East...................................	£7	7	–
Mrs East................................	£7	7	–
	£29	14	–

143. *Frances Stevenson to Scovell, 'Resignation', 29 November 1922*

Thank you so much for sending me a copy of Bulmer's letter.[341] It is a most interesting diagnosis of the political position and Mr. Lloyd George was very glad to have it. I am very sorry not to have written to you before regarding the letter you wrote to me about your personal position. I am awfully sorry you have decided to go and we shall all regret losing you very much. I hope we shall see you before you finally take your departure, and I wish you all good luck in the future.

341 Not located in the archive.

Select Bibliography

Printed Private Papers, Diaries and Memoirs

Boyce, George, [ed.], *The Crisis of British Unionism: Lord Selborne's Domestic Political Papers, 1885–1922*, (London: The Historians Press, 1987).

Clynes, J.R., *Memoirs 1869–1924*, (London: Hutchinson, 1937).

Gilbert, Martin, [ed.], *Winston S Churchill: Companion Vol. 4*, part 3, (London: Heinemann, 1977).

Hoare, Samuel, *Empire of the Air*, (London: Collins, 1967).

Middlemas, Keith, [ed.], *Thomas Jones: Whitehall Diary*, Vols.1–3, (London, Oxford: University Press, 1969–71).

Ramsden, John, [ed.], *Real Old Tory Politics: The Political Diaries of Robert Sanders, Lord Bayford 1910–1935*, (London: The Historians Press, 1984).

Riddell, Lord, *Lord Riddell's Intimate Diary of the Peace Conference and After 1918–1923*, (London: Victor Gollancz, 1933).

Self, Robert, [ed.], *The Austen Chamberlain Diary Letters: The Correspondence of Sir Austen Chamberlain with His Sisters Hilda and Ida, 1916–1937*, (Cambridge: Cambridge University Press, 1995).

Taylor, A.J.P., [ed.] *Lloyd George: A Diary by Frances Stevenson*, (London: Hutchinson, 1971).

Thorpe, Andrew and Toye, Richard, [eds], *Parliament and Politics in the Age of Asquith and Lloyd George: The Diaries of Cecil Harmsworth MP, 1909–1922*, (Cambridge: Cambridge University Press, 2016).

Wilson, Trevor, [ed.], *The Political Diaries of C.P. Scott 1911–1928*, (London: Collins, 1970).

Books

Adams, R.J.Q., *Bonar Law* (Stanford: Stanford University Press, 1999).

Ball, Alan R., *British Political Parties: The Emergence of a Modern Party System*, (London: Palgrave: 1987).

Ball, Stuart, *The Conservative Party and British Politics 1902–1951*, (New York: Routledge, 2013).

Bentley, Michael, *The Liberal Mind, 1914–1929*, (Cambridge: Cambridge University Press, 1977).

Beaverbrook, Lord, *The Decline and Fall of Lloyd George*, (New York: Duell, Sloan and Pearce, 1963).

Blake, Robert, *The Conservative Party from Peel to Churchill*, (London: Fontana, 1972).

Blake, Robert, *The Unknown Prime Minister. The Life and Times of Andrew Bonar Law 1858–1923*, (London: Eyre and Spottiswoode, 1955).

Cook, Chris, *The Age of Alignment: Electoral Politics in Britain 1922–1929*, (London: Macmillan, 1975).

Cook, Chris and Stevenson, John, *A History of British Elections Since 1689*, (London: Routledge, 2014).

Maurice, Cowling, *The Impact of Labour, 1920–1924. The beginning of Modern British Politics*, (Cambridge: Cambridge University Press, 1971).

Cowling, Maurice, *The Impact of Hitler: British Politics and British Policies 1933–1940*, (Cambridge: Cambridge University, 1975).

Cregier, Don M., 'Lloyd George's lucre: the National Liberal Fund', in Krieger, Don M., [ed.], *Chiefs without Indians: Asquith, Lloyd George and the Liberal Remnant*, (Washington D.C.: University Press of America, 1982), 113–47.

Cuthbert, D.D., 'Lloyd George and the Conservative Central Office, 1918–22' in Taylor, A.J.P., [ed.], *Lloyd George: Twelve Essays*, (London: Hamilton, 1971). 167–87.

Dutton, David, *A History of the Liberal Party Since 1900*, 2nd Edition (Basingstoke: Palgrave, 2013).

Gilbert, Martin, *Winston S. Churchill. Official Biography*, vol. 4, (London: Heinemann, 1975).

Jenkins, Roy, *The Chancellors*, (London: Papermac, 1999).

Kinnear, Michael, *The Fall of Lloyd George: The Political Crisis of 1922*, (London: Macmillan, 1973).

Laybourn, Keith, Reynold, Jack, *Liberalism and the Rise of Labour 1890–1918*, (London: Croom Helm, 1984).

McKibbin, Ross, *The Evolution of the Labour Party 1910–1924*, (Oxford: Oxford University, 1974).

Morgan, Kenneth O., *Consensus and Disunity: The Lloyd George Coalition Government 1918–22*, (Oxford: Clarendon, 1979).

Morgan, Kenneth O., 'Lloyd George's Stage Army: The Coalition Liberals, 1918–22', in Taylor, A.J.P., [ed.], *Lloyd George: Twelve Essays*, (London: Hamilton, 1971), 225–54.

Owen, F., *Tempestuous Journey, Lloyd George His Life and Times* (London: Hutchinson, 1954).

Powell, David, *British Politics, 1910–35*, (London: Hutchinson, 2004).

Pugh, Martin, *Speak for Britain! A New History of the Labour Party*, (London: The Bodley Head, 2010).

Ramsden, John, *The Age of Balfour and Baldwin, 1902–1940*, (London: Longman, 1978).

Rees, Rosemary, *Britain, 1890–1939*, (London: Heinemann, 2003).

Searle, G.R., *The Liberal Party: Triumph and Disintegration 1886–1929*, (New York: St Martin's Press, 1992).

Searle, G.R., *A New England? Peace and War 1886–1918*, (Oxford: Oxford University Press, 2004).

Tanner, Duncan, 'Class voting and radical politics: the Liberal and Labour parties, 1910–31', in Lawrence, Jon & Taylor, Miles, [eds] *Party, State and Society. Electoral Behaviour in Britain since 1920,* (Aldershot: Scolar, 1997), 106–30.

Thorpe, Andrew, *The British General Election of 1931*, (Oxford: Oxford University Press, 1991).

Wilson, T., *The Downfall of the Liberal Party 1914–1935*, (London: Collins, 1966).

Wrigley, Chris, *Lloyd George and the Challenge of Labour. The Post-War Coalition 1918–1922*, (Hemel Hempstead: Harvester Wheatsheaf, 1990).

Wrigley, Chris, 'Coalition Blues: The Conservatives, the Liberals and Conservative-Liberal Coalitions in Britain since 1895', in Hart, Bradley W. and Carr, Richard [eds], *The Foundations of the British Conservative Party: Essays on Conservatism from Lord Salisbury to David Cameron*, (London: Bloomsbury, 2013).

Articles

Beers, Laura D., 'Punting on the Thames: Electoral Betting in Interwar Britain', *Journal of Contemporary History*, 45, 2, 2010, 282–314.

Close, David, 'Conservatives and Coalition after the First World War', *Journal of Modern History*, 45, 2, 1973, 240–60.

David, Craig, 'High Politics and the "new political history"', *Historical Journal*, 53, 2, 2010, 240–260;

Steven Fielding, 'Looking for the "new political history"', *Journal of Contemporary History*, 42, 2007, 515–524.

Crowcroft, Robert, 'Maurice Cowling and the writing of British political history', *Contemporary British History*, 22, 2008, 279–286.

Douglas, Roy, 'The background to the "Coupon" election arrangements', *English Historical Review*, 86, 1971, 318–36.

Freeman, G., 'The Liberal Party and the impact of the 1918 Reform Act', *Parliamentary History*, 89, 2018, 47–63.

Graham Jones, J., 'The "Coaly Libs" and the "Wee Frees": Cardiganshire politics 1920-24' in *Ceredigion*, Part 1 in 17, 3, 2015, 129–70, and Part 2 in 17, 4, 2016, 83–112.

Jarvis, David, 'Mrs Maggs and Betty: The Conservative Approach to Women Voters in the 1920s', *Twentieth Century British History*, 5, 1994, 129–52

McEwen, John M., 'The coupon election of 1918 and Unionist members of parliament', *Journal of Modern History*, 34, 3, 1962, 294–306.

McGill, Barry, 'Lloyd George's timing of the 1918 election', *Journal of British Studies*, 14, 1974, 109–24.

Sloan, Geoffrey, 'Hide seek and Negotiate: Alfred Cope and Counter Intelligence in Ireland 1919–1921', *Intelligence and National Security* 33, 2, 2018, 176–95.

Stanley, Luke, 'The Rebel Chief Whip: The Role of Leslie Wilson in the Fall of the Lloyd George Coalition, 1922', *Parliamentary History*, 38, 2, 2019, 224–43.

Wilson, Trevor, 'The Coupon and the British General Election of 1918', *Journal of Modern History* 36, 2 (1964), 28–42.

Index of Westminster Constituencies

General Index

Printed and bound by CPI Group (UK) Ltd, Croydon, CR0 4YY

17/03/2026

14845004-0001